Computational and
Quantitative Studies

The Collected Works of M. A. K. Halliday

Volume 1: *On Grammar*

Volume 2: *Linguistic Studies of Text and Discourse*

Volume 3: *On Language and Linguistics*

Volume 4: *The Language of Early Childhood*

Volume 5: *The Language of Science*

Volume 6: *Computational and Quantitative Studies*

Volume 7: *Studies in English Language*

Volume 8: *Studies in Chinese Language*

Volume 9: *Language and Education*

Volume 10: *Language and Society*

Volume 6 in the Collected Works of M. A. K. Halliday

Computational and Quantitative Studies

M. A. K. Halliday

Edited by Jonathan J. Webster

continuum
LONDON • NEW YORK

Continuum
The Tower Building 80 Maiden Lane
11 York Road   Suite 704
London SE1 7NX New York, NY 10038

First published 2005
This paperback edition published 2006

British Library Cataloguing-in-Publication Data
A catalogue record for this book is available from the British Library.

ISBN: 0–8264–5872–6 (hardback)
ISBN: 0–8264–8826–9 (paperback)

Library of Congress Cataloging-in-Publication Data
A catalog record for this book is available from the Library of Congress.

Typeset by YHT Ltd., London
Printed and bound in Great Britain by MPG Books Ltd, Bodmin, Cornwall

CONTENTS

Preface   vii

Acknowledgements   ix

PART ONE   **MACHINE TRANSLATION: THE EARLY YEARS**   1

Editor's Introduction   3

1   The Linguistic Basis of a Mechanical Thesaurus   6

2   Linguistics and Machine Translation   20

PART TWO   **PROBABILISTIC GRAMMAR AND THE CORPUS**   37

Editor's Introduction   39

3   Towards Probabilistic Interpretations   42

4   Corpus Studies and Probabilistic Grammar   63

5   Language as System and Language as Instance: The Corpus as a Theoretical Construct   76

6 [with Z. L. James] A Quantitative Study of Polarity and Primary Tense in the English Finite Clause 93

7 Quantitative Studies and Probabilities in Grammar 130

8 The Spoken Language Corpus: A Foundation for Grammatical Theory 157

PART THREE TOWARDS 'INTELLIGENT COMPUTING' (COMPUTING WITH MEANING) 191

Editor's Introduction 193

9 On Language in Relation to Fuzzy Logic and Intelligent Computing 196

10 Fuzzy Grammatics: A Systemic Functional Approach to Fuzziness in Natural Language 213

11 Computing Meanings: Some Reflections on Past Experience and Present Prospects 239

Appendix: Systems of the English Clause: A Trial Grammar for the PENMAN Text Generation Project [Information Sciences Institute, University of Southern California] 268

Bibliography 285

Index 295

PREFACE

The works presented in this volume on language in relation to computing should not be read simply as a retrospective on Professor Halliday's work in this area over the last fifty years. Rather, this volume is better thought of as a prospective from a scholar whose foresight has grown out of decades of experience working with language, first as a language teacher, then as a grammarian, never seeking to tame its 'ferociously complex' (Chapter Eleven) nature, only wanting to 'engage with it seriously and in appropriate theoretical terms' (Chapter Nine). For Halliday, this has meant modelling language paradigmatically, contextually, functionally, fuzzily and developmentally.

In the late 1950s, while working at the Cambridge Language Research Unit on a project concerned with machine translation, Professor Halliday realized the need to 'formalize paradigmatic relations, those of the system', but as he recalls, 'I did not know how to do it – and I totally failed to persuade anyone else of this!' (Chapter Seven). Since then, however, as the chapters in this volume clearly evidence, he has succeeded in advancing our knowledge of how one can indeed 'model language paradigmatically: that is, as choice, with the system network as organizing concept' (Chapter Nine).

With the advent of the spoken-language corpus and advances in computing technology, it has become possible to conduct quantitative studies of naturally occurring, spontaneous speech, taking us beyond what can be recovered by introspection to discover language as it is actually used in the context of situation (Chapter Eight). Speech in situ opens a window to the soul of language – 'as semiotic system-&-process'. The ranks and levels, properties and functions of an underlying, invisible system are revealed as one interrogates the corpus to find out who is doing what with language, where, when, why and how. Corresponding to the representation of context in terms of field (what is going on), tenor (who is involved), and mode (in what medium) are metafunctions associated with processes of construing human experience (ideational), enacting social relationships (interpersonal), and creating discourse (textual). It is not surprising given the complexity of human experience and dynamics of social relationships that language is 'inherently fuzzy', and 'perhaps the single most complex phenomenon in nature' (Chapter Eleven). Language is not dysfunctional because it is fuzzy. Rather, precisely because of its dynamic character, its potential 'is indefinitely large – it is always capable of growing further, without any limits that we are aware of' (Chapter Nine). Language never ceases to amaze.

While the focus of study may be on 'everyday discourse as contextualized in real life' – what some might call the 'commonplace', the system underlying that discourse cannot be adequately described only in commonsense terms, without reference to designed systematic knowledge. As Professor Halliday puts it, 'One would not expect to design a robotic system on the basis of Year Six mathematics!' (Chapter Nine). Whether the endeavour is machine translation, corpus linguistics or intelligent computing, what is needed is a theory of language which will provide a fuller, more realistic picture of language as a system rich in meaning potential. Systemic-functional grammar accomplishes just that.

Professor Halliday foresees the day when computing – 'the most future-oriented of all present-day human activities' – becomes computing with meaning, 'when language comes to function not just as the object of computing but as its instrument' (Chapter Eleven). Before this can happen, however, two 'noticeable disjunctions' must be addressed: (i) the disjunction between 'language and knowledge', which needs to be reconceptualized as a single unified semiotic system with two related levels of representation, the lexico-grammatical and the semantic; and (ii) the disjunction between 'the instance and the system of which it is an instance' (Chapter Eleven), recognized as simply different perspectives on the same phenomenon.

The lasting significance of the chapters in this volume comes from the fact that their insights are grounded in a theory which neither idealizes nor trivializes the object of study, but diligently strives to paint a picture of language which captures its true character.

ACKNOWLEDGEMENTS

We are grateful to the original publishers for permission to reprint the articles and chapters in this volume. Original publication details are provided below, and also at the beginning of each chapter.

'The linguistic basis of a mechanical thesaurus, and its application to English preposition classification' from *Mechanical Translation*, 3:3, December 1956, pp. 81–8. © Massachusetts Institute of Technology. Reprinted by permission.
'Linguistics and machine translation' from *Zeitschrift für Phonetik, Sprachwissenschaft und Kommunikationsforschung*, Band 15, 1962, Heft 1/2. Reprinted by permission of Akademie Verlag, Berlin.
'Towards probabilistic interpretations' from Eija Ventola (ed.), *Trends in Linguistics: Functional and Systemic Linguistics: Approaches and Uses*, Berlin and New York: Mouton de Gruyter, 1991.
'Corpus studies and probabilistic grammar' from Karin Aijmer and Bengt Altenberg (eds), *English Corpus Linguistics: Studies in Honour of Jan Svartvik*, London and New York: Longman, 1991. Reprinted by permission of Longman Group Limited.
'Language as system and language as instance: the corpus as a theoretical concept' from Jan Svartvik (ed.), *Directions in Corpus Linguistics: Proceedings of Nobel Symposium 82*, Berlin: Mouton de Gruyter, 1991.
'A quantitative study of polarity and primary tense in the English finite clause' from John M. Sinclair, Michael Hoey and Gwyneth Fox (eds), *Techniques of Description: Spoken and Written Discourse*, London: Routledge, 1993. Reprinted by permission of Routledge.
'Quantitative studies and probabilities in grammar' from Michael

Hoey (ed.), *Data, Description and Discourse: Papers on the English Language in Honour of John M. Sinclair on his Sixtieth Birthday*. London: HarperCollins, 1993. © 1993 Michael Hoey.

'The spoken language corpus' from Karin Aijmer and Bengt Altenberg (eds), *Proceedings of ICAME 2002: The Theory and Use of Corpora*, Göteborg 22–26 May 2002, Amsterdam: Editions Rodopi. Reprinted by permission of Editions Rodopi.

'On language in relation to fuzzy logic and intelligent computing' © 1995 IEEE. Reprinted, with permission, from *Proceedings of 1995 IEEE International Conference on Fuzzy Systems. The International Joint Conference of the Fourth IEEE International Conference on Fuzzy Systems and The Second International Fuzzy Engineering Symposium*. IEEE: Piscataway NJ, 1995.

'Fuzzy grammatics: a systemic functional approach to fuzziness in natural language' © 1995 IEEE. Reprinted, with permission, from *Proceedings of 1995 IEEE International Conference on Fuzzy Systems. The International Joint Conference of the Fourth IEEE International Conference on Fuzzy Systems and The Second International Fuzzy Engineering Symposium*. IEEE: Piscataway NJ, 1995.

'Systems of the English clause: a trial grammar for the PENMAN text generation project' reprinted by permission of Information Sciences Institute, University of Southern California.

PART ONE

MACHINE TRANSLATION: THE EARLY YEARS

EDITOR'S INTRODUCTION

This first section includes two works from Professor Halliday's early years, the first *The Linguistic Basis of a Mechanical Thesaurus*, presented at the October 1956 Conference on Mechanical Translation, and published in 1957 in MIT's *Mechanical Translation*. The second, *Linguistics and Machine Translation*, appeared five years later in *Zeitschrift für Phonetik, Sprachwissenschaft und Kommunikationsforschung*. While computer technology has drastically changed since the time when these commentaries first appeared, nevertheless, they continue to be as relevant today to those working in this area as they were nearly half a century earlier. This is because the principles and methodology which they discuss are grounded in a theory of language "as a unique, patterned form of human social activity, operating in the context of other social activities" and not dependent on the current state of computer technology. "Machine translation," states Professor Halliday, "is a problem in applied linguistics, specifically a problem requiring the application of those parts of General Linguistic theory which deal with the systematic description and comparison of languages."

The basic premise is that "description must precede translation", in particular at the levels of grammar and lexis on the one hand, and context on the other. Moreover, the description must be "anchored in sound and scientific theory", and "the methods used in description [should be] derived from and answerable to, this theory". In the case of machine translation, the computer needs to perform "a complex operation of comparative descriptive linguistics", which means that it "has to digest not only the descriptions of two languages but also the rules for the systematic relating of these two descriptions one to the other".

3

Translating between two texts involves a comparative description of two languages, not in terms of linking two languages, each as a whole, but rather by relating items in two languages to each other in terms of translation equivalence linked to grammatical rank scale. Professor Halliday outlines three stages in the translation process:

> First, there is the selection of the "most probable translation equivalent" for each item at each rank, based on simple frequency. Second, there is the conditioning effect of the surrounding text in the source language on these probabilities: here grammatical and lexical features of the unit next above are taken into account and may (or may not) lead to the choice of an item other than the one with highest overall probability. Third, there is the internal structure of the target language, which may (or may not) lead to the choice of yet another item as a result of grammatical and lexical relations particular to that language: these can be viewed as brought into operation similarly by step-by-step progression up the rank scale.

The difference, Professor Halliday notes, between "literal" translation and "translation in the accepted sense", can be explained with reference to the rank scale. Literal translation occurs at group rank or below, possibly also a mixture of group and word, whereas translation in the accepted sense occurs at the rank of the clause, "and a good translation needs to be based on the sentence as its unit". This highlights the importance of the second stage in which "grammatical and lexical features of the unit next above are taken into account and may (or may not) lead to the choice of an item other than the one with highest overall probability". Similarly, in the third stage, when dealing with the grammatical and lexical relations particular to the target language, there must be a corresponding "step-by-step progression up the rank scale". Unlike the human translator who performs all three stages as a single process, the computer "will need to shunt up and down among the different units of the rank scale as the translation advances towards the final choice of equivalent". All this assumes the availability of a detailed description of "the ordering of elements into systems within which determination operates and the working out by descriptive linguistic methods of the criteria governing choice among the elements ranged as terms in one system". Also needed is a thesaurus – "the lexical analogue of the grammatical paradigm". In a thesaurus, "words are arranged in contextually determined series" thereby making it possible to achieve not only translation equivalence but also contextual equivalence.

Summing up at the end of the first chapter, Professor Halliday has this to say about what he refers to as "the thesaurus method": "The method is far from having been worked out in full; the principle on which it rests, that of 'make the language do the work', can only be fully applied after the linguists have done the work on the language." The same principle applies irrespective of rank throughout the grammar. While we no longer call it "mechanical translation", nevertheless the principles and the methods outlined in these two chapters continue to point the way forward in an endeavour where success depends more on advancing our knowledge of language than on machines.

Chapter One

THE LINGUISTIC BASIS OF A MECHANICAL THESAURUS⋆ (1956)

Abstract

The grammar and lexis of a language exhibit a high degree of internal determination, affecting all utterances whether or not these are translated from another language. This may be exploited in a mechanical translation program in order to cope with the lack of translation equivalence between categories of different languages, by the ordering of elements into systems within which determination operates and the working out by descriptive linguistic methods of the criteria governing the choice among the elements ranged as terms in one system. Lexical items so ordered form a thesaurus, and the thesaurus series is the lexical analogue of the grammatical paradigm.

Introduction

A fundamental problem of mechanical translation, arising at the levels of both grammar and lexis, is that of the carry-over of elements ranged as terms in particular systems; i.e., systems established non-comparatively, as valid for the synchronic and syn-topic description of what is regarded for the purpose as 'one' language. The translation process presupposes an analysis, generally unformulated in the case of

---

⋆ This is one of a series of four papers presented by the Cambridge Language Research Unit to the October 1956 Conference on Mechanical Translation (for abstracts see MT, Vol. III. No. 2, pp. 36–7).

human translation, of the source and target languages; and it is a commonplace that a one-to-one translation equivalence of categories – including not only terms within systems but even the systems themselves – does not by itself result in anything which on contextual criteria could be called translation. One might, for example, be tempted to give the same name "aspect" to two systems set up in the description respectively of Chinese and English, on the grounds that both systems are the grammatical reflection of contextually specified categories of a non-absolute time-scale in which components of a situation are ordered in relation to one another; not only would the terms in the systems (e.g. Chinese and English "perfective") not be translationally identifiable: not even the systems as a whole (unless a neutral term was introduced to universalize them) could be assigned translation equivalence.

Syntax

Where translation is handled as a function between two given languages, this problem can be met by a comparative description of the kind that has come to be known as "transfer grammar", in which the two languages are described in mutually (or unilaterally) approximating comparative terms. For mechanical translation this is obviously unsatisfactory, since each language would have to be analysed in a different way for every new language on the other end of the translation axis. On the other hand the search for categories with universal translation validity, or even with validity over a given limited group of languages, whether it is undertaken from within or from outside language, could occupy many years; and while the statistical survey required for the intralinguistic approach would be, for the linguist, perhaps the most pleasing form of electronic activity, the pursuit of mechanical translation cannot await its results!

In practice, therefore, we compromise, and make a descriptive analysis of each language which is at the same time both autonomous and geared to the needs of translation. We then face the question: what is the optimum point at which the source language and the target language should impinge on one another? Let us suppose we possess two documents: one consisting of a descriptive analysis of each of the two languages, the other a body of texts in the two languages, the one text a translation of the other. In the first document we find that in Language 1 there is a system A with terms m, n, o, p, and in Language 2 a system B with terms q, r, s, t. The second document reveals a translation overlap between these systems such that we can make a synthesis as follows: Language 1, system A_1, terms n_1, o_1, p; Language 2, system A_2, terms n_2, o_2, q, r, where the use of the same letter indicates probability greater than a certain arbitrary figure that translation equivalence exists. Meanwhile document one has specified what are the determining features (contextual, grammatical, etc.) of the two systems, and the pro-portional overlap between the two sets of determining features represents the **minimum** probability of translation equivalence. The actual probability of translation equivalence is always greater than the determining features show, because although (a) if a contextual feature X determines both n_1 and n_2, there is predictable equivalence since by definition if X is present for one text, it is present for its translation, yet (b) if n_1 is determined by a grammatical feature Y of Language 1 and n_2 by a grammatical feature Z of Language 2, there is no predictable equivalence though equivalence will arise when-ever Y is found to be the translation equivalent of Z.

Since translation, although a mutual **relation**, is a unilateral **process**, what we are interested in is the choice of forms in the target language, let us say Language 2. Document one (which is presumed for this purpose to be ideal, though it must be stressed that at present there is no language which does not still require to be swept by many maids with many (preferably electronic) mops before such an ideal description is obtained) has given us the determining features of all forms in Language 2, and document two has shown us what forms of Language 2 can be predicted with what probability to be the translation equivalents of what forms of Language 1. (However ideal document two, there can never be certainty of equivalence throughout; the reason will be clear from document one, which shows that it is not the case that all languages are determined by the same features differently distributed, but that features which are determining for one language are nondetermining for another.) The final output of the translation process is thus a result of three processes, in two of which the two languages impinge upon one another. First we have translation equivalence, second, equivalence of determining features, third, operation of particular determining features in the target language. This is not necessarily a temporal order of procedure, but it may be illustrated in this way: suppose a Chinese sentence beginning *ta zai nali zhu-le xie shihou jiu ...* Translation equivalence might give a positive probability of

Chinese non-final perfective = English simple past perfective: *zhu-le* = *lived*. (This identification is chosen for the sake of example, and is based merely on probability.) Equivalence of determining features overrules this by showing that some feature such as "past time reference relative to absolute past time" determines English past in past perfective: *zhu-le* = *had lived*. A particular determining feature of English, however, connected with the non-terminal nature of the time reference (which is irrelevant in Chinese) demands the imperfective: so we get *When he had been living there for some time* ...

Now the 'ideal' translation may be thought of as the contextual one: it is that in which the form in Language 2 operates with identical effect in the identical context of situation as the form in Language 1. Theoretically, the one thing which it is not necessary to have to arrive at such a translation is the original: the first of the three processes above can be left out. But in translation in practice, one always has the original (the text in the source language), and what one does not have is the complete set of its determining features. The human translator may implicitly abstract these from the text, but this may not be wholly possible in any given instance, since the text may not contain indications of them all; and in any case the computer cannot do this until we have the complete ideal linguistic description. In mechanical translation the second of the three processes becomes the least important because it can be least well done; and the computer must concentrate on the first and the third: that is, the translation equivalence between source and target language, and the particular determining features of the latter. The less use made of comparative systematization, the more use must be made of the particular systematization of the target language. In translation as in any other linguistic composition a great deal is determined internally, by the structure of the target language; if the source language is going to yield only, or mainly, translation equivalence (as it must unless, as said above, we are to have a different description for each language in each pair in which it occurs) maximum determination must be extracted from within the target language.

For this we require a systematic description of the target language, which will be the same whatever the source language, since it is accounting for features that are quite independent of the latter. It is quite clear what this means for the grammar: a formal grammatical analysis which covers the description of the relations between grammar and context to the extent of those contextual features which can be abstracted **from the language text** (not those which are dependent on situational features not themselves derivable from the text). In the example given above, we have to get both the past in past (*had lived*) and the imperfective (*been living*) from English context-grammar alone (if you try to get them through the source language text the procedure will be immensely complicated and will depend on transfer grammar, thus losing generality, since each source language will then have to have a different treatment for every target language, i.e. the Chinese of Chinese-English will be different from the Chinese of Chinese-Russian, without in any way simplifying the treatment of the target language): to get the English tense-aspect complex out of the English is relatively simple, whereas to get it out of the Chinese is absurdly complicated. There will be in other words a mechanical grammar of target English to account for the internally determined features of the language. One has only to think of source texts in Italian, Russian, Chinese and Malay to realize how much of the grammar of the English output would be left undetermined by the highest common factor of their grammatical translation equivalences.

Lexis

The problem has been discussed so far in terms of grammar, but it arises in the same way with the lexis. The first stage is likewise one of translation equivalence, the second stage is the use of the determining features of the target language. The question is: how can the lexis be systematized so as to permit the use of **particular** (non-comparative) determining features, and especially, is it possible to operate the second stage to such an effect that the first stage can be almost restricted to a one-to-one translation equivalence (in other words, that the number of translation homonyms can be kept to a minimum, to a number that will be as small as, or smaller than, the number of historically recognized homographic (or, with a spoken input, homophonic) words in the language), which would clearly be of great advantage to the computer?

What is required is a systematic arrangement of the lexis which will group together those words among which some set of "particular" determining features can be found to operate. Any arrangement based on orthography or phonology is obviously useless, since orthography plays no, and phonology very little, part in determining the choice of a given word at a given time. A grammatical arrangement by word classes adds nothing if, as is proposed, grammatical features are to be carried over separately as non-exponential systems, since classification is also in the main irrelevant to word determination, and where it is not, the grammar will do all that is required. (This merely amounts to saying that we cannot use grammar to determine the lexis because grammar will only determine the grammatical features of the lexis.) The form of grammatical systematization suggested above gives the clue: what is needed is a lexical arrangement with contextual reference. The lexis will be ordered in series of contextually related words, each series forming a contextually determined system, with the proviso that by context we mean (a) collocation, that is specifically word context, the statistically measured tendencies for certain words to occur in company with certain others, and (b) those non-collocational features of the context which can be abstracted from the language text.

The lexis gives us two points of advantage over the grammar, in reality two aspects of the same advantage, which arise from the fact that lexis reflects context more directly than does grammar. In the first place, one-to-one translation equivalence has a higher probability of resulting in translation in lexis than in grammar – there are whole regions of the lexis, especially in technical vocabulary, where it works with near certainty; and in the second place, where there is no *term* (word) equivalence there is usually at least *system* (series) equivalence. So we exploit the first advantage by giving one-to-one equivalence at the first stage, and the second advantage by the "series" form of arrangement.

Thesaurus

The type of dictionary in which words are arranged in contextually determined series is the thesaurus. Each word is a term in one, or more than one, such series, and the translation equivalents provided by the first stage of the dictionary program function as **key-words** leading in to the second, the thesaurus, stage. Each word will pass through the thesaurus, which will either leave it unchanged or replace it by another word in the series.

Each thesaurus entry, that is one series with its key-word(s), thus forms a closed system among whose terms a choice is to be made. We are already in the target language as a result of the translation equivalence of the first stage, and a pre-thesaurus output would be an interlingual form of the target language including some elements which were not words – since some key-words are in fact non-verbal symbols introduced to deal with the "partial operator" sections of the lexis, to which we shall return later.

By the time the thesaurus stage of the dictionary program is reached we have one word in the target language (more than one word in the case of homonyms, and a symbol in the case of partial operators). We may also have a general context indicator from the source language of the type that most mechanical translation programs have envisaged, giving a clue to the generalized class of discourse in which we are operating. How much is still left to be provided from the resources of the target language itself can be gauged from a few specimens of non-technical railway terminology given below. Only four languages have been used, English, French, Italian and Chinese; and three of these are in close cultural contact; and yet there is so much overlap that we have a sort of unbroken "context-continuum" ranging (in English) from *railway station* to *coach*. It is admittedly something of a *tour de force*, in that the words used are not the only possible ones in each case, and adequate translation would result, at least in some instances, from the use of other words. But if we consider each language in turn as a source language, each one is a possible non-translation form, and a one-to-one word equivalence would clearly not result in translation between any pair of languages, let alone among the whole four. Moreover, the sentences used were not chosen as containing words especially liable to overlap, but merely because the present writer happens to be interested in railways and in the linguistics of railway terminology.

Each sentence is given in English, because it is the language of this chapter, together with a brief indication of situational or linguistic context where necessary. The underlined English words, and the words in the French, Italian and Chinese lists, are contextual translations of each other: that is, words which a speaker of each language would be likely to use in an utterance having the same 'meaning' (i.e. the same place in the same sequence of linguistic and non-linguistic activity) in the same situation. They are considered as operating in a spoken text, where much of the context is situational; but in a written text, which we envisage for mechanical translation at present, the absence of "situation" is compensated by a fuller linguistic context, which is what the computer can handle. It should be stressed that, although only one word is given in each case, this is not

12

regarded as the only possible word but merely as one which would not be felt to be out of place (this is in fact implicit in the criterion of 'the same meaning', since if it was felt to be out of place it would alter the context-sequence).

Finally, the English is British English; I do not know the American terms, but I suspect that even between British and American English there would be no one-to-one translation equivalence!

As with grammar, the systematization of the features determining the choice among terms in a lexical series requires a vast amount of statistical work, the result of which will in fact be the simplest statement of the lexical redundancy of the language. This redundancy is reflected in the fact that the terms in the commutation system operating at any given point in a context sequence are very restricted. (Two terms in a system are said to commute if one can be replaced by the other in identical context with change of meaning. If no such replacement is possible, or if replacement is not accompanied by change of meaning, they do not commute.) The restrictions can be systematized along a number of different dimensions, which will vary for different languages. The sort of dimensions that suggest themselves may be exemplified from the sentences below.

(i) Chinese *huochezhan, chezhan* and *zhan* in (2), (3) and (4) do not commute; they might commute elsewhere (e.g. *huochezhan* and *chezhan*, to a bus driver) but here they are contextually determined along a dimension which we may call "specification", ranging from the most general term *zhan* to the most specific *huochezhan*. In mentalist terms, the speaker or writer leaves out what is rendered unnecessary by virtue of its being either "given" in the context (linguistic or situational) or irrelevant. The computer does not know what is irrelevant – in any case irrelevance is the least translatable of linguistic phenomena – but it does know what is given, and would select *zhan* here if certain words are present in the context (railway terms such as *huoche*, and the *ting* ('stops') of (5)), *chezhan* if there is some reference to a specific form of travel, and *huochezhan* otherwise.

(ii) English *track, line, railway*: the choice in (12), (14) and (16) is not a matter of specification but of classification. Like the three Chinese words, they may denote one and the same physical object; but their connotations are as it were respectively 'ential', functional and institutional. A purely locational context could give *track*, a proper

NON-TECHNICAL RAILWAY TERMINOLOGY

	Situational or Linguistic Context	English	French	Italian	Chinese
1.	Here's the <u>railway station</u> (pointing it out on a map).	railway station	gare	stazione ferroviale	huochezhan
2.	How do I get to the <u>station</u>? (inquiry in the street)	station	gare	stazione	huochezhan
3.	<u>Station</u>, please! (to taxi driver)	station	gare	stazione	chezhan
4.	There's one at the <u>station</u> (on the way to the station, to companion who inquires e.g. about a post office).	station	gare	stazione	zhan
5.	How many <u>stations</u> does it stop at? (on the Underground)	station	station	stazione	zhan
6.	It's two <u>stops</u> further on.	stop	arrêt	fermata	zhan
7.	It doesn't stop at the <u>halts</u> (i.e. only at the staffed stations).	halt	halte	fermata	xiaozhan
8.	Travel in this coach for the country <u>platforms</u>.	platform	point d'arrêt	fermata	yuetai
9.	They're mending the <u>platform</u>.	platform	quai	marciapiede	yuetai
10.	He's waiting on the <u>platform</u>.	platform	quai	marciapiede	zhantai
11.	The train's at <u>Platform</u> 1.	platform	quai	binario	zhantai
12.	I dropped my cigarettes on the <u>track</u> (while waiting at the station).	track	voie	binario	guidao
13.	Don't walk across the <u>line</u>.	line	voie	binario	tiegui
14.	The trains on this <u>line</u> are always late.	line	ligne	linea	lu
15.	There's a bridge across the <u>line</u>.	line	ligne	linea	tielu
16.	He works on the <u>railway</u>.	railway	chemin de fer	ferrovia	tielu
17.	I'd rather go by <u>rail</u>.	rail	chemin de fer	ferrovia	huoche
18.	Let's go and watch the <u>trains</u>.	train	train	treno	huoche
19.	Get onto the <u>train</u>! (standing on platform)	train	train	treno	che
20.	There's no light in this <u>coach</u>.	coach	voiture	vettura	che

name *railway; line* overlaps with both (cf. (13) and (15)) and might be limited to functional contexts such as *main line*.

The word as a term in a thesaurus series is grammatically neutral: it is neutral, that is, as to all grammatical systems, both categories of the word (e.g. number) and word class itself. Since we cannot carry over the classes and other categories of the source language as one-to-one equivalences (e.g. Chinese verb ≠ English verb, Chinese plural ≠ English plural, even if both languages are described with categories named "verb" and "plural"), these are dealt with in the grammatical part of the program and only after having reached the target language do they re-enter the range of features determining word choice. The attempt to handle such categories lexically leads to impossible complexity, since every word category in each source language would have to be directly reflected in the thesaurus.

All mechanical translation programs have carried over **some** word categories non-lexically, word-inflections obviously lending themselves to such treatment. If in the thesaurus program the word is to be shorn of all grammatical features, including word class, the whole of the grammar must be handled autonomously, and the method proposed for this is the lattice program originated and developed by Margaret Masterman and A. F. Parker-Rhodes. The lattice program, which is a mathematical generalization of a comparative grammar (i.e. a non-linguistic abstraction from the description of a finite number of languages), avoids the necessity of the comparative (source-target) identification of word (and other grammatical) categories. The word class of the target language is determined by the L(attice) P(osition) I(ndicator), derived from the grammar of the source language; class is thus not a function of the word as a term in the thesaurus series, nor does the choice of word class depend on comparative word class equivalences.

The autonomy thus acquired by the lexis of the target language allows the thesaurus stage of the dictionary to be the same for one target language whatever the source language, and at the same time permits the maximum use of the redundancy within the target language by allowing different treatment for different sections of the lexis. This would be impossible if word classes were based on translation equivalence, since the thesaurus series could not form closed systems within which determination can operate. If for example one identified particularly (i.e. non-comparatively) a word class "conjunction" in the target language, the redundancy of the conjunction system can only be fully exploited if it is determined (as it is by the LPI) that the choice word must be a term in this system. If we attempted to carry over to Chinese word classes from, say, English, where we could not identify any grouping (let alone class) of words which would have valid translation equivalence with Chinese "conjunction", we should forfeit the redundancy of the Chinese system since the words among which we should have to choose could not be ordered as terms in any lexical series.

The thesaurus admits any suitable grouping of words among which determination can be shown to operate; the grouping may be purely lexical or partly grammatical (i.e. operating in the grammatical system of the target language). It might be that a word class as such, because of the redundancy within it, was amenable to such monosystemic treatment. This is clearly not the case with the "non-operator" (purely lexical) sections of the lexis, such as verbs and nouns in English, but may work with some partial operators. (Pure operators, i.e. words not entering into lexical systems, which are few in any language (since their work is usually done by elements less than words) – Chinese *de* is an example – will not be handled by the thesaurus, but by the lattice program.) The nouns in the above sentences enter into lexical series, but no determination system can be based on their membership in the word class of "noun"; prepositions, on the other hand, which are few in number – and of which, like all partial operators, we cannot invent new ones – can in the first instance be treated as a single lexical grouping.

It is simply because partial operators (which in English would include – in traditional "parts of speech" terms – some adjectives (e.g. demonstratives and interrogatives), some adverbs (those that qualify adjectives), verbal operators, pronouns, conjunctions and prepositions) are in the first instance grammatically restricted that they have a higher degree of overall redundancy than non-operators. Knowing that a noun must occur at a certain point merely gives us a choice among several thousand words, whereas the occurrence of a verbal operator is itself highly restrictive.

An idea of how the thesaurus principle might be applied in a particular instance may be given with respect to prepositions in English. In dealing with the English prepositions we can begin by considering the whole class as a lexical series. We can then distinguish between the **determined** and the **commutable**. Most prepositions are determined in some occurrences and commutable in others. The "determined" prepositions are simply those which cannot commute, and they are of two types: the pre-determined – those determined by what precedes (e.g. *on* in *the result depends on the temperature at* ..., which cannot be replaced, or *to* in ... *in marked contrast to the development of* ..., which could be replaced by *with* but without change of meaning), and the post-determined – those determined by what follows (e.g. *on* in *on the other hand*, or *to* in *to a large extent*). In the system of each type we may recognize one neutral term, pre-determined *of*, and post-determined *to*.

Determined prepositions will be dealt with not as separate words but as grammatical forms of the word by which they are determined. The combination of pre-determining word plus preposition will constitute a separate entry, a transitized form of the determining non-operator (verb, noun or adjective, including adverb formed from adjective), of which the occurrence is determined by the LPI. The features determining the occurrence of these forms are grammatical features of the determining word; they are connected in varying ways with the presence or absence of a following noun (group): *depends / depends on A, a contrast / a contrast with A, liable to A*; but *wake up / wake A (up)*. Which form of the word (with or without preposition) corresponds to which lattice position will be indicated if necessary in the same way as other word class information; in the absence of such indication the transitized form of words which have one is used before a noun. If a verb is not assigned a marked transitized form, it is assumed not to have one, and will be left unaltered in a lattice position that would require a transitized form if there was one; but if a noun or adjective without transitized form occurs in the corresponding lattice position the neutral term *of* is to be supplied. Thus *depend, contrast* (noun) have the transitized forms *depend on, contrast to*; *display, production, hopeful* have no transitized forms, and will thus give *display of (power), production of (machinery), hopeful of (success)*.

Post-determined prepositions are always treated as part of a larger group which is entered as a whole. These are forms like *at least, on the whole, to a large extent*, and are single words for thesaurus purposes. The exception is the neutral term *to* before a verb (the "infinitive" form). This is treated as a grammatical form of the following word (the verb) and will be used only when required by the LPI, e.g. in a two-verb or adjective-verb complex where the first element has no predetermined (or other) preposition: *desires to go* but *insists on going* – all other prepositions require the -ing form of verbs –, *useless to go* but *useless for* (commutable) *experiment*.

Determined prepositions in the English version of the Italian pilot paragraph are:

Pre-determined: of 1–6
Post-determined: at least; on the other hand; in fact; for some time past; above all; to mechanize.

Commutable prepositions operate in closed commutation systems of varying extent (e.g. *plants with / without axillary buds* (two terms only), *walked across / round / past / through / towards* etc. *the field*), and each one may enter into a number of different systems. Those which are lexical variants of a preceding verb are treated as separate lexical items, like the pre-determined prepositions (e.g. *stand up, stand down*, and favourites like *put up with*). The remainder must be translated, and among these also use is made of contextual determination.

The overlap in this class (i.e. among words in source languages which can be translated into words of this class in English) is of course considerable, as one example will show:

Sentences:	English	Italian	Cantonese
He went to London	to	a	
He lives in London	in	a	hai
He came from London	from		hai

We can however set up systems limited by the context in such a way that the terms in different systems do not commute with one another. For example, concrete and abstract: *to / in / from* commute with each other but not with *in spite of / for / without*. Within the concrete we have motion and rest: *to / from* commute with each other but not with *at / on / under*; and time and place: *before / after / until* commute with each other (in some contexts *before / until* do not commute but are grammatically determined) but not with *under / at*.

Commutable prepositions of this type will go through the usual thesaurus program in which they form series on their own (whereas determined prepositions and the "lexical variant" type of commutable prepositions do not); the context will specify in which system we are operating. If the source language has words to which English prepositions are given as translation equivalents, these will as usual be one-to-one (with limited homonymy where necessary: Cantonese *hai* would have to give *be at* (English verb or preposition according to LPI); *from* (preposition only), since on grounds of probability the motion context equivalent of *at* will be motion toward, not away from). Each key-word will in the usual way lead into a series the choice within which will be determined by the context category.

Commutable prepositions in the Italian pilot paragraph are:

Lexical variants:	none	
Free commutables:	with	(It. a, abstract 'with (/without)')
	for	1–4 (It. per, abstract)
	in	(It. in, abstract)

This paragraph is typical in that the freely commutable prepositions are a minority of the total prepositions in the English output.

Thus the thesaurus method, which uses the contextual determination within a language, is applicable to partial operators through the handling of redundancy at the level at which it occurs: where the use of a preposition depends on grammatical or lexical features (considering English forms like *put up with* to be lexical, not contextual, variants) it will be handled accordingly, and not as a term in a lexical preposition series. The method is far from having been worked out in full; the principle on which it rests, that of 'make the language do the work', can only be fully applied after the linguists have done the work on the language.

Chapter Two

LINGUISTICS AND MACHINE TRANSLATION
(1962)

Linguists often like to speak of linguistics as a science. It is true that each one of us may have his own view of exactly what that implies; but it must mean at least that linguistics is to be scrutinized according to some general criteria by which scientific theory and scientific methods are assessed. We should like linguistics to satisfy these criteria, not because the term "science" is a kind of status symbol for an academic subject but because we want to be able to account for linguistic events in a way that is, and can be shown to be, both valid and useful. In the "pure" side of the subject, that known frequently as "general linguistics", what is being sought is a valid and powerful theory, and rigorous methods; while for applied linguistics we need to be able to say things about language that are useful in any field of activity where the study of language is central. It is fair to say, I think, that linguistics has gone some way towards both these goals.

One important area for the application of linguistics is machine translation (for which I will use the affectionate abbreviation MT). Rather surprisingly, it has not always been obvious that MT is, among other things, applied linguistics. In part, this has been because linguistics, or at least that side of linguistics that is relevant to MT, was a fairly new subject without other known applications; in part it is due to the history of MT itself. It is convenient to date MT from the famous 1949 memorandum by Warren Weaver; but its origins include such sources as wartime work on code-breaking, the theoretical study of communication and the development of information theory, and the design and construction of electronic digital computers. It was probably these origins that gave to the early work on MT its particular slant: most of the effort was directed towards problems in electronic engineering and in the coding and transmission of information. This in turn determined the approach of many of those working in the field.

The solution of the relevant engineering and mathematical problems is of course a prerequisite of success in any MT project. But there is another side to the subject, as recognized already in the discussion at the VIIth International Congress of Linguists in London in 1952. This is the application of theory from linguistic science. MT is a problem in applied linguistics, specifically a problem requiring the application of those parts of General Linguistic theory which deal with the systematic description and comparison of languages: descriptive linguistics (known often in America as "synchronic linguistics" and by some people on both sides of the Atlantic as "structural linguistics"), and its recent derivative, comparative descriptive linguistics.

This body of theory is neither "an approach" nor "just common sense", any more than it was common sense which sent Major Gagarin into space, but a specialized scientific theory which, like any other of its kind, has to be learnt. From it are derived the methods for the description and comparison of languages, methods demanding rigorous and consistent application. Since the theory has been worked out and applied by linguists working on a large number of different languages in different parts of the world there are, as in a lot of subjects, divergent "schools"; but the area of agreement among them is far wider and more fundamental than are the divergencies.

The name "linguistics" reflects the independent and autonomous status of the subject as the science of language, that is to say, its categories and methods are not drawn from philosophy or logic or psychology or anthropology or mathematics or communication theory, but from language itself: from, that is, a theory founded on hypotheses that were set up to explain the way language works. Language, for this purpose, is regarded as a unique, patterned form of human social activity, operating in the context of other social activities; and the job of descriptive linguistics is to state the patterns of a language and show how it works. This inevitably gives the linguist a standpoint different from that of his colleagues in any of the other disciplines which study language as part of the material of their own research: his object is to throw light on language, not to use language to throw light on something else. This particularity of the linguistic study of language is especially marked in the study of

21

meaning: this is an essential and inseparable part of linguistic description and is not the same thing as, for example, the psychological or philosophical study of meaning.

Work on MT has brought out very clearly the contrast between the linguistic view of language and some of the views arrived at by looking at language through the lenses of other disciplines. Two opinions current in MT writings on language are that language is a code and that the code is fundamentally binary. Both these views are, from the standpoint of a communication engineer, tenable and useful. From the linguistic standpoint, however, these views are both questionable and unhelpful; and they have hampered MT work because they misrepresent the functioning of language both in its internal relations and in its relations to non-language. A code implies encoding and decoding processes, and a systematic relationship between code and message, which must be a relation between two distinct entities since the message exists independently of the code and does not determine the type of the code. Language, however, does not yield this dichotomy: in language, code and message are one, and there is no relation between two entities one of which can be chosen independently of the other. One may force an analogy, but I do not think it has been shown to be a fruitful one, between the categories of code and message on the one side and those of form and content (or concept) on the other; but concepts are not accessible to study except through linguistic forms and are not present as independent parts of the material, the *text*, that the linguist – or any other student of language – has to work with. The one linguistic process which could be regarded as a special instance of the coding process is that of translation, where a language Ly, the target language, can be said to stand in the relation of a code to a language Lx, the source language; but this is an entirely different point and is clearly not what is meant by those who say that language is a code.

Nor, to take the second point, do the patterns of language operate exclusively in binary oppositions. Grammatical systems, like all closed systems, can of course be stated in binary terms, and this is a convenience for statistical and electronic linguistics. But it is not a general truth about language, and to treat it as such will complicate any piece of work in which language data are being processed. If it is to be capable of rigorous definition and application to natural languages, a linguistic system, which is a pattern of a particular type with certain specific characteristics, must be allowed to have any number of terms. Language is like that. The attempt to force all language systems into binary mould has required recourse to the extreme of saying that the choice of any linguistic item is in binary opposition to the nonchoice of the same item; which is of some significance as a logical proposition but to linguistics is an irrelevant platitude. There happens to be one type of binary opposition that is fundamental to language, that of marked and (formally or contextually) unmarked terms in a grammatical system, or indeed in an open lexical set: an example from grammar would be English

	formally	**contextually**
student	unmarked	marked (=singular)
students	marked (+/s/)	marked (=plural)

which contrasts with Chinese

xuesheng	unmarked	unmarked (=singular or plural)
xueshengmen	marked (+/men/)	marked (=plural).

But not all systems have an unmarked term, and those that do often have more than one marked term; so that this feature, important as it is, is not by itself adequate as a primary dimension for the definition and description of language systems.

To describe a language meaningfully it is necessary to replace the vague generalizations and random observations transported ad hoc from other disciplines with a consistent and comprehensive theory of language; the methods used in description are derived from, and answerable to, this theory. This is no new idea: descriptive linguistics in ancient India was already a specialized study in its own right, and attained a sophistication of theory and rigour of application which were not surpassed in Europe until the present [twentieth] century, and which some descriptions used by learners of languages still fall far short of. It is impossible to describe language without a theory, since some theory, however inadequate, is implicit in all descriptions; but it is quite possible to make a description that is in practice unsystematic, with categories neither clearly interrelated nor consistently assigned. Such a description, however, is difficult to program on a computer, since the computer has no native language (and has had no classroom Latin) to which to relate an agglomeration of ad hoc categories. If the computer is to be expected to translate, then it is all the more essential that it should be provided with descriptions that are both accurate and theoretically valid, since it has to digest not only the descriptions of two languages, but also the rules for the systematic relating of these two descriptions one to the other. It is expected in fact to perform a complex operation of comparative descriptive linguistics, of which translation can be regarded as a special instance.

There are a number of things that can be said about translation from the linguistic point of view. For this it will be necessary to introduce some categories from linguistic theory, the technical terms for which are usually disguised as ordinary words, like "level" and "unit" and "form" and "rank" – linguists, especially European linguists, tend to prefer redefining old terms to coining new ones. *Levels* are the different types of pattern found in language: the two major types are *form*, the meaningful organization of language, and *substance*, the raw material of language; but the total range of levels, with subdivisions, is more complex. We need two levels of form, *grammar* and *lexis*, two of substance, *phonic* and *graphic*, two levels for patterns of the arrangement of substance in form, *phonology* and *graphology* (the two latter pairs, unlike grammar and lexis, being in "either/or" relationship, since language text is either spoken or written), and one level for patterns of the reflection by language of things that are not language, namely *context*. Form and context are the principal levels for the statement of meaning; form is the internal aspect of linguistic patterning, the relation of the parts to each other, context the external aspect, the relation of the formal items to other features of the situations in which language operates. Within form, grammar is the operation of items in closed system contrast, characterized by very complex relations with a small number of terms; lexis the operation of items in open set contrast, very simple relations with large numbers of terms. Much more abstraction is therefore possible in the statement of grammar than in the statement of lexis; in grammar we can recognize not only grammatical *items* but also abstract categories such as *units*, the stretches of differing extent which carry patterns, *structures*, the patterns of arrangement, and *classes*, the groupings of items that behave alike. In lexis, on the other hand, only the items themselves enter into patterned relations.

Translation, as a process, is unidirectional; but a translation, which is the end-product of such a process, is in mutual relation with the original: either of the two texts could replace the other as language activity playing a given part in a given situation. Taken together the two texts constitute a type of comparative description of the two languages, in which the two languages impinge on each other at a number of different levels. We can leave aside phonology and graphology, since these relate the form of a language to its spoken or written substance and are only accidentally relevant to translation within certain pairs of languages. For translation the important levels are those of form, namely grammar and lexis, and that of context. At these levels we have as it were two types of evidence, or two bodies of source material, for the comparison – that is, for the bringing into relation with one another – of the two languages.

On the one hand, there are actual translations; texts in the two languages, the one being translated from the other. These display probabilities of equivalence between items occurring in them. Such probabilities may be stated as simple, unconditioned probabilities, or as conditioned either in sequence or in combination. So one can ask, for example, "what is the most probable tense of the English verbal group in translation of the Russian past tense?"; or "what is the most probable tense of the English verbal group in translation of the Russian past tense if the latter is (a) in a clause preceded by a clause in which the verbal group also had past tense, or (b) combined with perfective aspect?" And of course one can state such probabilities in gradation, from most to least probable, and in quantified form; and one can take into account sequences and combinations of three, four and more features.

On the other hand, there is the material furnished by a comparative analysis of the two languages, in which their formal and contextual features are described by means of a single set of categories. Since descriptive categories are not universals – just because we find something we want to call a "verb" in one language this does not necessarily mean we shall find such a thing in another language – categories used for the comparison of two languages are drawn from the separate description of each. When they are conflated into a single set, degrees of likeness can be stated and measured. By stating the formal and contextual equivalents of grammatical structures and items, and of lexical items, with one set of categories, the comparison brings out the likeness and unlikeness between the two languages. This takes account also of partial equivalence, where correspondence is not one to one but systematic statement is still possible.

For lexis the statement of equivalence between two languages is traditionally made by a bilingual dictionary. The aim of the ideal dictionary could be said to be to state under what circumstances a word in Ly is the contextual equivalent of a word in Lx. The bilingual dictionary faces, in the main, two difficulties. One is the nature of "equivalence": the contextual equivalent is not necessarily the translation equivalent, since the latter is determined not only by contextual meaning but also by formal meaning, that is by the tendency to occur in collocation with other words. This difficulty can be met by extending the concept of a citation to cover not just **a word** in a given collocation but **a collocation** of words: the item for the statement of equivalence would not be *to climb (mountains &c.)*, since the contextual equivalent of *climb* here might not in fact collocate with all the words that are the contextual equivalents of *mountain* (still less with those of the "&c."), but would rather be *to climb a mountain*.

The other difficulty is that the category of ***word*** is not a universal constant. The term "word" is in fact highly misleading. In the first place, even within one language it is used to cover, and thus to conflate, two and sometimes three quite different categories, whose members only partially coincide. The name "word" is given to one of the units in grammar; this unit is then taken as the unit for dictionary entry. But the dictionary exists to state lexical, not grammatical, meaning; what the dictionary should be describing is the ***lexical item***, which is not always coextensive with the grammatical word. In those languages, such as English, which also have an orthographically defined "word" – defined as "that which occurs between two spaces in the script" – the "word" is now a unit on **three** levels and the probability that all three will exactly coincide is even lower. In the second place, even when the dictionary is freed from the tyranny of the grammatical word and allowed to handle the unit that is appropriate to it, the "lexical item", this latter is not a constant across languages. Languages vary very much in their organization of lexical meaning – that is, in how much and what they put into the items that operate in open sets and in collocation relations. This makes it all the more important in comparative description that the lexical item should be properly identified and its meaning stated according to how it works in the language. Since in a dictionary the order of items is linguistically almost random, for comparative purposes the thesaurus, which groups lexical items in their sets, may be a more useful method of lexical description.

In grammar we have as yet no complete comparative descriptions of any pair of languages, since these cannot be produced without prior statistical descriptions of each language, which require facilities that linguists are only just beginning to secure. Such descriptions are now both necessary and possible: necessary to the more effective **application** of linguistics, in MT and elsewhere, but made possible by advances in linguistic **theory**. The distinction is important: the move from qualitative to quantitative description is of no value whatever unless description is anchored in sound and scientific theory. This is why so much work that has gone into the counting of orthographic words in isolation, or into the laborious compilation of tables of occurrences of ill-defined, shifting, supposedly universal and often entirely non-linguistic categories, is sadly unrewarded. No doubt the uselessness of such work has influenced those MT workers who have denied the value of statistical descriptions of language. But once it is realized that linguistic theory can ensure that statements about language are meaningful, and thus turn MT from the hit-and-miss subject it has tended to be into a scientific discipline, such descriptions fall into place. It is not merely that statistical descriptions are needed for future progress in linguistic theory and method; they are of direct value in application. This is true even in the application of linguistics to language teaching: for example, all textbook accounts of the English so-called "phrasal verbs" are unsatisfactory, their operation being such that only quantitative analysis will yield an adequate classification. How much the more is it true of MT: translation is essentially a 'more likely / less likely' relation, and if a computer is to translate adequately it cannot operate on yes/no evidence alone.

Grammatical equivalence between two languages can be displayed most adequately, therefore, by means of quantitative studies of the grammar of each. Such equivalence must furthermore be related to the *rank* scale: the scale of grammatical units, of which the *word* is one. These units are the stretches into which language text is cut when grammatical statements are being made about it. Again they are not universals: they must be recognized afresh for each language. When we compare two languages we cannot link the languages as a whole; we select for comparison items from within them – and not only items, of course, but abstract categories (classes, structures and so on) of which the items are *exponents*. These items, and the categories set up in abstraction from them, must be related to the grammatical units of which they are members.

So for comparative purposes we need first to relate the *units* of the two languages to each other on the basis of probability of translation equivalence. If we can say, for example, that a "sentence" in Lx can usually be translated by a sentence in Ly – this being implied when we call the two units, one in Lx and the other in Ly, by the same name – then we can try to make a systematic statement to account for the occasions when this does not work. Suppose for illustration that we can describe Lx and Ly, separately, each with a system of five grammatical units, which we will call, in descending taxonomic order, "sentence, clause, group, word, morpheme". Then a clause, for example, in Lx will normally, but not always, be translated by a clause in Ly. Grammatical equivalence, in a comparative description, can be sought and stated at the rank of any one of these units: each must be taken by itself, since each has its own structures, classes and systems through which to display the formal similarities and differences between the two languages, and its own set of items as possible translation equivalents. If Lx, for example, makes a class distinction at the rank of the group between verbal group and nominal group, does Ly make the same distinction? And if so are the items which are exponents of the verbal group in Lx always translated by items which are exponents of the verbal group in Ly?

Lexical equivalence is not to be sought exclusively at any rank in the grammar. While the reason why, in the grammar of any language, we call one of the units "word" is that that unit, more than any other, yields lexical items, what defines the lexical item is not the fact that it is grammatically a word – it may not be – but the fact that it cannot be fully described by the grammatical categories. The latter account for the **closed systems** of language, and the items entering into them, this being the essential characteristic of grammar. One important consequence of the difference between grammar and lexis is that information theory, which is entirely appropriate to the statement of grammatical meaning – since information is a property of closed systems – is at present no use for the study of lexis: there is no way of quantifying the information carried by an open set.

As an illustration of the translation process, in the Appendix are given two sentences, each in both a Chinese and a Russian version. These sentences are shown segmented into their successive lower units: clauses, groups, words and morphemes, with each boundary implying all those below it (a group boundary must also be a word and morpheme boundary, and so on). The segmentation has been made to display maximum likeness, as in a comparative description of the two languages; it is also oversimplified in two ways: first, lineally discrete segments have been recognized throughout, though in fact grammatical units overlay one another (e.g. the English word *ran* consists of two morphemes, but these do not occur as one following the other), and second, **rank-shifting** has been avoided where possible. **Rank-shift** is the operation of one unit in the structure of a unit of lower rank: e.g. a clause by definition operates in sentence structure, but in *the man who came to dinner, who came to dinner* is a rank-shifted clause operating inside a nominal group.

Each sentence is then "translated" at each rank into English: first each morpheme is taken separately, then each word, and so on. In each case the English equivalent **item** is one which might turn out – at a guess: the counting has not been done – to be the most frequent translation equivalent **at that rank**: the one which would be the first choice for entry in a bilingual "dictionary" of morphemes, words, groups &c. Similarly the grammatical **pattern** chosen is that which might be the most frequent translation equivalent at the rank concerned. (The concept "most frequent translation equivalent" for a ***grammatical item*** in isolation, such as English *the* or *-ing*, is however inapplicable; such items are here symbolized "X" until their incorporation into higher units.) If we start from the morpheme, we can follow the translation step by step up the rank scale, each equivalent being adjusted as it finds itself co-occurring with certain other items, in a certain grammatical relation, in the unit next above. So for example, Chinese *tie*, as a morpheme, would most frequently be translated *iron*; when it is taken as part of the word into which it enters, this translation is the one most likely to appear (as when it is a word on its own, or in the words *tieqi = ironware* or *shengtie = cast iron*); elsewhere other equivalents must be chosen (*gangtie = steel, tielu = railway*). Each step can be regarded as a process in which the equivalent is retained unless positive contrary indications are found in the next unit.

It appears clearly that, while equivalence can be stated, in terms of probabilities, for all ranks, translation in the accepted sense does not occur below the rank of the clause, and a good translation needs to be based on the sentence as its unit. So-called "literal" translation is, roughly, translation at group rank, or at a mixture of group and word.

Theoretically, it would be possible for MT to proceed by means of a sentence dictionary, all possible sentences of Lx being entered, together with their translation equivalents in Ly. Since, in the scientific and other registers that we are interested in translating, a sentence is hardly ever repeated in its lexico-grammatical entirety, this is a practical impossibility. By the separation of grammar from lexis it becomes, with present-day computer storage, at least conceivable. Sentences containing identical sequences of lexical items (but differing in grammar) might recur, and sentences with identical sequences in grammar (but differing lexically) certainly do: regularly in the sense of 'having the same primary grammatical **structure**', at least down to the rank of the word; even the same sequences of grammatical **items** probably turn up now and again.

The illustration in the Appendix shows, for one of the English sentences, the grammatical and lexical material separated out. I (a) is a linear statement of the grammatical structures at all ranks; I (b) shows the grammatical items which are the exponents of each of the elements of structure. II gives the sequence of lexical items. From the point of view of linguistic theory, such separation is quite justified: indeed grammatical description and lexical description must proceed independently at first, since different relations (and therefore different theories) are involved – though description is not complete until the two levels have been related. The weakness from the point of view of MT, however, would be that in translation there must be constant cross-reference between the grammar and the lexis, since in all languages some grammatical items can only be identified by reference to lexical ones, and vice versa. For example, only the grammar of the English sentence shows which of a number of lexical items *part* is; conversely only the lexical identification of *part* allows us to say whether it is singular noun or plural verb.

In general, however, the unit selected as the basis for MT has been way down the rank scale, far below the sentence: usually the word or the morpheme, or a combination of both (especially where the source language is Russian). The use of the word or morpheme yields, by comparison with the sentence or clause, inventories of manageable size. At the same time it involves complex programs for the selection among possible equivalents, usually based on items in the immediate environment (though where grammar is involved **structures** are far more powerful, because more general), plus routines for reordering the components of the units above the translation unit. So for example the morpheme/word *chang* must be identified both lexically, as translatable by *long* – e.g. by collocation with *gong-li* 'kilometre'; and grammatically, as a finite intransitive verb 'is/are long' – which can be shown by its association with the item *gong* 'altogether', a member of a small class of words which can only precede a finite verb, but is more usefully shown (since this will cover a much greater number of instances) by the identification of the clause structure.

In fact there is no reason why any one unit should be taken as the sole basic unit for translation. In describing a language we give no special priority either to the morpheme or to the sentence: all units are equally "basic". In translation too we can handle each of the units, and "shunt" from one to another, taking advantage of the highly specific way in which the units can be shown, in the theory of grammar, to be interrelated.

If we analyse the translation process with "translation equivalence" regarded as linked to the grammatical rank scale, we can distinguish three stages in it. These are not of course discrete steps taken one after the other, but rather abstractions useful to the understanding of the translation process and of "a translation" as its end-product. First, there is the selection of the "most probable translation equivalent" for each item at each rank, based on simple frequency. Second, there is the conditioning effect of the surrounding text in the source language on these probabilities: here grammatical and lexical features of the unit next above are taken into account and may (or may not) lead to the choice of an item other than the one with highest overall probability. Third, there is the internal structure of the target language, which may (or may not) lead to the choice of yet another item as a result of grammatical and lexical relations particular to that language: these can be viewed as brought into operation similarly by step-by-step progression up the rank scale. Stage three is purely descriptive; the source language no longer plays any part here. The weighting of these (descriptive) factors from the structure of the target language against the (comparative) factors drawn from the source language is one of the major theoretical problems, analogous to the weighting of input against internally conditioned probabilities in automatic speech analysis.

As an example, consider the translation of the item *duo* in the Chinese version of the first sentence in the Appendix. As a morpheme it is most likely to require, in written English, the rendering *many*, though there are a number of other possible equivalents. When it turns out, by reference to the unit next above, that *duo* is here a complete word, not part of a word, it becomes more likely that it is a verb, to be rendered *are many*. This version is clearly unlikely to survive for long, and in many examples would be replaced at clause rank by *there are many*, on internal grounds: English would transform *the problems are many* into *there are many problems*. In this example, however, when we go one further up the rank scale, the place of *duo* in group structure shows that it stands to the numeral in a relationship rendered in English by the addition of *than* : *many than 23,000*. The rules of English require that in the structure

31

of which this is an example the comparative form (which has no item equivalent in Chinese) should be selected: *more than*. A more sophisticated program might alter this at clause rank to *over*, but this could not be generalized to all such occurrences of *duo* : *over three o'clock* is not acceptable. What is as it were left over to stage three will in any case depend on the comparison of the target language with the source language: if one was translating *trois jours* from (written) French, the English plural form *days* could be arrived at by translation from *jours*, whereas in the translation of the Chinese equivalent *san tian* the use of the plural form *days* in concord with numeral form *three* would appear as an internal feature of English.

The human translator performs all stages of the operation at all ranks in a single process. A computer program, if it is to achieve a reasonable degree of generality even in one pair of languages in one direction, may have to handle them separately. Whether it does so or not, in either case it will need to shunt up and down among the different units of the rank scale as the translation advances towards the final choice of equivalent. Units and their grammatical structures have to be identified; and this means that a lot of prior linguistic research needs to be done. For a long time it was not recognized by many workers in MT that description must precede translation: that the main function of computers for the first few years was to produce detailed descriptions of the languages between which it was proposed to translate. This is now well known, and we have centres of machine research where descriptive work is being done which will make large-scale MT a possibility in practice, as it always has been in theory.

The studies required are on these lines. First, particular descriptions, including quantitative statements, of each of the languages concerned: both (a) formal statistics, especially grammatical – e.g. occurrences of classes, and of sequences of classes, of each unit, but also lexical – occurrences of lexical items **in collocation** (most linguistic statistics to date has been lexical and has ignored sequences) and (b) statements linking the formal occurrences to the contextual meanings of the forms concerned. (Contextual meaning itself cannot be stated in quantitative terms, but – since it is dependent on form – it requires for MT to be based on statistical analysis in grammar and lexis.) Second, comparative descriptions, of pairs or groups of the languages concerned: either (a) direct comparison, suitable for a program concerned with only one pair of languages such as Russian-English, or (b) indirect comparison via a machine interlingua, for a general program to be adapted, with insertion of appropriate dictionaries, to an increasing number of different languages. The machine interlingua would be not a natural language nor an artificial language but a mathematical construct serving as a transit code between any pair of natural languages. It would of course have no output, and would reduce the total number of programs very considerably – for example from 90 to 20 if it was desired to translate each way between each pair from among ten different languages. The interlingua approach, though not generally favoured in the past, has much to recommend it for long-term application, giving as it does more scope for exploiting the power of linguistic theory. It is also likely to be of great benefit to that theory, since it could yield – not universal descriptive categories, which would be so weak as to be useless, but – a general frame of reference for the comparative categories which have to be set up when two languages are formally compared. It is not only MT which needs comparative descriptions; they are essential to other applications of linguistics, and nowhere more than in foreign-language teaching. So far, however, only MT has had the necessary facilities. It would be a pity if specialists in this important subject failed to make maximum use of the achievements of all its contributory disciplines.

Appendix

A. "Rank by rank" English translation of Chinese and Russian sentences.

Conventions:

///	sentence boundary
//	clause boundary
/	group boundary
(space)	word boundary
–	morpheme boundary
[[ ]]	boundary of rank-shifted clause
[ ]	boundary of rank-shifted group
1	morpheme equivalents
2	word equivalents
3	group equivalents

4   clause equivalents

5   sentence equivalents

X   grammatical item

(PN)   proper name

/// [Zhong-guo	di]	tie-lu /		gong	chang /
1 (PN) country	X	iron	way	altogether	long
2 China	X	railway		altogether	is/are + long
3 of China		railway		is/are altogether long	
4 the railways of China are altogether more than 23,000 kilometres in length					
5 The railways of China are altogether more than 23,000 kilometres in length, of which the greater part is in the Northeast Provinces.					

2	wan	3		qian	duo	gong-li //
1 2	ten + thousand	3		thousand	many	metric	mile
2 20 + thousand		3 + thousand			are + many	kilometre
3 more than 23,000 kilometres						

qi	da	bu-fen /		shi /	zai	dong-bei ///
1 thereof	great	part	share	X	at	east	north
2 thereof	is/are+ great	part		X	is/are + at	northeast
3 the greater part thereof				X	is/are in the northeast	
4 the greater part thereof is/are in the northeast						

/// Obšč-aja		dlin-a /	železn-ych dorog /		Kita-ja /	
1 general	X	long X	iron	X	(PN)	X
2 general		length	of + iron	of + ways	of + China	
3 the overall length			of railways		of China	
4 the overall length of the railways of China is over 23,000 kilometres						
5 The overall length of the railways of China is over 23,000 kilometres, of which the greater part is in the Northeast Provinces.						

ravn-a /		23 [	s	ličn-im]	tysjač-am /	
1 equal	X	23	with	extra X	thousand	X
2 is + equal		23	with	with + extra	to + thousand	
3 is equal		to 23	over		thousand	

kilometr-ov //	bol'š-aja ich	část' /	na-chod-it-sja /
1 kilometre X	great X	their	part X	on go/come X X
2 of + kilometres	great	their	part	is + found
3 kilometres	the greater part of them		is found
4	the greater part of them is in the Northeast Provinces		

v provinci-jach /	Sever-o-vostok-a ///
1 in	province X	north X east X
2 in	province	of + northeast
3 in the provinces	of the Northeast

/// wo-men /	suo kan-jian di //	bi-jiao /
1 I X	X	look see X	compare	compare
2 we	X	see X	compare
3 we	what / which see	compare with
4 what we see		compared with what we
5 What we saw was even more interesting than what we had heard before.		

wo-men /	yi-qian /	suo ting-jian	di //
1 I X	X	before	X	listen see X
2 we	before	X	hear X
3 we	before	what / which hear
4 heard before		

geng	you /	yi-si	///
1 X	have	mean	think
2 still + more	have	significance
3 have even more	significance
4 is/ are even more interesting		

/// vs-jo	to //	č-to /	my	u-vid-el-i //
1 all X	that	what X	we	by	see X X
2 all	that	what	we	saw
3 all		what	we saw	
4 all that		what we saw		
5 All that we saw was far more interesting than what we had heard before.				

gorazd-o	interesn-eje	/	to-go
1 good + at | X	interesting | X		that | X
2 far	more + interesting		of + that
3 is / are far more interesting			of that
4 is / are far more interesting than that			

[[č -to /	my	slyš-al-i /	ran-še]] ///
1 what | x	we	hear | X | X	early X
2 what	we	heard	earlier
3 what	we heard		earlier
4 what we heard before			

B. Grammatical and lexical features of an English sentence

/// The railway-s [of [China]] are / altogether /

more [than [23,000 kilo-metre-s [in [length]]]] //

[of [which]] the great-er part /is /in [the North-east Province-s] ///

I (a): Linear statement of sentence, clause and group structure

/// α/S dhq (/pn (/h)) /P h /A h /C e = hq (/pn

(/ohq (/pn (/h)))) // β / B = S q (/pb = n (/d=h)) deh

/ P h /A = C pn (/dsh) ///

I (b): Sequence of grammatical items

The ( )s of ( ) are ( ) more + than (numeral) ( )s in ( )

of which the ( )er ( ) is in the ( ) ( ) ( )s

II: Sequence of lexical items

railway China altogether 23,000 kilometre length great part northeast province

PART TWO

PROBABILISTIC GRAMMAR AND THE CORPUS

EDITOR'S INTRODUCTION

The chapters in this section were published fairly recently, in the period between 1989 and 2003. However, their basic premise, i.e. that a linguistic system is inherently probabilistic in nature, originated much earlier on when as a young language teacher in his twenties, Professor Halliday became interested in the probabilities associated with grammatical choices. Subsequently, his early work in the late 1950s on Chinese grammar took this interest a step further. Drawing on the fourteenth-century Chinese version of the *Secret History of the Mongols*, he "counted every instance of those grammatical categories that [he] had been able to resolve into systems". The basis for undertaking this quantitative work was "the principle that frequency in text instantiated probability in the system".

Chapter Seven gives an excellent account of the development of Professor Halliday's interest in "the quantitative aspect of grammatical systems" from these early beginnings, on to his work in machine translation at the Cambridge Language Research Unit, through to the early 1990s when he spent some time working with the COBUILD project at the University of Birmingham. It was there he collaborated with one of their research staff, Zoe James, in a study whose findings are reported on in a paper which appears as Chapter Six in this present volume: *A quantitative study of polarity and primary tense in the English finite clause* (1993). Their aim, as Professor Halliday explains, was not simply to count things, but to test "the hypothesis that grammatical systems fell largely into two types: those where the options were equally probable – there being no 'unmarked term', in the quantitative sense; and those where the options were skew, one term being unmarked". They carried out their investigation by looking at the two systems of polarity and primary tense in the COBUILD corpus.

If indeed the linguistic system is inherently probabilistic then, as Professor Halliday notes in Chapter Three of this volume, *Towards probabilistic interpretations* (1991), originally a paper presented at the Sixteenth International Systemic Congress, "the grammar (that is, the theory of grammar, the **grammatics**) has to be paradigmatic: it has to be able to represent language as **choice**, since probability is the probability of 'choosing' (not in any conscious sense, of course) one thing rather than another". Just as Firth's concept of system provides the kind of paradigmatic model of grammar required for a prob-abilistic interpretation of linguistic phenomena, so too corpus lin-guistics supplies the methodological means for collecting "evidence of relative frequencies in the grammar, from which can be estab-lished the probability profiles of grammatical systems" (Chapter Four, *Corpus studies and probabilistic grammar* 1991).

Corpus linguistics is as much about theory-building as it is about data-gathering. "Interrogating the corpus," as Halliday calls it in Chapter Five, *Language as system and language as instance: the corpus as a theoretical construct* (1992a), can extend beyond finding simple fre-quencies, to investigating how those frequencies break down according to register – register variation being defined as systematic variation in probabilities in the environment of some specific con-figuration of field, tenor, and mode; or to asking "how far the probability of selecting one term in a given system is affected by previous selections made within the same system" – e.g. "what is the effect on the probability of active/passive of choosing either declarative or interrogative in the same clause?"; or even to looking into whether there is an increase in complexity over time.

In Chapter Eight, *The spoken language corpus: a foundation for grammatical theory* (2002), Professor Halliday explains what it is about the spoken language corpus that makes it "a primary resource for enabling us to theorize about the lexicogrammatical stratum in language – and thereby about language as a whole". Not only is casual, spontaneous speech processed "at furthest remove from conscious attention", it is also "the most complexly intertwined with the ongoing socio-semiotic context". Because there are patterns that occur in speech and not in writing, "the fuller picture" of the sys-temic, creative potential in language "will only emerge from more corpus studies of naturally occurring spoken language". Each and every instance that together constitutes the corpus reveals the potential of the underlying system of language – the 'langue'. "The instance," writes Professor Halliday, "is valued as a window on to the system: the potential that is being manifested in the text."

Chapter Three

TOWARDS PROBABILISTIC INTERPRETATIONS (1991)

At the 13th International Systemic Workshop in Sydney in 1987, Jay Lemke spoke about cladistics, the study of how systems change through time; and he outlined models of two of the fundamental processes of change: the evolution of species, and the growth cycle of individual specimens. Here I want to follow up on two aspects of Lemke's observations, one general and the other specific. (His paper was entitled "Semantics, ideology and change".)

Let me begin with a very general point. The twentieth century has been the age of the disciplines, when knowledge was organized into subjects each having its own domain, its own concept of theory, and its own body of method. As usually happens in history, what began as a strength, as the opening up of a new potential, gradually – as the potential was realized – became a constraint; and the energy that had gone into creating these structures has had to be diverted into tearing them down again. But all systematic knowledge implies some form of structure; so something has to take their place; and what are emerging are structures of another kind, this time not disciplinary but thematic. Here the organizing concept is not the object that is being investigated – the "field" of study – but the kinds of question that are being asked. Cladistics is one such theme. In cladistics, the questions are about how systems change; the systems being studied might be cells, or human societies, or galaxies, but the same questions can be raised with reference to them all.

The thematic organization of knowledge is not a new idea; the earliest instance in Western thought was mathematics, where the theme was that of measuring things. Whatever you were investigating, if you studied it by using measurement you were doing mathematics. In the nineteenth century, evolution became a theme of this kind; it embodied the concept of history, the "arrow of time" which had been missing from the physical sciences and which they were now ready to bring back. But the human sciences were not ready for it. They still lacked the sense of a **system**, a model of how any form of organization persists; so in the following period they developed their own theme, that of structuralism. Change had to be taken off the agenda so that we could study how human systems were organized. Next came the theme of semiotics, the investigation of how things mean; this was clearly a relevant theme for the study of language, one which added a new dimension by contextualizing it within a wider universe of semogenic phenomena. (I am less certain about the status of cognitive science, which seems to me more like a generalized discipline than a theme – macro rather than meta in its relation to the subject-based categories of knowledge.) And then, of course, cladistics, the example from which I started.

So in packing up for the move into the twenty-first century we are changing the way knowledge is organized, shifting from a disciplinary perspective towards a thematic one; and this takes me into the more specific line of argument that I want to develop out of Lemke's discussion. This concerns the cladistics of language: the way language persists, and also changes, over the course of time.

From the point of view of European structuralism, a human system was a nexus of paradigmatic and syntagmatic relations that could be construed from the way they were manifested in patterns of behaviour. Saussure's langue/parole was one of the first formulations of this view. This clearly puts the system itself in a synoptic perspective. It is "held together" by various metaphors: equilibrium, functional load, and the like. By contrast, the behaviour – the text, if we are talking about language – is viewed dynamically. This contrast is made explicit in Hjelmslev's "system/process" interpretation. Obviously the system changes; but it moves slowly along the time track, like a glacier, so the synoptic perspective, which enables us to examine it in fine detail, does not noticeably distort it. The text, on the other hand, is like the glacier stream, the water flowing out of the glacier; the natural perspective on text is a dynamic one, especially if our prototype of it is spoken rather than written text.

It is clear that there is a complementarity here, and that each terminal – the code, and the behaviour – can be viewed from either perspective; and ultimately have to be, as Martin has pointed out

(Martin 1985), if the structuralist model is to be retained. Of course, the synoptic and dynamic positions cannot be fixed and determinate; they are acted out in too many ways. As soon as one admits syntagmatic relations into the system (as opposed to modelling it purely paradigmatically), one is taking on a dynamic commitment; while on the other hand syntagmatic relations in text are usually represented as constituent structure, which is a synoptic concept. To take another example, the metafunctional categories can be viewed synoptically as the form of organization of the semantics and lexicogrammar; or else dynamically as currents flowing through a stratified semiotic system. But questions about change suggest a predominantly dynamic perspective. How do we incorporate **change** into the structural linguistic concept of a system?

Lemke (1984) has characterized human, social systems as *dynamic open systems* which have the property of being metastable: that is, they persist only through constant interaction with their environment, and hence are in a constant state of change. It seems clear that a language is a system of this kind. In what senses, then, does a language interact with its environment? This can only be through its instantiation in text. The "environment" of the system is its context of culture; but the processes whereby it can be said to "interact with" this environment are just those of people talking and listening.

There are three different dynamics involved in these processes (Halliday 1988). One is that just referred to: the history of the system itself, as it persists by changing through time. This would presumably be change of an evolutionary kind. The second is the history of the individual construing the system: the dynamic of ontogenesis. This seems to be change in the form of growth, maturation and eventual death. Then, thirdly, there is the history of the instance: the dynamic of the unfolding of a text. The text is a semiotic event, not a system in the way that a language, and an individual "languager", can be said to be kinds of systems. But it is precisely this event, or rather the universe of countless such events, that **constitute** the system of language and give it its metastable form.

But of course these events are not countless. The system may have infinite potential; but it engenders a finite body of text, and text can be counted. Thus, we can make a reasonable assessment of the quantity of text that is typically involved in ontogenesis: how many instances a child of a given age, growing up in a given environment (say, a monolingual family) will have heard of a given phenomenon (say, syllables, or clauses). This provides an insight into how the system is construed by an individual learner: how text becomes system where the dynamic is one of growth.

This is one context – that of construing a semiotic system in the sense of learning it, as a child learns its mother tongue – for which we need to know about frequency in text. The other is so that we can explain how the system changes: the mechanism of metastability in a semiotic system, where the dynamic is one of evolution. Consider a physical system such as that of climate. This is instantiated in the form of weather: climate is the langue, weather the parole. Take any one component of climate: say, temperature. The exact temperature at any one place at any one moment of time seems to be of little significance; but when at many different places the daily minimum and maximum go up by an average of one degree a decade for five decades, we say that the climate is changing. This is not because no such temperatures had ever occurred before; no doubt they had. But now the probability has changed. In fact, every single instance alters the probabilities of the system in some measure; but such perturbations are too small to be taken account of, and mostly cancel each other out. When they build up to form a trend, however, we recognize that the **system** is undergoing change.

Frequency in text is the instantiation of probability in the system. A linguistic system is inherently probabilistic in nature. I tried to express this in my early work on Chinese grammar, using observed frequencies in the corpus and estimating probabilities for terms in grammatical systems (1956, 1959). Obviously, to interpret language in probabilistic terms, the grammar (that is, the theory of grammar, the *grammatics*) has to be paradigmatic: it has to be able to represent language as **choice**, since probability is the probability of "choosing" (not in any conscious sense, of course) one thing rather than another. Firth's concept of "system", in the "system/structure" framework, already modelled language as choice. Once you say "choose for polarity: positive or negative?", or "choose for tense: past or present or future?", then each of these options could have a probability value attached.

Shannon and Weaver, in their *Mathematical Theory of Communication* (1963 [1949]), had provided a formula for calculating the information of a system, which I used in an exploratory way for a paper, "Information theory and linguistics", in 1968. This was a valuable concept for linguistics; but structuralist linguists had dismissed it because they had no paradigmatic model and had therefore attempted to relate it to representations of syntagmatic structure, to which it has no relevance at all. Information is a property of a system (in the Firthian sense); not of its individual terms. The system with maximum information is one whose terms are equiprobable; any skewness (departure from equiprobability) involves a reduction in information. Hence a minimally redundant system network would be one in which all systems tended towards equiprobability.

Systems of this kind can be designed; but they do not normally evolve. In a human system, minimally redundant does not mean maximally efficient; and human systems, like evolved systems in general, always incorporate a certain redundancy in some form or other, the skewing of probabilities being one. When I was constructing my original system networks for English in the early sixties (Kress (ed.), 1976[1]), I counted some grammatical frequencies, noting the occurrences of different terms in some of the primary systems, to see if any general principles of frequency distribution suggested themselves.

It was necessary at the start to distinguish between systems of two different kinds: recursive systems, and non-recursive systems.

(1) Recursive systems: those interpreted in metafunctional terms as *logical* – that is, in which the meaning is construed as a generalized semantic relation between pairs of elements, and thus can be selected iteratively. Languages differ (within limits) as regards which meanings they construe as "logical" in this sense; the typical ones are presumably those in the areas of expansion (*i.e., e.g., and, or, then* (time), *so, then* (condition), *yet,* etc.) and, perhaps, projection (*says,*

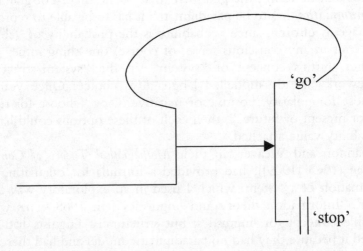

Figure 3.1 General notation for recursive systems

thinks). English is unusual in also treating tense in this way, as a serial relationship in time (present relative to past relative to . . .).

Such systems could generate indefinitely long strings. In fact they are fairly restrained. But while there may sometimes be a qualitative factor involved in limiting their output, as there seems to be in the case of English tense, in general the restraint is quantitative. If we represent the iterative choice as in Figure 3.1, then there is a probability attached to these options, and it is skew: one is more likely to stop than to go around again. Counting English tenses in some conversational texts, I found that the ratio was of the order of magnitude of one in ten. Very roughly approximated, for every occurrence of a 4-term tense (e.g., *had been going to be working*) there were ten 3-term tenses, a hundred 2-term tenses and a thousand 1-term tenses. So I formulated this as a general hypothesis about recursive systems, representing it in a network as Figure 3.2, where system (I) is the logical-semantic relation (e.g. past/present/future) and system (II) is the option of iterating the choice.

(2) Non-recursive systems: those of the other metafunctions. In principle these should be able to range over all probability

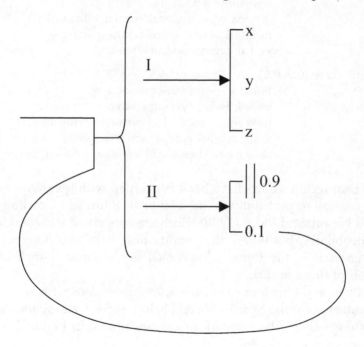

Figure 3.2 Recursive system with probabilities shown

distributions from 0.5/0.5 to approximating 0/1. But this kind of spread seemed to me to be highly unlikely. It would be unlikely for all systems to be equiprobable, since this would not leave enough redundancy. (In fact it could be shown to be impossible, since a network is not a simple taxonomy; there are conjunct and disjunct entry conditions in it.) But it would equally be unlikely for systems to take up all possible distributions of probabilities along the whole continuum from equiprobable to maximally skew.

On the basis of what little counting I had done, I suggested a bimodal distribution. The hypothesis was that systems tended towards one or other of just two types, (i) equiprobable and (ii) skew, with the skew tending towards a ratio of one order of magnitude (which I represented for obvious reasons as nine to one, i.e., 0.9/0.1). This corresponds to one interpretation of the concept of marking: type (i), the equiprobable, have no unmarked term, while type (ii), the skew, have one of their terms unmarked. Expected examples of each type, in English, would be:

(i) equiprobable (0.5/0.5)
        number: singular/ plural
        non–finite aspect: '*to*'/ '*ing*'
        process type: material/mental/relational
        nominal deixis: specific/non–specific
        verbal deixis: modality/tense

(ii) skew (0.9/0.1)
        polarity: positive/negative
        mood: indicative/imperative
        indicative mood: declarative/interrogative
        voice (verbal group): active/passive
        declarative theme: Subject-theme/other theme

Two recent studies have been concerned with text frequency and its relation to probability in the grammar: Plum and Cowling (1987) and Nesbitt and Plum (1988). Both are concerned with conditioned probabilities, but where the conditioning is of two different kinds: interstratal in the former, intrastratal in the latter. I shall consider each of these in turn.

Plum and Cowling examined 4,436 finite clauses from interviews conducted for the Sydney Social Dialect Survey, taking into account (among others) the network of options shown in Figure 3.3.

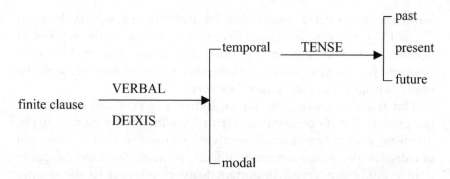

Figure 3.3 Network for example from Plum and Cowling (1987)

Of the total, 3,294 selected temporal deixis and 1,142 modal. These were distributed by social class of speaker as shown in Table 3.1.

Table 3.1 Selection of temporal and modal deixis by social class of speaker [from Plum and Cowling 1987]

	temporal deixis	modal deixis	Total
Lower working class	891	213	1,104
Upper working class	1,323	603	1,926
Middle class	1,080	326	1,406
Total	3,294	1,142	4,436

Thus there is a slight skewing by social class: lower working class favour tense more strongly than the others, and middle class slightly more strongly than upper working class, although the difference is hardly significant. But when they take the 3,294 having temporal deixis and examine the selection of primary tense, excluding a very small number of futures (27 in all, so leaving 3,267 past or present), the results are as in Table 3.2:

Table 3.2 Selection of primary tense (past/present) by social class [after Plum and Cowling 1987]

	past	present	Total
Lower working class	306 (35%)	579 (65%)	885 (100%)
Upper working class	789 (60%)	515 (40%)	1,304 (100%)
Middle class	752 (70%)	326 (30%)	1,078 (100%)
Total	1,847 (57%)	1,420 (43%)	3,267 (100%)

So while the overall probability of past/present was fairly even (57%/43%), the conditioning effect of social class, in the register in question, skewed this in opposite directions: the middle class favoured past and the lower working class favoured present, with the upper working class located in between.

This is a classic manifestation of Bernstein's principle of code, or (to give it the more accurate term) "coding orientation". If the linguistic system was not inherently of a probabilistic kind it could not display these sociolinguistic effects. As it is, this kind of quantitative study can reveal important features relevant to the deeper social order.

An example of such a study, but one with a considerably broader scope, is that of Ruqaiya Hasan, who has been conducting research into how the linguistic interaction between mothers and children shapes the way children learn: their forms of reasoning and of knowing, the ways in which they construe experience in language, and the dimensions of the semiotic space within which their consciousness is constituted and enabled to develop. She has assembled a database of some 21,000 messages (using that term to label the semantic unit typically realized as a mood-selecting clause), consisting of spontaneous conversation, in the home, between mothers and their children of 3–4 years. There are 24 such dyads, 12 with boys and 12 with girls. Hasan has used systemic theory to construct a semantic network representing the total paradigm of significant options, and the entire corpus has been analysed in respect of the features incorporated in that network.

She has then used principal components analysis, as this has been adapted to variation theory, to study the systematic patterns of variation in semantic choice; for example, in the way the mothers answer their children's questions. What the program does is to cluster those sets of features that contribute most to variation in the data (the principal component factors); for example, in parts of the discourse where the mothers are answering their children's questions, a factor consisting of some six semantic features is found to account for a large amount of the variance among the individual dyads. Interestingly, three of these features relate to the children's questions and three relate to the mothers' answers. Once these features are identified it is possible to examine what extra-linguistic variables in the population are being reflected in this semantic variation.

For these enquiries Hasan has been able to use research methodology developed in variation theory; but her theoretical stance is very different from that of Labov. Labov's variants are by his own definition meaningless; they are phonological or morphological realizations of an assumed semantic constant – and hence arbitrary, in that there is no significance in which group selects which variant (to take the classic example, the prestige variant is +r in America, −r in England). By contrast, Hasan is concerned with the statistical properties of **meaningful** choice. The key concept here is Hasan's "semantic variation", the selection of different meanings **which are themselves the realization of some constant at a higher level** (hence this is code variation, not register variation where there is no higher-level constant). But here the higher-level constant is located in the social contexts, specifically the socializing contexts of mother-child interaction; so the options differentially favoured by one or other social group are alternative realizations of the same semiotic activity, for example, that of controlling the child's behaviour, or of helping in the search for explanations. See Cloran (1989); Hasan (1988); Hasan and Cloran (1990).

The predominant extralinguistic variables that are found to correlate with this semantic variation are the sex of the child and the social-class position of the family. Hasan's results thus strongly support Bernstein's original findings and his general theory, derived as they are from an entirely different database and underpinned by a much more elaborated linguistic model than was available to Bernstein in the 1960s. But the significance of Hasan's work for the present discussion is that the semantic features involved in this variation are realized, non-arbitrarily, through grammatical systems to which probabilities can be assigned. Hasan is showing that the semantic choices made by the mother affect the child's ways of reasoning and of learning; that this is possible is because the lexicogrammatical features that carry these semantic patterns are quantitatively foregrounded, and **such foregrounding affects the probabilities of the child's own system**. If text frequency was a so-called "performance" phenomenon, it would have no effect on the "competence" of a listener. But the child's potential is affected; not in the sense that it becomes a direct copy of the mother's, but in the sense that the probabilities in the child's system collectively constitute a meaning style that is semiotically and ideologically compatible with that of the mother.

Part of the meaning of a grammatical system is the relative probability of its terms. This is so even if these probabilities remain constant across all environments – as in some instance no doubt they do. Where they do not, there may be systematic variation that can be interpreted as the conditioning of these probabilities "from above". This may be either from code or from register; in either case, it is exploiting the potential of language as a stratified probabilistic system.

Let us now consider the situation where probabilities are being investigated from the point of view of their conditioning **within the grammar itself**. Nesbitt and Plum (1988) investigated the relative frequency of options in the clause complex system, using data from Plum's sociolinguistic interviews with dog fanciers. The relevant system network is given in Figure 3.4.

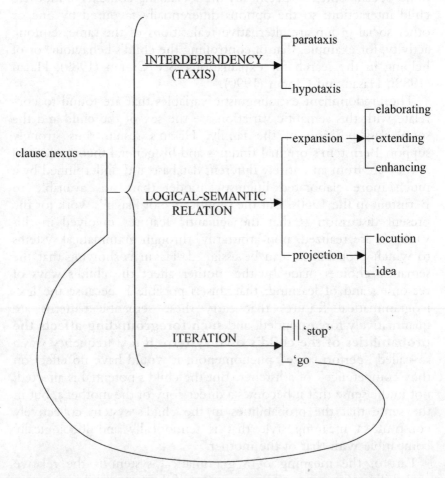

Figure 3.4 Network for example from Nesbitt and Plum (1988)

The total sample was 2,733 clause nexuses. The raw scores and percentages for each of the two systems taken separately, (i) inter-dependency, or "taxis"; (ii) logical-semantic relations, were as set out in Table 3.3.

Table 3.3 Figures and percentages for taxis and logical-semantic relations [after Nesbitt and Plum 1988]

INTERDEPENDENCY (TAXIS)		LOGICAL-SEMANTIC RELATIONS	
parataxis	1,918 (70%)	expansion	2,284 (84%)
hypotaxis	815 (30%)	projection	449 (16%)
Total	2,733 (100%)	Total	2,733 (100%)

When these are intersected, the figures are as given in Table 3.4.

Table 3.4 Taxis (parataxis/hypotaxis) by logical-semantic relations (expansion/projection) [after Nesbitt and Plum 1988]

LOGICAL-SEMANTIC RELATIONS / TAXIS	expansion	projection	Total
parataxis	1,656	262	1,918
hypotaxis	628	187	815
Total	2,284	449	2,733

Expressing these as percentages, and summing along both axes, we get Table 3.5.

Table 3.5 Taxis by logical-semantic relations, with percentages both ways [after Nesbitt and Plum 1988]

LOGICAL-SEMANTIC RELATIONS / TAXIS	expansion	projection	Total
parataxis	86% 1,656 73%	14% 262 58%	100% 1,918
hypotaxis	77% 628 27%	23% 187 42%	100% 815
Total	2,284 100%	449 100%	2,733

Thus, if we ask whether the proportions remain the same when the two systems are intersected, the answer is that, on the whole, they do. The effect is slightly exaggerated along both dimensions: that is, the combination of "parataxis × expansion" is 73% of all taxis and 86% of all logical–semantic relations. But the difference between these and the simple proportions (70%, 84%) is not significant.

When they take the next step in delicacy, however, the picture changes. Table 3.6 shows the raw scores for taxis intersected with the subcategories of expansion, namely elaborating, extending, and enhancing.

Table 3.6 Taxis by expansion (elaborating/extending/enhancing) [after Nesbitt and Plum 1988]

EXPANSION / TAXIS	elaborating	extending	enhancing	Total
parataxis	386	1,117	153	1,656
hypotaxis	128	42	458	628
Total	514	1,159	611	2,284

Nesbitt and Plum sum these as percentages along one dimension only, as in Table 3.7.

Table 3.7 Taxis by expansion, with percentages showing proportions of taxis within each type of expansion [after Nesbitt and Plum 1988]

EXPANSION / TAXIS	elaborating	extending	enhancing
parataxis	386 / 75%	1,117 / 96%	153 / 25%
hypotaxis	128 / 25%	42 / 4%	458 / 75%
Total	514 / 100%	1,159 / 100%	611 / 100%

They then argue as follows. If you choose "extending", then there is virtually no choice of taxis; we can treat this as "all extending are paratactic". (This corresponds to the traditional category of "co-ordination", which is a complex of parataxis × extending. The small group of hypotaxis × extending, such as clauses introduced by *as well as, besides, rather than, instead of,* would be ignored.) These can therefore be left out of consideration, leaving just the intersection of parataxis/hypotaxis with elaborating/enhancing. If you choose "elaborating", you are more likely to choose parataxis (the traditional category of "apposition"); while if you choose "enhancing", you are more likely to choose hypotaxis (the traditional "adverbial clauses", plus equivalent non-finites). In other words, as Plum and Nesbitt (1988: 21) express it, "elaborating favours parataxis, enhancing favours hypotaxis".

This is certainly true – although it would be relevant to point out that elaborating favours parataxis just in the proportion in which parataxis is favoured over hypotaxis in expansion as a whole (75% : 25% ::: 73% : 27%). But this time if we sum the rows instead of the columns we obtain rather a different picture, as in Table 3.8:

Table 3.8 Taxis by expansion, with percentages showing proportions of expansion within each type of taxis [based on Nesbitt and Plum 1988]

TAXIS \ EXPANSION	elaborating	extending	enhancing	Total
parataxis	23% 286	67% 1,117	10% 153	100% 1,656
hypotaxis	20% 128	7% 42	73% 458	100% 628

From this point of view, parataxis and hypotaxis are identical in their effects on (i.e., as environments for) elaborating, which remains at between a fifth and a quarter of the total (23% in the environment of parataxis, 20% in that of hypotaxis). What changes, in this perspective, is the effect on extending and enhancing; thus:

  parataxis: favours extending (67%), disfavours enhancing (10%)
  hypotaxis: disfavours extending (7%), favours enhancing (73%)

– with elaborating bubbling along as a minor motif in both.

When systems are intersected in this way, one is being treated as the conditioning environment of the other; and since either system can take either role, this gives two complementary perspectives. Nesbitt and Plum's interpretation is: first choose your logical-semantic relation, and that will help to determine the taxis. But it also makes sense to say: first choose your taxis, and that will help to determine the logical–semantic relation. The picture may look rather different from each of the two perspectives, and for a robust interpretation it may be necessary to take account of both.

When taxis is intersected with projection, the picture looks the same whichever system is chosen as environment of the other, as in Table 3.9.

Table 3.9 Taxis by projection, with percentage summed both ways [after Nesbitt and Plum 1988]

PROJECTION TAXIS	locution	idea	Total
parataxis	87% 227 86%	13% 35 19%	100% 262
hypotaxis	20% 37 14%	80% 150 81%	100% 187
Total	264 100%	185 100%	449

In other words:

  locution: favours parataxis (86%), disfavours hypotaxis (14%)

  idea: disfavours parataxis (19%), favours hypotaxis (81%)

  parataxis: favours locution (87%), disfavours idea (13%)

  hypotaxis: disfavours locution (20%), favours idea (80%)

These figures, which are very robust, give a clear account of the association between these two systems; they show up the two prototypical kinds of projection, (i) direct speech and (ii) indirect thought. Of course, the figures relate only to this register; but if the pattern turns out to be repeated across other functional varieties then it can be regarded as a feature of the system of the English language at its present stage. Now, this kind of **partial association** between systems could be perfectly stable; but it could also, as Nesbitt and Plum point out, be a symptom of a change in progress. The hypothesis would be that at some earlier time there was only one system, say, "projected speech/projected thought", the contrast between the terms being realized by two variables: "projected speech" by direct deixis plus a verbal process, "projected thought" by indirect deixis plus a mental process. Subsequently, these realizations were deconstructed so as to be able to vary independently of each other; but the association between them remained in a probabilistic form. This "dissociation of associated variables" is, as I have pointed out elsewhere, an important semogenic resource; and it is virtually inconceivable that it should be other than a gradual process. That is to say, whether or not the situation would eventually evolve to one where the two systems were entirely independent of one another, it would not reach that stage in one catastrophic leap.

Let me summarize here the principal types of relationship that we may expect to find between two simultaneous systems. It should be remembered that "simultaneous" means 'treated as independent', i.e., networked as in Figure 3.5.

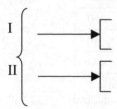

Figure 3.5 Simultaneous systems

From the point of view of a probabilistic grammar, this signifies 'anything **other than** one being fully dependent on the other', which is networked as in Figure 3.6 (i.e., as a relationship in delicacy).

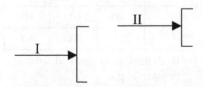

Figure 3.6 System II dependent on system I (related in delicacy)

In other words, simultaneous systems may be statistically associated – that is, only partially independent, their intersection being governed by probabilities which are not simply the product of the separate probabilities of each. In such a case, one system acts as a conditioning environment on the other, so that a term in System I "favours" the choice of a term in System II.

Tables 3.10 a and 3.10 b (i)–(vii) show some possible distributions

Table 3.10 a (i)–(iii). Intersection of systems I and II where both are (fully) independent systems

II \ I	m	n	T
p	100	100	200
q	100	100	200
T	200	200	400

II \ I	m	n	T
p	324	36	360
q	36	4	40
T	360	40	400

(i) Both systems have no unmarked term

(ii) Both systems have one term unmarked

II \ I	m	n	T
p	180	180	360
q	20	20	40
T	200	200	400

(iii) System I has no unmarked term, system II has one term unmarked

Table 3.10 b (iv)–(vii). Intersection of systems I and II where the two are associated (partially dependent)

II \ I	m	n	T
p	140	60	200
q	60	140	200
T	200	200	400

II \ I	m	n	T
p	140	100	240
q	60	100	160
T	200	200	400

(iv) Both have no unmarked term, but m p favoured, n q favoured

(v) Both have no unmarked term, but m favours p

II \ I	m	n	T
p	140	60	200
q	100	100	200
T	240	160	400

II \ I	m	n	T
p	180	20	200
q	20	180	200
T	200	200	400

(vi) Both have no unmarked term, but p favours m

(vii) Stronger variant of (iv), "reversal of marking"

of text frequencies that would reflect typical relationships between a pair of simultaneous systems. In (i)–(iii), the two systems are unassociated (fully independent); in (iv)–(vii) there is some association between them. The figures are constructed for binary systems; they can be intrapolated for systems that are ternary or beyond.

By investigating this kind of internal conditioning within the grammar, using a large-scale corpus of text, we can greatly improve on the present purely qualitative interpretation, according to which systems are either dependent or simultaneous, and recognize intermediate degrees of partial association between systems in a system network. The corpuses are now readily available, for example the COBUILD corpus at Birmingham (see Sinclair 1987), but the analysis still has to be manual, because no parser can yet assign enough feature descriptions to be usable for the purpose. However, one such pass through a corpus, tagging it for the principal systems in some grammar such as the "Nigel" grammar networks developed at the Information Sciences Institute (ISI), would yield material for a great number of valuable studies. It would also be useful, for example, to study transitional probabilities: how the choice of a/b is affected by the choice made in the same system in the preceding clause, or other relevant unit, in the text.

The objection has sometimes been raised that, while it is perfectly possible to establish frequencies of occurrence of grammatical features in a corpus of text, these cannot be interpreted as probabilities in the system because every text is in some particular register. This is a spurious objection. Of course, every text is in some register, just as every text is in some dialect – that is, every text is located somewhere in dialectal and diatypic space. This means that the greater the variety of texts examined, the more accurate the picture will be; it requires a lot of observations to approximate to a quantitative profile of the grammar of a language – but that does not render it a meaningless concept. To return to the earlier analogy with climate, every set of temperature readings is made under certain specific conditions – latitude and longitude, height above sea level, time of day, on land or on water, and so on; but it is perfectly meaningful to talk, as everyone is doing, about global temperatures, provided one takes a broad enough sample. These are the probabilities in the climatic system. It is interesting that nobody disputes lexical probabilities; it is accepted that words can be compared for their relative probability of occurrence in the language as a whole, and that this is achieved by examining word frequencies in a wide variety of registers. It is the same principles that are being invoked for prob-abilities in grammar. In fact lexis and grammar are not different phenomena; they are the same phenomenon looked at from dif-ferent ends. There is no reason therefore to reject the concept of the overall probability of terms in grammatical systems, on the grounds of register variation. On the contrary; it is the probabilistic model of lexicogrammar that enables us to explain register variation. Register variation can be defined as the skewing of (some of) these overall probabilities, in the environment of some specific configuration of field, tenor and mode. It is variation in the tendency to select certain meanings rather than others, realizing variation in the situation type.

This relates register variation (diatypic) to diachronic variation, since the latter is also variation in the probabilities of the linguistic system – variation along the arrow of time. Sometimes, in the course of this process, a probability will achieve certainty (a value of 0/1), which is a categorical change; and sometimes there will be cata-strophic change, as happens when the entire system is creolized. These are the limiting cases (and as such, both have analogies in diatypic variation). In terms of the cladistic model, linguistic change through time is evolutionary; and this also seems to apply, at least in the case of examples such as the language of science, to the history of particular registers.

One of the recurrent motifs of structuralism was the warning against transferring evolutionary concepts onto language; and it was a wise warning, because in many ways, as these had usually been applied, they clearly did not fit. But the concepts are now under-stood and applied rather differently; and evolution – like other fundamental issues, such as the origins of language, or the relation between language and culture – can be readmitted onto the agenda. It goes without saying that, if we draw on general concepts about systems, and system change, in our interpretation of language, we recognize that semiotic systems differ in important ways from phys-ical systems, and also from biological systems. These differences need to be re-problematized: how, and why, are semiotic systems different?

The two critical vectors are surely those of instantiation and realization. The first is the relation between the system and the instance; the second is the relation between strata. If we are talking specifically about language, then the first is the relation between language as system and language as text; the second is that relating semantics, lexicogrammar and phonology. Saussure conceptualized the first in terms of the opposition between langue and parole, the second in terms of that between signified and signifier. At the same time, Mathesius introduced the concept of "oscillation": variation in language that was both diatypic and diachronic. With a probabilistic interpretation of the system we are, in a sense, combining the Saussurean and the Mathesian perspectives. What is special about semiotic systems is the nature of these two relationships, and in particular, the way they combine qualitative and quantitative effects.

This is obviously not something to be discussed in a few closing paragraphs; so I shall just make one point about each. With regard to instantiation, I have used the probabilistic interpretation to try to show how text becomes system, bringing in the analogy from the physical system of climate. So let me emphasize the difference: namely that, in a semiotic system, instances have differential qualitative value, so that one **highly valued** instance can by itself lead to a change in the system. We might call this the "Hamlet factor", since the main context in which such value accrues is that of literature, and Hamlet is, as the (no doubt fictitious) old lady said, "full of quotations". The Hamlet factor is probably operative only in semiotic systems.

With regard to realization, all I shall try to do is enumerate some steps in what is inevitably a rather complex argument. The natural sciences, especially theoretical physics, are characterized by very high orders of abstraction. This abstraction, however, is located in the **interpretations** of physical processes (i.e., the metalanguage), not in the processes themselves; in other words, the systems characterized in this way are semiotic systems, not physical systems. Physical and biological systems are typically compositional, their processes governed by cause-and-effect. (They may include some of the semiotic type also – Jakobson used to cite the genetic code; and some very recent theories treat physical systems as semiotic systems.) Semiotic systems are characterized by stratification, their (internal) "processes" being realizational.

Linguistic systems are typically treated as if they were of this compositional, cause-and-effect type: "a consists of $b_1 + b_2 + \ldots$; b consists of $c_1 + c_2 + \ldots$", or "a causes b; b causes c; $\ldots$". (A common outcry against stratal models is "but which stratum causes which?") Thus in generalizing the signified ↘ signifier relationship across the system, we have treated the strata as if they were entities in a universe of this kind: "a is realized by b; b is realized by c; $\ldots$" Then, in order to avoid a crude cause-and-effect interpretation, we have tried to remove all directionality from the system, using constructivist metaphors that are made to face both ways: the context constructs the grammar, and the grammar constructs the context.

A more promising interpretation of realization is, in my view, Lemke's (1984) concept of "metaredundancy". This is, quite explicitly, a directional model, and there has to be a lower bound: let us call it stratum z. Stratum y is realized by stratum z; y ⟍ z. But stratum x is realized, not by stratum y but by the realization of stratum y by stratum z: x ⟍ (y ⟍ z). For stratum w, likewise: w ⟍ (x ⟍ (y ⟍ z)); and so on. Such a relationship is not reducible to a chain of dyadic, cause-and-effect type relations.

This makes sense of Hjelmslev's notion of the connotative semiotic, as used by Martin (1985, and elsewhere). It also enables us to escape the contructivist trap, which seems to force an unreal choice between "language expresses reality" and "language creates reality". (I have been using "construe" to try to suggest the upward relationship in the Lemkean model.) I also find it helps me to understand how we can change reality by getting busy on language. There must be some reason why so much of our interaction with our environment begins and ends in grammar.

This last section has been, clearly, a trailer; not a systematic presentation of ideas coherently thought through. It is intended mainly to contextualize what went before, since it seems to me that in order to understand the special properties of semiotic systems it is necessary to show that such systems can be represented in probabilistic terms.

Note

1. (Kress (ed.), 1976: 101–35 / Halliday, 2002: Section 1, Appendix)

Chapter Four

CORPUS STUDIES AND PROBABILISTIC
GRAMMAR (1991)

In the Preface to his book *On Voice in the English Verb*, which was published a quarter of a century ago, Jan Svartvik wrote that "corpus-studies will help to promote descriptively more adequate grammars" (Svartvik 1966: vii). This modest claim ran against the ideology prevailing at that time, according to which corpus studies had nothing to contribute towards an understanding of language. Chomsky's theory of competence and performance had driven a massive wedge between the system and the instance, making it impossible by definition that analysis of actual texts could play any part in explaining the grammar of a language – let alone in formulating a general linguistic theory.

Explicitly rejected was the relevance of any kind of quantitative data. Chomsky's sarcastic observation that "*I live in New York* is more frequent than *I live in Dayton Ohio*" was designed to demolish the conception that relative frequency in text might have any theoretical significance.[1] Svartvik recognized, however, that the significance of linguistic frequency measures was not something that could be trivialized out of court in this way. As well as using data from the corpus to establish a taxonomy of classes of the passive in English, and to set up the "passive scale" in the form of a serial relationship (implicational scaling), he also calculated the ratio of passive to active clauses and compared the frequency of passives across a range of different registers. Such patterns could not be reduced to accidental effects like the population of American cities, or people's preferences in the personal names they bestowed on their children.

There is no longer any need to argue for the importance of corpus studies as a source of information about the grammar of a language, and indeed as a source of insight into the nature of grammar in general. Svartvik's own subsequent work, and that of the Survey of English Usage quartet of which he has been a permanent member, has shown beyond doubt how much can be learnt from what the corpus contains. But the theoretical status of corpus frequencies is still an open issue, and it is to this topic that I would like to return here.

It had always seemed to me that the linguistic **system** was inherently probabilistic, and that frequency in text was the instantiation of probability in the grammar. In working on Chinese grammar, in the 1950s, I used such text frequencies as I had available and assigned crude probabilities to the terms in the grammatical systems.[2] Firth's concept of "system" provided the necessary paradigmatic base. It seemed to me self-evident that, given a system "polarity" whose terms were "positive/negative", the fact that positive was more frequent than negative was an essential property of the system – as essential as the terms of the opposition itself. Analytically, of course, it was necessary to separate the statement of the terms of the system from the statement of their relative probabilities; but what was involved was a single phenomenon, not two.

It turned out that some people felt threatened by this suggestion, regarding it as an attack on their freedom as individuals to choose what they wanted to say. It was rather as if by stating people's probable sleeping behaviour one would be denying them the freedom to lead a nocturnal existence if they chose. But there was an interesting contrast here. Occurrences in vocabulary had been being counted for some time, and the results had been used, by Zipf (1935), to establish general principles such as the relationship between the relative frequency of a lexical item and its place in the rank order; and while it could be questioned what significance such generalizations might have, the fact that word frequency patterns could be systematized in this way was accepted as a property of language.[3] It was a systematic feature of English that *go* was more frequent than *walk* and *walk* was more frequent than *stroll*, and nobody was particularly upset by it. Why, then, the resistance to quantitative patterns in the grammar?

This might be explained if there was some fundamental difference between lexis and grammar; but this seemed to me unlikely. I have always seen lexicogrammar as a unified phenomenon, a single level of **wording**, of which lexis is the **most delicate** resolution.[4] In a paradigmatic interpretation, the "two" form a continuum: at one end are the very general choices, multiply intersecting, which can readily be closed to form a paradigm, such as **polarity: positive/ negative, mood: indicative (declarative/interrogative)/imperative, transitivity: material/mental/relational**, and these are best illuminated by being treated as grammar; while at the other end are choices which are highly specific but open-ended, with each term potentially entering into many term sets, e.g. *run* contrasting (i) with *walk*, (ii) with *hop, skip,* (iii) with *jog,* etc., and these are best illuminated by being treated as lexis. Midway along the continuum are things like prepositions and modals which do not yield a strong preference to either form of treatment. But both lexicographer and grammarian can occupy the whole terrain: "lexis" and "grammar" are names of complementary perspectives, like the synoptic and dynamic perspectives on a semiotic process, or wave and particle as complementary theories of light, each explaining different aspects of a single complex phenomenon.

Given this concept of lexicogrammar, it does not make sense to condone relative frequency in lexis but deny its validity in grammar. Admittedly, grammar is the 'deeper' end of the continuum, less accessible to conscious attention, and this may be why the treatment of grammar (in any form) always engenders more resistance. But the concept of the relative frequency of positive : negative, or of active : passive is no more suspect than the concept of the relative frequency of a set of lexical items. It is, on the other hand, considerably more powerful, because the relative frequencies of the terms in a grammatical system, where the system is closed and the number of choices is very small (typically just two or three), can be interpreted directly as probabilities having a significance for the system of language as a whole.

It is clear that the significance of such probabilities is not that they predict single instances. What is predicted is the general pattern. We might establish that, for any clause in English, the probability of its being negative is (say) one in ten; but that will not enable us to specify in advance the polarity of any one particular clause. However, this is not to say that probability has no significance with regard to the single instance. It has; but its relevance lies not in predicting but in interpreting. Part of the meaning of choosing any term is the probability with which that term is chosen; thus the meaning of negative is not simply 'not positive' but 'not positive, against odds of nine to one'. This is one of the reasons why grammatical choices may mean different things in different registers, where the odds may be found to vary.

For register variation, in fact, probability is the central concern. As Svartvik found in his study of voice in English, corpus studies suggest that grammatical frequencies will vary across the diatypic varieties, or registers, of a language but that they will vary within certain limits. Thus for his main corpus of novel and science texts the overall proportion among finite clauses was 88 per cent active to 12 per cent passive. When the frequency of passive was expressed as the number of passive clauses per thousand words, the figure, obtained from a large corpus, came out at 11.3; this corpus consisted of eight text sets in different registers, within which the number of passives per thousand words varied from 23 in the science texts to 3 in the advertising ones. Four out of the eight clustered between 12.7 and 8.2, with the one sample of speech showing 9.2.[5] Svartvik did not give the active : passive ratio for the different text sets; but assuming that the average figure of 11.3 passives per thousand words corresponds to the 12 per cent of passive clauses in the smaller corpus, this would suggest that, while the overall probability of active : passive is 0.88 : 0.12, it would vary between 0.76 : 0.24 and 0.96 : 0.04 in a range of different registers, with all but science and advertising falling between 0.84 : 0.16 and 0.94 : 0.06. This is the sort of picture that is borne out by subsequent investigations – with the stipulation, of course, that passive is not always identified in the same way.[6] But the critical observation that Svartvik made was that "the frequencies for most of the texts of a text group are remarkably similar". Register variation can in fact be defined as systematic variation in probabilities; *a register* is a tendency to select certain combinations of meanings with certain frequencies, and this can be formulated as the probabilities attached to grammatical systems, provided such systems are integrated into an overall system network in a paradigmatic interpretation of the grammar.

Diachronically, frequency patterns as revealed in corpus studies provide explanations for historical change, in that when interpreted as probabilities they show how each instance both maintains and perturbs the system. "System" and "instance" are of course not different things; they form yet another complementarity. There is only one phenomenon here, not two; what we call language (the system) and what we call text (the instance) are two observers of that phenomenon, observing it from different distances. (I have used the analogy of "climate" and "weather".) To the "instance" observer, the **system** is the potential, with its set of probabilities attached; each instance is by itself unpredictable, but the system appears constant through time. To the "system" observer, each **instance** redefines the system, however infinitesimally, maintaining its present state or shifting its probabilities in one direction or the other (as each moment's weather at every point on the globe redefines the global climate). It is the system which has a history – that is, it is the system-observer who perceives depth in time; but the transformation of instance into system can be observed only through the technology of the corpus, which allows us to accumulate instances and monitor the diachronic variation in their patterns of frequency.

Now that it is possible to store and process massive quantities of text, and programs of great elegance are available for quantitative studies, the main limitation on the use of corpuses for probabilistic grammar is the familiar catch that what is easy to recognize is usually too trivial to be worth recognizing. It is not that the categories we have to retrieve are necessarily very delicate ones – that would merely increase the size of the corpus needed in order to retrieve them, which is hardly a problem these days. On the contrary; at this stage we still need statistics for very general categories of the grammar. But they have to be categories with real semantic power, not distorted so as to suit the capabilities of a typically simplistic parser.[7] For example, the clause *it occasionally happens* would be positive, *it rarely happens* negative; the clause *a replay would be your only hope* active, *your only hope would be a replay* passive. With systems such as voice and polarity it is fairly easy to parse mechanically so as to identify perhaps 70–75 per cent of instances; but it then becomes exponentially more costly as one approximates 100 per cent. A human parser, of course, does not attain 100 per cent, because some instances are inherently indeterminate and humans also make mistakes; but there is still a critical gap between what the machine can achieve and what the human can achieve. So in deriving grammatical probabilities from a corpus we still depend on human participants for carrying out the text analysis.

Given, then, a paradigmatic grammar, based on the concept of the "system" in Firth's sense of the term, frequency information from the corpus can be used to establish the probability profile of any grammatical system. From this profile – the probabilities of each of the terms – we can derive a measure of the information that is generated by that system, using Shannon and Weaver's formula (1963 [1949]: 8–16)

$$H = - \Sigma p_i \log_2 p_i$$

where p_i is the probability of each term in the system taken separately. The value of H (information) will vary from 1, where all terms are equiprobable, to a vanishingly small number as they become more and more skew, but reaching 0.08 when the ratio of two terms is 99 : 1. (The formula can be applied to systems with any number of terms.) $1 - H$ (1 minus the information value) gives the value R (redundancy).

It has been shown that those who know a language can make an informed guess about the relative frequency of its words – to return to the example above, they will recognize that *go* > *walk* > *stroll*. This is just an aspect of 'knowing the language'. Provided they have some understanding of grammatical concepts and categories (and do not feel threatened by being asked to reflect on them), they can do the same for the grammar. Speakers of English can recognize that active is more frequent than passive, positive than negative, declarative than interrogative, *the* than *this* or *that*, simple tenses than compound tenses. They will be uncertain, on the other hand, of the relative frequency of singular and plural, *this* and *that*, *a* and *the*, past and present. This suggests that some systems tend towards being equiprobable and hence have a higher information value, while others are notably skew and thus display a greater degree of redundancy (in the technical sense of that term in information theory).

I had found some such pattern emerging when I counted instances in Chinese, where it seemed that very general grammatical systems fell into two such broad types. This seemed to account for our sense that some systems have an **unmarked term**, whereas others have not. An unmarked term is a default condition: that which is selected unless there is good reason for selecting some other term. It is not **defined** by frequency, but it is likely to correspond to the more probable term in a system whose probabilities are skew.

When I started counting occurrences of comparable features in texts in English, a similar pattern appeared. For example, simple past and simple present, while they might be very unequal in any given register, appeared roughly equal in their frequency overall. Likewise the three major process types of material, mental and relational; these form a transitivity system of three terms whose occurrence in any particular text type is liable to be quite skew, but the three terms show up as fairly evenly distributed when the figures for the different types are combined. Some systems, on the other hand, remained skew over a wide register range: positive was more frequent than negative, active than passive, declarative than interrogative, simple tenses than compound tenses. My figures were not large; I counted simply until the least frequent term had reached 200 occurrences. But as far as they went they suggested that grammatical systems vary in their probability profiles.

But the variation was not random, and the more interesting feature was the particular bimodal pattern that seemed to emerge. In principle, any set of systems might distribute themselves evenly over the whole scale of probability values, from 0.5 : 0.5 to 0.99 : 0.01 (from equiprobable to maximally skew). But we are considering semiotic systems, which are systems of a particular kind. We know they are unlikely all to be equiprobable; such a grammar would have no redundancy at all, and no human semiotic could work with such restraint.[8] On the other hand, it seems equally unlikely that they could be spread over all possible values; a semiotic system of this kind would be virtually impossible to learn. The figures suggested, rather, that grammatical systems fall into two main types: (i) the equiprobable, those tending towards 0.5 : 0.5, and (ii) the skew – and that these latter tended towards a ratio of one order of magnitude, which we could represent ideally as 0.9 : 0.1. Svartvik's frequency figures for active and passive defined a system of this second type (probabilities 0.88 : 0.12).

It is interesting to note that this skew profile of 0.9 : 0.1 is just at the point where, in Shannon and Weaver's theory of information, the redundancy measure works out at 50 per cent. (To be exact, $H = R = 0.5$ where the probabilities are 0.89 : 0.11.)[9] This, as it happens, was the value they had calculated for what they rather quaintly referred to as "the redundancy of English", meaning by this the redundancy of English orthography interpreted as a system of twenty-seven symbols (twenty-six letters and a space) and calculated up to strings of "about eight" letters. As a property of English orthographic sequences this made only a very limited appeal to linguists, since it was not clear what implications it had for other languages or for other linguistic levels – and in any case it rested on a not very adequate characterization of the orthography of English. But it would be a matter of some significance if it turns out that grammatical systems tend towards a bimodal probability distribution where one mode is that of almost no redundancy and the other is that where redundancy is around 50 per cent. The actual values showing up in my own informal frequency counts would be defined by the following limits:

(i) equiprobable

p $0.5 : 0.5 \sim 0.65 : 0.35$

H 1 ~ 0.93

(ii)   skew

p $0.8 : 0.2 \sim 0.89 : 0.11$ $\sim 0.95 : 0.05$

H 0.72 ~ 0.5 ~ 0.28

In other words, the redundancy was either (i) less than 10 per cent or (ii) somewhere in the region of 30–70 per cent, and often towards the middle of that range, close to 50 per cent. If this is in fact a general pattern, it would suggest that the grammar of a natural language is organized around the interaction between two modes of quantizing information: one where each act of choice – each instance – is maximally informative (it might equally well have been the opposite), and one where it is largely uninformative (since you could pretty well have guessed it already). Furthermore, it might be the case that these two kinds of system occur in roughly equal proportion.

A semiotic of this kind would have enough 'play' in it to allow for functional variation in register, but enough constraint to ensure that such variation was systematic – without which it could not, of course, be functional. Svartvik's figures showed both effects: the global probabilities, those of the grammar of English, and the locally conditioned probabilities, those of this or that particular register. To refer again to the analogy of the climate, it is entirely meaningful (as we all know today) to establish probabilities for the global climate as well as the local probabilities conditioned by season, latitude, height above sea level, time of day and so on. It is equally valid to talk of global probabilities in a language while still recognizing that every text is located somewhere or other in diatypic space. And just as we define regions of the globe by reference to their weather patterns, so (as suggested above) we can define registers by reference to their grammatical probabilities: register variation is the resetting of the probabilities in the grammar. But it seems likely that these probabilities will typically remain within the values defined by the system type; and that only in rather specialized registers (Firth's "restricted languages") should we expect a categoric shift such as a reversal of marking – for example in predictive texts like weather forecasting, where future leaps over past and present and becomes the most frequent tense. Generally, this external conditioning of the probabilities, realizing variation in the context of situation, is probably not such as to perturb the overall profile of the system.

A corpus which is organized by register, as all the great first-generation ones have been, makes it possible to study such external conditioning of probabilities, and to show how the grammar of doing science differs quantitatively from that of telling stories, advertising and so on. But the corpus also enables us to study the conditioning effects from within the grammar itself: to ask what happens if we intersect the frequency patterns of two simultaneous systems (that is, systems that have the same point of origin but such that neither is dependent on the other), like voice and polarity as systems of the clause. Are they truly independent? Are the probabilities for active : passive the same whether the clause is positive or negative, and are the probabilities for positive : negative the same no matter whether the clause is active or passive?

Table 3.10 showed some possible effects, with typical values attached, using two imaginary systems: system I with terms m, n, and system II with terms p, q (see Chapter 3 Tables 10 a, b, p. 58). In (i)–(iii) the two systems are unassociated; in (iv)–(vii) there is some association between them. Where two systems are associated in this way, there may be one-way favouritism, such that m favours p but p does not favour m, as in (v), or vice versa, as in (vi); or two-way favouritism, such that m favours p and p favours m, as in (iv). There may also be a reversal of marking, as in (vii), where the two favoured combinations are m with p and n with q. A real situation of type (vii) is described by Nesbitt and Plum (1988), working with a corpus of spoken English texts. Overall, the system of interdependency, or "taxis" (parataxis : hypotaxis), is within the equiprobable range (0.6 : 0.4), as is that of projection (locution : idea). But there is an association on the one hand (a) between parataxis and locution, such that:

(a) within parataxis, locution : idea   = 0.87 : 0.13
     within locution, parataxis : hypotaxis   = 0.86 : 0.14

and on the other hand (b) between hypotaxis and idea, such that:

(b) within hypotaxis, idea : locution   = 0.80 : 0.20
     within idea, hypotaxis : parataxis   = 0.81 : 0.19

In other words, the favoured combinations are those of "direct speech" and "indirect thought", and the reverse combinations appear as marked terms.

We can also use the corpus to establish transitional probabilities within the text. Given a system of the clause, how are its probabilities affected by choices in the preceding clause – both within the same system and in other systems? Sinclair has shown that the probabilities of lexical items are affected transitionally by collocation within a span (lexical distance) of up to about four (Sinclair *et al.* 1970, Sinclair 1985); and we may find similar effects obtaining in the grammar. It seems likely that the kinds of predictions we make as listeners and readers would depend on Markov properties of the lexicogrammar as a whole.

There are good reasons for thinking that an important semogenic process, whereby new meanings are created in the evolution of the system through time, is that of the dissociation of associated variables, whereby one system of two terms with complex realizations evolves into two simultaneous systems:

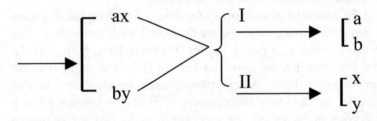

Where this happens, it is highly likely that systems I and II would, initially at least, be partially associated; the pattern of parataxis : hypotaxis and locution : idea described by Nesbitt and Plum is suggestive of just such a change in progress, as they point out. In other words, one may postulate an earlier stage consisting of a single system, "direct speech/indirect thought" (paratactic locution/ hypotactic idea), from which the present pattern has evolved. The pattern might stabilize in its present form, or it might evolve further to one in which the two systems become fully independent, with neither conditioning the choice within the other. One can think of many other systems which might have had this kind of history; for example, tag questions, where in present-day English the tag may select either "polarity reversed" or "polarity constant", the latter being the marked term, may have evolved through a stage where the only possible form was that with polarity reversed. This same process, whereby associated variables gradually become dissociated from one another, is also a characteristic feature of children's language development. The most favoured combinations are construed first, forming a system on their own; these are then deconstrued, and the remaining, less favoured combinations introduced as additional choices.[10]

Corpus studies have a central place in theoretical investigations of language. There are many ways in which a corpus can be exploited, of which the one considered here – by no means the only one – is that of providing evidence of relative frequencies in the grammar, from which can be established the probability profiles of grammatical systems. These in turn have implications for at least five areas of theoretical enquiry: developmental, diatypic, systemic, historical and metatheoretic. Children construe the lexicogrammar, on the evidence of text frequency, as a probabilistic system; a probabilistic model can help to explain the growth of their meaning potential. Diatypic variation, or register, is variation in the probabilities of the grammar; this is the major resource for systematically construing variation in the environment (the *situation*). Systemically, the grammar of a language can be represented paradigmatically as a network of choices, each choice consisting of a small number of alternatives related by probability; these probabilities appear to form a pattern related to the construing of "information". Historically, both semogenesis, the creation and maintenance of meaning, and its opposite, the destruction of meaning, can be explained in terms of probabilities, in the way grammatical systems evolve towards more, or less, informative states. Metatheoretically, the key concepts for interpreting a semiotic system, as a stratified dynamic open system, are those of realization and instantiation; the corpus shows how a system of this kind persists through being constantly perturbed, with each instance reconstructing the potential of the whole. The immense scope of a modern corpus, and the range of computing resources that are available for exploiting it, make up a powerful force for deepening our awareness and understanding of language. The issues raised in this chapter relate to a small fraction of this whole domain.

Notes

1 Made in the course of a denunciation of corpus studies in a lecture at the Linguistic Society of America Summer Institute, Bloomington, July 1964.

2   See Halliday (1959), especially Chapter 6 and Appendix C; also Halliday (1956).

3   Cf. however Gross's (1972: 154) comment that Zipf's law "has been found to be of such generality that no precise use of it can be made in linguistics".

4   See Halliday (1961). The concept of lexis as most delicate grammar is developed by Hasan (1987a) and exemplified in detail in Hasan (1987b).

5   Svartvik (1966) gives the following figures (Table 7:4, p. 155).

Text	No. of words	No. of passives	Passives per 1,000 words
Science	50,000	1,154	23.1
News	45,000	709	15.8
Arts	20,000	254	12.7
Speech	40,000	366	9.2
Sports	30,000	269	9.0
Novels	80,000	652	8.2
Plays	30,000	158	5.3
Advertising	28,000	83	3.0

6   Quirk *et al.* comment (1985: 166): "There is a notable difference in the frequency with which the active and passive voices are used. The active is generally by far the more common, but there is considerable variation among individual *text types*" (my italics).

7   There are, obviously, many forms of human-machine collaboration in retrieving grammatical frequencies from a corpus. An example would be Peter Collins's (1987) use of the London-Lund Corpus for his work on clefts and pseudo-clefts.

8   The most obvious reason for this is that there is too much noise. But there are other, more fundamental reasons to do with the nature of a dynamic open system: no system which persists through constant perturbation from its environment could remain in a state of almost zero redundancy.

9   It may be helpful to give values of H (information) and R (redundancy) for some probability profiles of a binary system, to two places of decimals:

Probabilities	H	R
0.5 : 0.5	1	0
0.6 : 0.4	0.97	0.03
0.67 : 0.33	0.91	0.09
0.8 : 0.2	0.72	0.28
0.9 : 0.1	0.47	0.53
0.99 : 0.01	0.08	0.92

The 'hinge' probability profile, where H and R become equal at 0.5, is 0.89 : 0.11 ($H = 0.499916$).

10 This appears clearly from Painter's (1984) systemic interpretation of child language development.

Chapter Five

LANGUAGE AS SYSTEM AND LANGUAGE AS INSTANCE: THE CORPUS AS A THEORETICAL CONSTRUCT (1992)

1. Grammatics and the corpus

It has always seemed to me, ever since I first tried to become a grammarian, that grammar was a subject with too much theory and too little data. (It was also a subject which had no proper name; it was confusing to have the same word *grammar* both for the object of study and for the science which studied it, which is why I have come to use "grammatics" to refer to the latter.) Back in 1949, when under the guidance of my teacher Wang Li I first put together a corpus of Cantonese sentences in order to study the grammar of the dialects of the Pearl River Delta (Wang Li was then conducting a survey of their phonology), I was struck by how little was known about how people actually talked. Of course, Cantonese had not been very much documented at the time; but Mandarin was not much better off. Wang himself, in his work on Chinese grammar, took all his examples from the C18 novel *Story of the Stone* (*Dream of Red Mansions*); and when I challenged him on this he said it was because the evidence of the modern language was *bù kě kào* ('unreliable')! And when I switched to working on English, ten years later, the situation there seemed hardly different. English was by that time coming to be written about as much as any language anywhere; but even those such as C. C. Fries who had recognized the need for authentic discourse and set out to obtain it had access only to small fragments of a rather specialized kind. (There were just two far-sighted scholars – Randolph Quirk and Freeman Twaddell – who had begun to design and make plans for a substantial corpus of English.)

Two points seemed to me to stand out. One was that we needed to have very large samples of real text. I considered that grammar had to be studied quantitatively, in probabilistic terms, and had shown (at least to my own satisfaction!) in my PhD study of an early Mandarin text how quantitative methods could be used to establish degrees of association between different grammatical systems. But the systems in question were clause systems, and one needed very large numbers of occurrences. If, as it appeared, there was typically a difference of about one order of magnitude (ten to one) in the relative frequency of unmarked and marked terms, such as positive / negative or declarative / interrogative, then to get anywhere beyond the least delicate grammatical categories we were going to need not thousands of clauses but hundreds of thousands for reliable numerical data.

The other consideration was a strong conviction I have always had that it is only in spoken language, and specifically in natural, spontaneous interaction, that the full semantic (and therefore grammatical) potential of the system is brought into play. If you listen grammatically, you will hear sentences of far greater complexity than can ever be found in writing – sentences which prove barely intelligible when written down, yet were beautifully constructed and had been processed without any conscious attention when they occurred in natural speech. I had heard verbal groups like *had been going to have been paying* and *will have been going to have been being tested* tripping off the tongue, at a time when structuralist grammarians were seriously wondering whether something as forbiddingly complex as *has been being eaten* could ever actually be said!

When David Abercrombie first invited me, in 1959, to teach on his British Council Summer School in the Phonetics of English, I asked him what he wanted me to teach. He said: "You know Chinese; teach intonation!" That appealed to me; I am no phonetician, but intonation was my strong point – I had been the one among Wang Li's research students who was charged with analysing the tone systems of the dialects covered by his survey. In Canton we had had one of the first new wire recorders, which seemed to me then the greatest single technological advance in the history of linguistics (at least, it was when wire gave way to tape); so having read what I could find on English intonation (Kingdon's (1958) book had not yet appeared) I set out to collect my own miniature corpus. My first one hour's tape of natural conversation took me just forty hours to transcribe, putting in my tentative intonation analysis; it proved to be an amazingly rich resource not only for intonation but for all manner of grammatical questions as well. A few years later Afaf Elmenoufy recorded and transcribed ten hours of conversation and was able to reveal significant discourse patterns in the grammatical functions of intonation (Elmenoufy 1969).

In the early 1960s John Sinclair and I plotted to collect a corpus of spontaneous English conversation; he did most of the work, and was able to organize the recording and transcription of a number of hours of casual speech. (The richest resource, from my own point of view, turned out to be the monological passages occurring within spontaneous dialogue.) We worked together on problems of grammar and lexis, and took the first steps towards designing a corpus as a theoretical resource for studying sentence structure and lexical collocation. By that time computers had been around long enough for it to be obvious that such work could be transformed by bringing in computational techniques, and we began looking at it from that point of view. But then we both moved and went in separate ways; and what John Sinclair has done since then is a matter of history – one of the most important chapters, I believe, in the history of linguistic research.

Sinclair is by nature a lexicographer, whose aim is to construct the grammar out of the dictionary. I am by nature a grammarian, and my aim (the grammarian's dream, as I put it in 1961) is to build the dictionary out of the grammar. There is a significant issue of complementarity here, which will also serve as a model for something I want to say later. There is in every language a level of organization – a single level – which is referred to in everyday speech as the "wording"; technically it is lexicogrammar, the combination of grammar and vocabulary. (I have always retained the linguists' term **grammar** in preference to the philosophers' term *syntax*, since syntax traditionally excludes the grammar of the word.) The point is that grammar and vocabulary are not two different things; they are the same thing seen by different observers. There is only one phenomenon here, not two. But it is spread along a continuum. At one end are small, closed, often binary systems, of very general application, intersecting with each other but each having, in principle, its own distinct realization. So for example all clauses are either positive or negative, either indicative or imperative, either transitive or intransitive (in the traditional analysis), and so on; all verbal groups are either active or passive, either past or present or future; &c. &c. At the other end are much more specific, looser, more shifting sets of features, realized not discretely but in bundles called "words", like *bench* realizing 'for sitting on', 'backless', 'for more than one', 'hard surface'; the system networks formed by these features are local and transitory rather than being global and persistent.

We name the two ends of the continuum as different things, calling the first **grammar** and the second **vocabulary**. This is because they look very different; or rather, more significantly, because they lend themselves to different techniques of analysis. We have always had "grammars" and "dictionaries". Now it is perfectly possible to treat the whole phenomenon grammatically; indeed in my way of talking about it just now I was doing just that. It is equally possible to treat the whole phenomenon lexically: at one end are content words, typically very specific in collocation and often of rather low frequency, arranged in taxonomies based on relations like 'is a kind of' and 'is a part of'; at the other end are function words, of high frequency and unrestricted collocationally, which relate the content words to each other and enable them to be constructed into various types of functional configuration. There are obvious advantages in adopting a unified approach; and of course there are the bits in the middle, areas such as are represented in English by circumstantial systems (prepositions), systems of modality and temporality (modal and temporal adjuncts) and so on, which can be illuminated more or less equally well from either end. But the phenomena at the two poles are qualitatively different; so that, while (to borrow the analogy from Dirac's quantum field theory, showing the dual nature of light as wave and particle (Polkinghorne 1990)) we have a general theory of lexicogrammar such that if you interrogate the system grammatically you will get grammar-like answers and if you interrogate it lexically you will get lexis-like answers, there are diminishing returns in each case. The amount of effort required to get grammar-like answers increases, and the payoff goes down, as you move towards the lexical end; and likewise with the search for lexis-like answers as you move towards the grammatical end.

Sinclair has shown what the corpus can do for lexical studies (Sinclair, Jones and Daley 1969; Sinclair (ed.) 1987; *Collins COBUILD English Language Dictionary*). He is now tunnelling through the system interrogating it lexically while moving further and further towards the grammatical end. That story I obviously leave to him, and return to my preferred stance as a grammar-observer. It seemed to me clear in 1960 that useful theoretical work in grammar was seriously hampered by lack of data; we depended on the corpus as a resource for further advance. Moreover it would have to be computerized, in the sense that some part of the work would be performed computationally to permit large-scale frequency studies. But here, of course, the grammar-observer faces an additional problem. The lexicologist's data are relatively easy to observe: they are words, or lexical items of some kind, and while their morphological scatter is a nuisance, involving some cumbersome programming and also some awkward decisions, it is not forbiddingly hard to parse them out. The grammarian's data are very much less accessible: I cannot even today ask the system to retrieve for me all clauses of mental process or marked circumstantial theme or high obligation modality. I have to choose between working on just those systems that can be retrieved by parsing, using a trawling strategy with a certain amount of clutter to be cleared away by subsequent manual inspection (there are a good number of these, but it is still a highly restrictive condition), and doing a massive job of manual analysis and simply using the system to crunch the numbers afterwards, which of course severely limits the size of the available sample. (The answer at this point in time, I think, is a modified version of the former, selecting systems that could be critical for a probabilistic grammatical theory.)

My own view of grammar has always been that it is to be treated as inherently probabilistic, and without any assumption of hidden variables. Thus, a grammatical system (say, polarity) is to be represented not as

polarity: positive / negative

but with a probability attached to each term, for example

polarity: positive$_{0.9}$ / negative$_{0.1}$

The clause grammar that I wrote at the start of the Penman project at the University of Southern California Information Sciences Institute in 1980 was of this kind (Appendix, pp. 268 ff.). It was a network of 81 systems each with a probability attached to the individual terms; this was then programmed for the project by Mark James. It was run as a random generator, without the probabilities attached; and it produced garbage, as unconstrained grammar generators always do. But when it was run with the probabilities also being implemented, then (as the Director of the project, Bill Mann, expressed it to me afterwards) it produced garbage that now actually looked like

English – it bore some family resemblance to possible human language.

The probabilities I had suggested were of course extremely crude. From my original studies in the grammar of Chinese I had derived the general proposition that grammatical systems were essentially of two types: (1) those with no unmarked term, and (2) those with one term unmarked. The former were characterized by roughly equal probabilities; the latter, by probabilities which were skew. In the mid-1960s, when working on English grammar, I had counted some samples of English grammatical categories, taking as my basis for each system a population of 2000 occurrences (so, for clause systems of primary delicacy like indicative / imperative, 2000 clauses; for those of secondary delicacy, e.g. (within indicative) declarative / inter-rogative, 2000 occurrences of indicative; and so on). The samples were thus very small and the number of categories extremely limited. But within that limited sample the same bimodal pattern seemed to emerge; and in the systems with one term unmarked, the frequency skewing tended to cluster around one order of magnitude. So in the grammar written for the Penman project – which later came to be called the "Nigel" grammar – I had assigned just those two values: "equiprobable" as 0.5 / 0.5, and "skew" as 0.9 / 0.1 (with analogous values for the ternary systems which, however, I had eliminated wherever possible). Svartvik's original work on voice in the English verb (Svartvik 1966) provided important further evidence: his overall figures showed just this kind of skewing, with active coming out on average about ten times as frequent as passive. (I will come to the question of variation between different registers later on.)

The skew value of 0.9 / 0.1 seemed rather an unmotivated artefact of decimalism, until I noticed that a possible explanation for it could be found in information theory. A system of probabilities 0.5 / 0.5 is of course minimally redundant. The values 0.9 / 0.1 incorporate considerable redundancy; but this is just the point at which redund-ancy and information balance out. In a binary system, H (informa-tion) = R (redundancy) = 0.5 when the probabilities are 0.89 / 0.11. It seems plausible that the grammar of a natural language should be constructed, in outline (i.e. in its most general, least delicate cate-gories), of systems having just these two probability profiles; rather than, say, having all systems equiprobable, which would be too easily disrupted by noise, or having systems distributed across all prob-ability profiles from 0.5 / 0.5 to 0.99 / 0.01, which would be practically impossible for a child to learn.

I have taken for granted, up to this point, that relative frequency in the corpus is the same thing as probability in the grammar. Let me now put this more precisely: frequency in the corpus is the instantiation (note, not realization) of probability in the grammar. But what in fact does this mean?

Let me invoke the same kind of reasoning as I used in talking about lexicogrammar. We are so accustomed to thinking about language and text in terms of dichotomies such as the Saussurean langue and parole, or Hjelmslev's system and process, that we tend to objectify the distinction: there is language as a system, an abstract potential, and there are spoken and written texts, which are instances of language in use. But the "system" and the "instance" are not two distinct phenomena. There is only one phenomenon here, the phenomenon of language: what we have are two different observers, looking at this phenomenon from different depths in time. If I may use once again the analogy drawn from the weather: the instance-observer is the weatherman, whose texts are the day-to-day weather patterns displaying variations in temperature, humidity, air pressure, wind direction and so on, all of which can be observed, recorded and measured. The system-observer is the climatologist, who models the total potential of a given climatic zone in terms of overall probabilities. What appears to the former as a long-term weather pattern becomes for the latter a defined climatic system. There is only one set of phenomena here: the meteorological processes of precipitation, movement of air masses and the like, which we observe in close-up, as text, or else in depth, as system. But one thing is clear: the more weather we observe, as instance-watchers, the better we shall perform as system-watchers when we turn to explaining the climate.

Thus there is no discontinuity when we rewrite frequency as probability. But there will be a progressive approximation such that the larger the corpus from which we obtain our picture of the frequencies, the more accurate our account of the system is going to be. With this in mind, let me outline some of the ways in which, if our concern is to model the system, we are likely to be interested in asking questions of the text.

2. Interrogating the corpus

1.   The first and most obvious type of question is one concerning simple frequencies. What are the overall relative frequencies of the terms in a number of low delicacy grammatical systems such as, in English, the following?

(clause)
mood: indicative (declarative / interrogative) / imperative
transitivity, process type: material / mental / relational
transitivity, participation: middle/ effective
theme: unmarked / marked (circumstance / participant)
polarity: positive / negative

(verbal group)
deixis: primary tense (past / present / future) / modality
secondary tense: none / one / two ...
voice: active / passive

(nominal group)
deixis: specific / non-specific
number: singular / plural

Many others could be enumerated; obviously, results on early counts will affect decisions about what is to be counted subsequently.

These figures would be used to test any general hypothesis, such as that of a probability "typology" of systems (0.5 / 0.5 and 0.9 / 0.1) already discussed. This would be a property only of low–delicacy systems, since it could not survive beyond one or two degrees of dependence (where systems intersect, and have conjunct entry conditions). An important component in this interrogation is that of recursive systems (such as secondary tense); these provide the paradigm case of 0.9 / 0.1 (one in ten chance of choosing to go round again; cf. no. 7 below).

Systems like voice and number need to be interrogated twice: once for the whole population (all verbal or nominal groups), and again for the population at risk (only verbal groups in effective clauses can be **either** active **or** passive; only nominal groups with count noun as Head can be **either** singular **or** plural). In other words, we would both exclude and include those instances where an unmarked feature like active or singular is assigned by default.

More delicate systems such as types of declarative and inter-rogative, subcategories of modality, subcategories of nominal deixis, more delicate process types and so on, would then be investigated in order to determine degrees of association between them (see no. 5 below).

These are "raw" frequencies calculated over the language as a whole, across its functional varieties (cf. no. 2 below). Such frequencies spread across many varieties of spoken discourse constitute the primary evidence that children have available to them in learning their mother tongue; they are reconstrued by children as an integral feature of the grammar of the language.

2.   Secondly we would investigate the same grammatical systems with the frequencies broken down according to register. The Survey of English Usage established the principle, essential for corpus studies, of keeping apart texts in different register; the "Quirk grammars" have always recognized that relative frequency in grammatical systems was register-dependent, and Svartvik's studies of voice in English already referred to served as a paradigm example.

The importance of this step is that, in my view, diatypic or register variation is, simply, variation in the setting of grammatical probabilities (cf. Biber 1992). That is how register is defined. Register, like dialect, is the name of a kind of variation; we are able to talk about "a dialect" because only certain of the possible combinations of variants are taken up and these form recognizable "syndromes", and the same applies to variation of the diatypic kind. What we call "a register" is a syndrome of lexicogrammatical probabilities. Sometimes, of course, a resetting of probabilities in just one system may be diagnostic, or nearly so: to cite obvious examples, in some recent work on computational semantics by Matthiessen and myself (1999), we have taken recipes and weather forecasts as experimental texts, and here imperative mood and future primary tense (respectively) leap into prominence as most highly favoured choices. But only a detailed corpus-based study can reveal the perturbations in frequency that are not obvious in the way that these ones are.

There has been some misunderstanding on this topic, with the argument being put forward that since every text is in some register or other, only register-based frequencies have any meaning, and it is meaningless to talk of global probabilities in grammar. This is rather like saying that since it is always spring, summer, autumn or winter a mean annual precipitation is a meaningless concept. Global probabilities are just that: global probabilities. I think they **have** a significant interpretation, as inherent properties of grammatical systems, in the context of language development; when children are learning the tense system, and all the other primary systems of the grammar, they are not sensitive to register variation. But we **give** such probabilities a significant interpretation once we talk about departing from them; if we recognize departure from a norm, then there has to be a norm to depart from. If we characterize register variation as variation in probabilities, as I think we must, it seems more realistic to measure it against observed global probabilities than against some arbitrary norm such as the assumption of equiprobability in every case. (Again there are obvious analogies with interpreting variations in climate.)

3. Thirdly there is the question of whether, and if so how far, the probability of selecting one term in a given system is affected by previous selections made within the same system. This is obviously a question that can be asked with reference to any system that can be identified for investigating independently.

On the face of it, there are some systems where it seems reasonable to expect that there would be transitional effects of this kind; for example tense, and type of process. In others it is hard to see why there should be, such as number or polarity. But the general conception of a text as a Markoff process seems highly plausible; our expectancies do play a significant part in our understanding of what we read and hear (for example in overcoming noise, as is demonstrated to every first-year student of phonetics). Sinclair's work on collocation has made it clear that transitional effects do take place lexically, up to a span of about four lexical items (Sinclair 1985); so it is certainly relevant to check them out in the grammar.

4. There is another question which is related to the last, since it is also a matter of text dynamics, but which cannot be reduced to *n*-gram frequencies of terms within a system. Rather, it is a form of dynamic in which there is (or seems to be) an increase in complexity over time: namely, the tendency for complexity to increase in the course of the text.

If we think of language process in cladistic terms, then the process of phylogenesis is one of **evolution**: the evolution of the language system through time. The process of ontogenesis is one of **growth**: each human being construes the system and maintains it in maturity, and then it decays. The unfolding of the text is a process of **individuation**; there is a beginning, a middle and an end. We might refer to this process as "logogenesis", using *logos* in its original sense of 'discourse'. (I owe to Jay Lemke this interpretation of the different kinds of change that may inhere in semiotic systems; cf. Lemke 1990.)

Both evolution and growth are characterized by increasing complexity. It seems that this might also be true of a text, in some respects and perhaps under some circumstances. There are some local increases in complexity; to return to the example of the multiple tense choice I cited at the beginning, I was unable to record the conversations in which I heard those tenses spoken, so the dialogue which follows is fictitious, but there was a build-up of this kind, and I doubt whether the verb form would ever be used without one:

– Can I use this machine?	[no tense
– Sorry; we use it ourselves in the mornings.	[present
– Are you using it now?	[pres. in pres.
– Yes we are.	
– Are you going to be using it this afternoon?	[pres. in fut. in pres.
– Well no; but it's going to be being tested.	[pres. in fut. in pres., passive
– What! It's been going to be being tested now for ages!	[pres. in fut. in past in pres., passive
It'll've been going to've been being tested every day for about a fortnight soon!	[pres. in past in fut. in past in fut., passive

This, as I said, is a purely local increase; such a thing is certainly of interest, but it could not be retrieved as part of the quantitative profile of a text. An example of a more general increase in complexity is provided by grammatical metaphor. In scientific and technical discourse the amount of grammatical metaphor seems to increase in the course of the text; much of it has to be built up instantly, by (in a typical case) gradually nominalizing processes and properties that have been brought in first in the form of verbs and adjectives. Thus, apart from preliminaries (headlines, titles and abstracts), nominal strings like *glass fracture growth rate* and *increasing lung cancer death rate* tend to accumulate throughout the text rather than being announced at the beginning. The logogenetic history of the first of these, spread over three or four pages of closely printed text, included the following ancestry:

how glass cracks	[*crack* Process; *glass* as Actor
the stress needed to crack glass	[*crack* caused Process, *glass* Goal
as a crack grows	[*crack* nominalized, as Carrier
the crack has advanced	[ditto, as Actor
will make slow cracks grow	[as caused Actor; + property *slow*
the rate at which cracks grow	[property nominalized as *rate*
the rate of crack growth	[second process *grow* nominalized
we can decrease the crack growth rate	[*crack growth rate* as complex nominal
glass fracture growth rate	[most nominalized form in this text

The text has now constructed a highly complex technical object with the characteristic grammatical structure of a **word complex**, here a string of four common nouns (see Michalske and Bunker 1987).

It should be possible to test the hypothesis that such grammatical metaphor tends to increase in the course of the text, at least in the case of certain registers. On the one hand we could use a general measure such as lexical density, the number of lexical items per ranking clause, perhaps weighted for their overall frequency bands; and on the other hand, certain more specific measures such as the length of nominal chains, or adjectival-nominal chains, and the selection of verbs that are typically associated with such grammatical metaphors.

There are other possible ways in which texts might tend to increase in complexity; for example, the average number of ranking clauses per sentence, or the number of phrases and clauses "rank-shifted" inside nominal groups. Equally, there might be compensating decreases in complexity, though it is harder to see how these could be motivated in themselves.

5.   Returning now to the overall probabilities, we would also seek from the corpus information about the degree of association between simultaneous systems. Suppose we take the systems of the clause: what is the effect on the probability of active / passive of choosing either declarative or interrogative in the same clause? There may be no association at all between the two, in which case the probabilities are unaffected; or there may be a tendency for (say) interrogative to favour active more strongly than declarative does.

We will refer to these as conditional probabilities. The two types of conditioning effect, the transitional and the conditional, are of course formally equivalent; but since the transitional probabilities are linear, the first choice always constitutes the environment for the second. With conditional probabilities, on the other hand, the two choices are being made simultaneously, and so either can be treated as the environment for the other; in the above example, we could equally well ask, what is the effect on the probability of declarative / interrogative of choosing either active or passive in the same clause? The two effects may be reciprocal, but they may not: the discussion by Nesbitt and Plum referred to below contains examples of both.

This sort of enquiry becomes particularly relevant when we are considering simultaneous systems sharing the same immediate entry condition, since they are especially likely to be associated. An extremely valuable pilot investigation was carried out by Nesbitt and Plum (1988), into the intersection between interdependency (hypotaxis / parataxis) and logical semantic relation (expansion / projection) in the English clause complex. I have discussed this in detail in another place (Chapter 3 this volume) and will not repeat the discussion here. They used a sample of 2,733 clause nexuses, and were able to show from the frequencies of the different feature combinations that certain pairs of systems were independent of each other whereas others had some degree of association between them.

6. There is, however, one further theoretical reason for investigating conditional probabilities as outlined in the preceding section, and that is for the insights they can give into historical linguistic processes. Chapter 3 Table 3.10 presented a set of tables showing the intersection of two simultaneous systems as demonstrated by text frequency; the examples were imaginary ones showing the kinds of possibility that arise. In Tables 3.10 a (i)–(iii), the figures show the two systems to be unassociated: in (i), both systems are equiprobable (no unmarked term), in (ii) both are skew (one term unmarked), while in (iii) there is one of each. In Table 3.10 b (iv)–(vi), on the other hand, the systems are equiprobable but there is some association between them: either reciprocal, as in (iv), or one-way, as in (v) and (vi). Thus in (iv), m favours p and p favours m, likewise n favours q and q favours n; whereas in (v) m favours p but not the other way round, and in (vi) p favours m but not the other way round. Finally, Table 3.10 b (vii) shows a variant of (iv), in which the conditioning effect (of p and m on each other, and of n and q on each other) is so strong that the result is as if each system had an unmarked term but with the marking reversed. The systems studied by Nesbitt and Plum yielded various types: the intersection of

hypotaxis / parataxis with expansion / projection is of type (iii), while that of hypotaxis / parataxis with the subcategories of projection, locution / idea, is of type (iv) – but tending towards (vii).

What this last example means, in terms of traditional grammar, is that, while the balance between "speech" and "thought" was roughly equal, and the balance between "direct (quoted)" and "indirect (reported)" was also roughly equal, there was a strong association of "speech" with "direct" and of "thought" with "indirect". This could reflect a process of the gradual dissociation of associated variables, if we reconstruct a stage in history at which there was only a single system of projection, "direct speech" versus "indirect thought". The figures in the corpus could suggest an ongoing change whereby the other two combinations had been opened up, but had not yet reached a point where the choices were entirely independent of one another.

It seems likely that this dissociation of associated variables, by which one complex system (typically, a system having a complex realization by two simultaneous features) is prised apart, evolving into two simultaneous systems with the features recombining, is the most powerful resource in language for the creation of new meanings. We could represent this situation as in Figure 5.1.

(2)

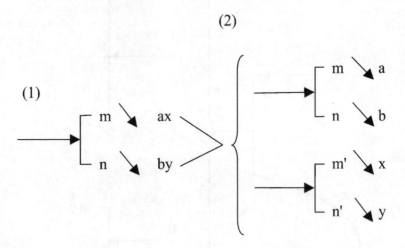

Figure 5.1 Evolution of a system into two simultaneous systems

Assuming that System (1), at time one, was inherently equiprobable, then the initial state of (2), at time two, would approximate to that described in Table 3.10 b (vii), with m and m' strongly favouring each other, and *n* and *n'* strongly favouring each other (i.e. the preferred realizations still being *ax* and *by*). The association might stabilize at this point; or it might evolve further, at time three, into that described in Table 3.10 b (iv); and even further, at time four, into that of Table 3.10 a (i), with two equiprobable systems entirely independent of one another.

Obviously it is only by observing such systems evolving over time that we can say whether a given state is stable or is part of an ongoing historical change; and such processes are likely to take place fairly slowly. It is possible that a diachronic corpus such as that at the University of Helsinki would contain enough instances for some patterns of this kind to be revealed. But even without being able to examine the historical evidence we would still find it worth while to show on quantitative grounds where something of this kind might be happening. One reason is that it corresponds to one of the major patterns in children's language development, whereby children first construe a single system formed of the most favoured feature combinations, and then later deconstrue it and reconstrue with new meanings introduced at the interstices.

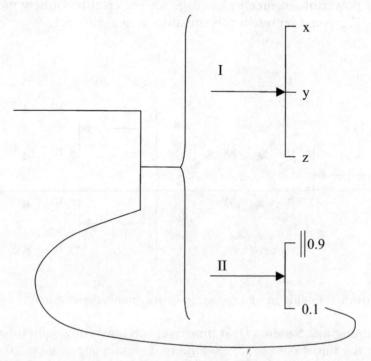

Figure 5.2 Recursive system, showing probabilities of re-entry

7. As a final example of queries to be addressed to the corpus, let me refer to the one type of system in the grammar which is inherently quantitative in nature: the choice between choosing and not choosing. These are recursive systems of the form shown in Figure 5.2. This represents a system such as the English tense system, with the choice of past / present / future combined with the simultaneous option of "going round again". My own very limited counting within such systems suggested that they were governed by the same skewness principle and that "stop" was always the unmarked term. Thus in the finite verbal group the proportion of one-term ("simple") tenses to those of more than one term was roughly ten to one; that of two-term tenses to those of more than two terms likewise (beyond that the numbers were too small to be significant). This result was irrespective of which tense was actually chosen any particular time round. It would be valuable to know whether a similar pattern occurs with "complexes" of all kinds: clause complexes, verbal group complexes and so on. Are sentences with two ranking clauses (one "clause nexus") one-tenth as common as those with only one clause? In other words, could there be a single pattern of frequency distribution covering all kinds of "marking"? In many systems having an unmarked term, that feature is unmarked also in the realizational sense: it is unexpanded, while the marked term involves some expansion, like positive / negative in English (*does / doesn't*). The choice of "going round again" in a recursive system is also a form of expansion. Thus we would be asking whether there was a general quantitative principle covering such cases as:

negative$_{0.1}$ / positive$_{0/9}$	didn't take / took
complex tense$_{0.1}$ / simple tense$_{0.9}$	has taken / took
phased verbal group$_{0.1}$ / unphased$_{0.9}$	began to take / took
clause nexus$_{0.1}$ / clause simplex$_{0.9}$	I took it because ... / I took it.

It may turn out that there are no such regularities of any kind. But it is that possibility that makes it interesting if they occur.

Every instance of a text that is spoken or written in English perturbs the overall probabilities of the system, to an infinitesimal extent (whether it has been recorded in a corpus or not! – hence the function of the corpus as a sample). To say this is to treat the system as inherently probabilistic. This has been the stance of the lexis-observer for the best part of a century; no one is surprised that children learning a language build up a probability profile of the vocabulary. For some reason, grammar-observers often find this stance distasteful, as if assigning probabilities in grammar was a threat to the freedom of the individual (perhaps because the grammatical end of the continuum is buried more deeply below the level of conscious attention?). But it would seem to me very surprising if children did not also construe a probability profile of the grammar; and I think there is considerable evidence that they do.

In order to approach the grammar in this way, we have to model it paradigmatically, as choice. (It should always be made clear that this has nothing to do with conscious processes of choosing. In this regard, a speaker, or writer, may always "choose" to subvert the probabilities of the system – which leads back to the same point: that this makes sense only if the probabilities are part of the system in the first place.) A major theoretical problem facing paradigmatic grammars, such as the "systemic" grammar that I have used throughout this chapter, is how to incorporate probability into the grammatics. In a system network, either two systems are independent, or they are associated; there are no degrees of association set up between them. The simple "probability tagging" that has been used so far is obviously a very crude affair. Fundamental work is needed on the probabilistic modelling of systems in a paradigmatic grammar of this kind. But in my view this effort is more likely to be successful if we first find out more of the facts; and that can only be done by interrogating the corpus.

Chapter Six

A Quantitative Study of Polarity and Primary Tense in the English Finite Clause (1993) [Co-Authored with Z. L. James]

1 Preliminaries

1.1 The corpus used

The aim of this study was to undertake some basic quantitative research in the grammar of Modern English.[1] To do this, we required a corpus which was:

1. made up of naturally occurring language;
2. readily available and easy to access;
3. large enough to provide a significant sample of the least common structures we were interested in;
4. drawn from specified genres.

We used the 18 million words of written text that formed the major part of the original COBUILD corpus, which appeared to meet these criteria. In particular, the texts making up the corpus had been chosen with learners in mind; texts in which language was used in untypical ways were excluded, so that the publications derived from the corpus would be maximally useful to students of English. Full details of the texts used are listed in the 'Corpus Acknowledgements' section of the COBUILD dictionary (Sinclair *et al.* 1987).

The new COBUILD corpus, known as the "Bank of English", which is currently being collected, will contain a similar quantity (approximately 20 million words) of spoken material which will be accessible independently, and this spoken subcorpus would be an obvious choice for a complementary study.

1.2 Theoretical framework

The relevant theoretical concept in grammar is that of the ***system***, as used by Firth (1957a) and subsequently developed in "systemic" grammar (Halliday 1976; Halliday and Martin 1981; Matthiessen 1988). A systemic grammar is a paradigmatic grammar in which the fundamental organizing concept is that of the system: that is, a set of options with a condition of entry, such that exactly one option must be chosen whenever the entry condition is satisfied. A system is thus a kind of 'deep paradigm' (Halliday 1966). A simple example would be: system of "number", options (or "terms", in Firth's terminology) "singular / plural", entry condition "nominal group: count–able". Traditionally in systemic theory, this has been represented schematically as

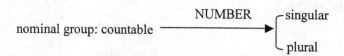

Such a representation is, however, incomplete, because it does not yet show how the options singular and plural are realized. Each term in the system carries with it a ***realization statement*** specifying what is to be done to construct the chosen form. To continue with the same example, we would write

$$\text{nominal group: countable} \xrightarrow{\text{NUMBER}} \begin{cases} \text{singular} \searrow [\ ] \\ \text{plural} \searrow \text{Thing: } + \hat{}(e)s \end{cases}$$

This would indicate that, if you choose singular, you take no action at this point, while if you choose plural you add -(e)s at the end of the word functioning as Thing in the nominal group. This functional element itself has been inserted in an earlier realization statement.

Quantitative work in grammar depends on some such concept of a system, such that one can ask: given (say) 100,000 instances of a nominal group that **could** be either singular or plural, but not both, and **must** be one or the other, how many were, in fact, singular and how many were plural? (See Halliday 1959; Svartvik 1966; Hasan and Cloran 1990.)

Note that if such a question can be asked, then set theory or other formal logic can be used as models, as the boundaries between sets are clearly defined. There is no cline between singular and plural; that is to say, if we represent the grammar with these as discrete categories we shall not be distorting the picture. In a quantitative study we are assuming that the categories to be counted (for example, classes of the clause, or of the group) form clearly defined sets of this kind. This does not mean, of course, that there is some simple criterion for recognizing each instance; but it does mean that we can assign instances to one class or the other with a reasonably close degree of approximation.

In a systemic grammar the entire grammar is represented as a network of systems, each of which is potentially a candidate for quantitative analysis; large systemic grammars have some 700–1,000 systems (Matthiessen 1989; Fawcett and Tucker 1990). Some of these, of course, are rather **delicate** systems, such as the contrast between straight and transferred negative in clausal modalities, for example between *I think not* and *I don't think so*; it will have to be a very large corpus before we find enough instances of this contrast in different environments to enable us to make any revealing generalizations about it. But we naturally want to establish quantitative profiles of the less delicate, more general systems first.

The main problem that arises is that of parsing. Hardly any of the major grammatical systems of English (or probably those of any language) have simple, consistent patterns of realization such that instances can be easily recognized by computer (computational analysis being necessary in practice to perform large-scale counting). One might almost formulate it as a general principle of language that the easier a thing is to recognize, the more trivial it is and hence the less worthwhile it is to recognize it. Some systems are thoroughly cryptotypic, and appear only in the form of complex reactances and differences in potential agnation; almost all the systems in the domain of transitivity in English are of this kind (see Davidse 1992a, b, c, 1994, 1996, 1999), as well as being further complicated by the pervasive presence of metaphor in the grammar (Halliday 1985; Martin 1991; Halliday and Matthiessen 1999). For example, there is no obvious way of writing a program to count the number of clauses which select material, mental or relational types of process. It is not that such systems have no realization statements attached to them; they have – but these involve complex chains of realization, and it is a slow and lengthy job to parse them out.

1.3 Setting up a hypothesis

We decided to try to access the corpus directly, using existing programs that had already been developed for COBUILD'S lexicographical, and more recently grammatical, research (Sinclair 1987). This meant that we had to identify grammatical systems whose instances we could recognize to a sufficient degree of approximation by reference to lexemes, and combinations of lexemes, represented orthographically – with original spelling and punctuation, as in the computerized corpus. At the same time, they had to be systems of a high level of generality (not too delicate, in systemic terminology); and they had to be interesting. In fact, once something has been shown to be a grammatical system, it is interesting *ipso facto*; but we wanted to go for systems that construe the main dimensions of experiential and interpersonal meaning, like mood and transitivity; and this meant working with systems of the clause, since it is largely in the grammar of the clause that such meanings are construed.

Our aim, however, was not simply to count things, but in doing so to test a hypothesis. Halliday had formulated the hypothesis that grammatical systems fell largely into two types: those where the options were equally probable – there being no "unmarked term", in the quantitative sense; and those where the options were skew, one term being unmarked. This was based on figures he had arrived at in the 1960s, by counting manually 2,000 instances each of a number of sets of systemic options across texts of different genres in modern English. If we assume a binary system (and it should be emphasized explicitly that **not** all systems are binary), this means that in an "equi" system, each term would occur with roughly the same frequency, while in a "skew" system one term would be significantly more frequent than the other. In his small–scale manual counting Halliday had found that the difference in frequency of the options in a skew system tended to be approximately one order of magnitude. In order to formulate a hypothesis in terms of probabilities he expressed this as

equi systems: 0.5 : 0.5
skew systems: 0.9 : 0.1

In other words, the prediction was that general grammatical systems would not be distributed evenly across the probability scale, with all values from 0.5 : 0.5 to 0.99 : 0.01, but that they would be distributed bimodally into these two probability profiles – with some approximation to these two values. A similar pattern would be predicted for ternary systems, except that it should be possible to find more than one type within the skew. We expect this overall picture to be generally true, although the exact distribution of probabilities may vary among different genres. Possible insights into why this pattern should exist have been discussed [elsewhere] (Halliday 1992; this volume, Chapter 5).

1.4 Choosing the systems

We decided to identify, for investigation, systems that would allow us to make a start towards testing this hypothesis. We could not, of course, start from the clause; that is, we could not take as given in the text any neatly bounded and recognizable unit corresponding to this abstraction. While punctuation originally evolved as a way of marking off linguistic units, no unit in the orthography (such as 'string of words between any two punctuation marks') corresponds exactly to a clause in the grammar. This is partly because punctuation is a mixture of the grammatical and the phonological; but partly also because, even in its grammatical guise, it has evolved to the point where it is used to set up an independent hierarchy of units in counterpoint to the 'original' constituent hierarchy, thus opening up for written language new systems of meaning analogous to the systems realized by intonation in the spoken language. We therefore had to work with systems whose realization did not depend on our being able either to count clauses or to identify locations within them (for example, 'clause-final'). The situation was rather the other way round: we hoped that we would be able to derive from the study of particular clause systems some estimate of the total number of clauses in the corpus, and perhaps also some pointers towards the mechanical construction of clause boundaries.

As our first task we took two systems: polarity and primary tense. Polarity has the two options "positive/negative", as in *It is. / It isn't.*, or *Is it? / Isn't it?*, or *Do! / Don't!* It is a system that is entered by all **major** clauses (clauses other than the **minor** ones of calls, greetings and exclamations), both finite and non-finite. Primary tense has the three options "past / present / future", as in *said / say(s) / will say*, or *didn't say / do(es)n't say / won't say*. Primary tense is the deictic component in the tense system, and hence is entered only by finite clauses – and not all of these, because in some clauses deixis is achieved by modality (for example, *should say / shouldn't say*); so that clauses where the Finite operator is a modal have no primary tense either. We restricted the investigation to finite clauses, partly because non-finites are outside the domain of primary tense and partly also because it is harder to recognize their polarity (for every *-ing* form you have to decide whether it is functioning as Predicator or not).

Fairly obviously, in the terms of the starting hypothesis, polarity was a skew system, with positive as the unmarked term; the relative frequency predicted by the hypothesis was therefore nine positive to one negative.

Primary tense was more complicated; it was a three-term system for which the prediction was that two terms (past, present) would be equally probable, the third term (future) much less so. But for the sake of simplicity we wanted to set it up as a binary system, and test just the "equi" part of the hypothesis for past and present. We therefore postulated a two-step system of primary tense as follows:

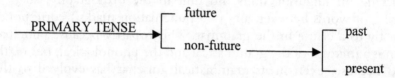

This leaves "past / present" as a binary system, with the two terms predicted to be equal in frequency. (An alternative hypothesis would have been "past / non-past"; the reason for preferring the first one was that futures are difficult to recognize, since every occurrence of *will* and *'ll* (and even of *would, should* and *'d*, because of "sequence of tenses") could be either future tense or modality. One could even justify postulating "present / non-present" as a first cut; but that would still be subject to the same practical objection. See 4.3.3 below.)

2 Methods of investigation

2.1 Defining the sets we wished to identify

Ideally, the strategy for investigating polarity would be something like the following:

1 Identify and count all finite clauses.
2 Within this set, identify and count all those that are negative.

3   Subtract the negative from the finite and label the remaining set positive.
4   Calculate the percentage of negative and positive within the total set of finite clauses.

If a diagrammatic representation of this is helpful, refer to Figure 6.1.

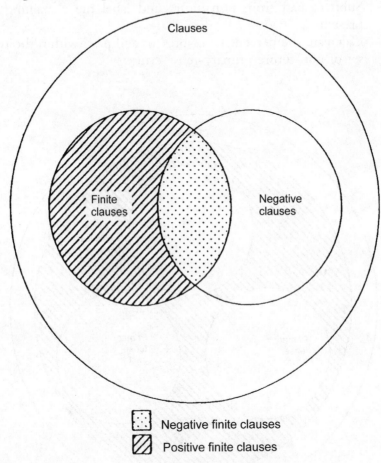

Figure 6.1 Diagrammatic representation of the sets involved in quantifying polarity

Similarly, an ideal strategy for investigating tense would be as follows:

1   Identify and count all finite clauses having modal deixis.
2   Within the set of finite clauses remaining (which therefore

have temporal deixis, that is, primary tense) identify and count those whose primary tense is future.

3   Subtract future from temporal deixis and label the remaining set non-future.

4   Within non-future, identify and count those whose primary tense is past.

5   Subtract past from non-future and label the remaining set present.

6   Calculate the percentage of present and past, within the total set of non-future primary-tense clauses.

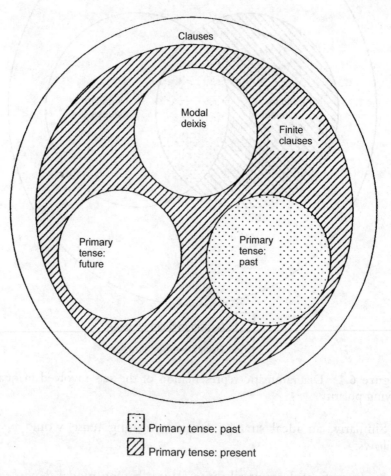

Figure 6.2 Diagrammatic representation of the sets involved in quantifying primary tense

The sets relating to the primary-tense system are indicated in Figure 6.2. In setting out the Venn diagrams we have assumed a particular order of procedure. Figure 6.1 suggests negative as the "marked" set (that which is to be identified as a subset of the total set of clauses), and this is consistent with treating it as the marked term in the system. In Figure 6.2, "primary tense: present" is suggested as the unmarked set, with the other primary tenses, and modality, as marked subsets; this corresponds to our idealized order of procedure (not one that could be closely followed in practice), but should not be interpreted as suggesting that "primary tense: present" is an unmarked option in the system.

2.2 Problems with identifying sets

We considered various ways to identify the relevant sets of clauses most accurately. No parser can yet identify instances of "finite clause" or "primary tense: past" with sufficient reliability; to attempt to adapt any existing parser to carry out this operation would be a major research project in itself, so we had to approximate the figures as best we could. We also considered using one or other of the available COBUILD taggers, especially in order to separate instances of finite verbs from their homographs (for example, *work* as finite verb from *work* as noun, *changed* as finite verb from *changed* as adjective and so on). However, as this particular task was one of their least successful operations, we decided against it.

What we had to do was to devise means of identifying the categories we were interested in to a reasonable degree of accuracy and in such a way as to minimize possible distortions (that is, distortions of the figures for polarity and primary tense). Thus if a number of non-finite clauses were going to slip under the net and be counted among the finite, then there should be some means whereby these also should be recognized to be either positive or negative.

2.3 Finite operators used to classify clauses

A clause is finite if its Predicator is deictic: that is, if its verbal group embodies a choice of deixis. Verbal deixis is either (a) modality or (b) primary tense. Semantically, deixis means having a reference point in the 'you and me, here, now' of the speech situation – that is, it means that the proposition is deemed as valid relative to that situation. In deixis by modality (modal deixis), the validity is made relative to the speaker's judgement, or the speaker's request for the listener's judgement; and this is a judgement in terms of probability or obligation, high, median or low, for example, *it could be dangerous* ('I think'), *could it be dangerous?* ('do you think?'). In deixis by primary tense (temporal deixis), the validity is made relative to the time of speaking, and this is in terms of orientation, past, present or future, for example *it was dangerous, it is dangerous, it will be dangerous*. In both cases, the deictic choice is associated with a choice of polarity, positive or negative. So to all the above examples correspond negative agnates: *it couldn't be dangerous, couldn't it be dangerous?; it wasn't dangerous, it isn't dangerous, it won't be dangerous*.

In many instances, the deixis is expressed by a Finite operator. Counting instances of these operators could therefore be helpful in classifying clauses. The Finite operators can be listed, and divided into two general categories as follows:

Modal operators						
can		could	may		might	will
can't	cannot	couldn't	mayn't		mightn't	won't
would	should	must	ought (+ to)		need	dare
wouldn't	shouldn't	mustn't	oughtn't (+ to)		needn't	daren't

Temporal operators[2]							
am	is	are	was	were	have	has	had
ain't	isn't	aren't	wasn't	weren't	haven't	hasn't	hadn't
will	would	shall	should	do	does	did	
won't	wouldn't	shan't	shouldn't	don't	doesn't	didn't	

In a more detailed consideration of these operators, there are some additional points to be taken into account:

1 *Do, does, did* and their negatives are strictly 'tense/polarity' operators, realizing negative and marked positive options in simple past and simple present tense, for example, *took – didn't take – did take, takes – doesn't take – does take*.

2 *Am, is, are, was, were* are strictly 'tense or voice' operators, realizing tense in combination with v-ng, voice in combination with v-n, for example, *is taking, was taking, is taken, was taken*. (For v-ng and v-n notation see page 110)

3 Temporal operators also occur in non-finite form (apart from

102

do, does, did). These forms are *be, being, been, have, having* and (the non-finite agnate of *will, shall*) *be, being, been* + *going to/ about to*. They occur in the secondary tenses, for example *will be taking, has been taking, will have taken, might have been going to take*, and in passive voice, for example *is being taken, had been taken*.

A few of these operators also occur as other lexemes, for example *can* = 'tin container', *will* = 'desire' or 'testament'. Inspecting 200 instances of each of these words, we found the following number of non-operator occurrences:

    can 0   may 7   might 1   will 10   must 0   am 3   do 0

(*am* occurs here because it also figured as 'a.m.' in reference to the time of day). In counting occurrences of the Finite operators, we extrapolated from these figures and disqualified a proportionate number from the total. Also, we eliminated from the list the forms *need* and *dare*, because these occur as full (lexical) verbs and it was impossible to separate the two conditions; *needn't* and *daren't* were left in, because they occur only as Finite operators. (Occurrences of *need* are counted elsewhere; see Section 4.2 below. *Daren't* is comparatively rare.)

The numbers of occurrences of each of the Finite operators in the 18-million-word corpus are given in Table 6.1.

2.4 *Limitations of counting operators*

Counting operators was the first step towards counting the number of finite clauses, resolving all of them into positive and negative, identifying those with non-future primary tense and resolving these into past and present. It left the following problems untackled:

1   It omitted instances of the two most frequent tense forms in the language, namely "simple past" and "simple present" in positive polarity and active voice: past *took*, present *take(s)*. In order to count finite clauses which do not contain one of the listed operators, the actual verb forms had to be counted. The simple past and simple present forms of the three most frequent verbs in the language, namely *be, have, do*, also function as finite temporal operators (*was, were; had; did; am, is, are; have, has; do, does*), and so did not need to be recounted.

103

Table 6.1 Finite operators

Positive	Number of instances	Spurious instances out of 200	Corrected count	Negative		
can	33,002	0	33,002	can't, cannot	9,568	
could	32,164		32,164	couldn't	4,102	
may	17,716	7	17,096	mayn't	3	
might	12,509	1	12,446	mightn't	85	
						modal, and
will	34,817	10	33,076	won't	2,818	future
would	48,882		48,882	wouldn't	3,094	temporal
shall	3,787		3,787	shan't	137	
should	16,053		16,053	shouldn't	700	
must	15,520	0	15,520	mustn't	296	
ought	1,547		1,547	oughtn't	40	
			213,573		20,843	
am	6,599	3	6,401	ain't	476	
is	149,514		149,514	isn't	3,037	
are	70,925		70,925	aren't	1,160	
						present
have	76,207		76,207	haven't	1,533	temporal
has	33,749		33,749	hasn't	501	
do	32,011	0	32,011	don't	16,737	
does	7,387		7,387	doesn't	3,069	Total present:
			376,194		26,513	402,707
was	186,839		186,839	wasn't	4,144	
were	60,276		60,276	weren't	839	past
had	109,835	8	105,442	hadn't	2,415	temporal
did	19,322		7,387	didn't	9,637	Total past:
			371,879		17,035	388,914
		Total positive	961,646	Total negative	64,391	

Results: For polarity, 961,646 clauses were found to be positive and 64,391 negative out of a total of 1,026,037. For primary tense, 402,707 clauses were found to have present primary tense and 388,914 were found to have past primary tense out of a total of 791,621.

Note: The "corrected count" is arrived at by deducting from the "number of instances" a number extrapolated from the figure of disqualified occurrences in a sample of 200. For example, out of the 200 instances of *may*, 7 were found to be other than Finite operator (the month of May, in some context or other). The raw count of 17,716 was therefore reduced by 7/200 (that is, 3.5 per cent) to 17,096. If no disqualified occurrences were found, the figure is shown as 0. Where there is no entry in the column, the test was not applied. For negative realized as Finite operator + *not*, see Table 6.2.

This might not greatly affect the figures for primary tense, since the proportion of past : present may remain the same with other verbs. But it seriously distorts the figures for polarity, since those omitted are, subject to 2 below, all positive.

2   It omits all instances where negative is realized by a separate word: most typically *not*, but also *never, nothing, no one/nobody,* as well as rarer forms such as *seldom* and *hardly*. This again distorts the figure for polarity, since those instances that are omitted are all negative.

3   It omits all abbreviated forms of the Finite operators, namely:
   (a) 'll (= will, shall)
   (b) 'd (= would, should; had)
   (c) 'm (= am)
   (d) 's (= is; has)
   (e) 're (= are)
   (f) 've (= have)

These are a mixture of temporals and modals: *'ll* and *'d* may be either, the remainder are temporal only. Of the temporals, *'ll* is future, *'d* may be either future (*would, should*) or past (*had*); the remainder are present. All are positive, but they may occur in a negative clause where negative is realized by a separate word as in 2 above; for example *they're not playing, I've never asked*. Note that *'s* occurs also as a possessive and that all abbreviated forms occur not only with pronouns as Subject but also with nouns. (The corpus includes such instances as *martini'd* and *whorehouse'll* – typically found where the Subject nominal group contains a prepositional phrase or relative clause as Qualifier.)

It also fails to separate temporal from modal instances of those operators which occur as both, namely *will, 'll*; and also *would, should, 'd*, which occur as "sequenced" variants of temporal *will, shall: he'll (will) do it: he said he'd (would) do it; shall I do it?: I asked if I should do it*. This is irrelevant when we are counting the total number of finite clauses, but it matters if we want to separate modality from primary tense as a whole (that is, with future included in primary tense).

Note, however, that *am, is, are, was, were + to*, and *have, has, had + to*, although they express modality, have **temporal, not modal** deixis: *I had to / have to / will have to tell them; that was / is / will be to* *throw away*; in other words they are like *be able to, be supposed to* and suchlike forms, where the modality is non-finite. These therefore are adequately accounted for.

4   It counts the mood tag (tag questions) as a separate finite clause; thus, *Mary would know, wouldn't she?* would count as two occur-rences, one positive and one negative. But the mood tag is not a separate clause; and while it might be argued that, since some are negative and some positive and all retain the finite feature (modality or primary tense) of their parent clause, this does not matter, in fact it does distort the picture, because the **choice** of polarity in the mood tag is not independent of that in the parent clause. In the tag, you do not choose "positive / negative"; you choose "polarity reversed / polarity constant", with "polarity reversed" as the unmarked option. Hence tagged positives are overwhelmingly likely to be negative, and vice versa; so if tags are counted separately, they exaggerate the figure for negative instances.

2.5 Filling the gaps

The above problems are listed in order of importance; but as they get less important they also get easier to deal with. So we dealt with them in reverse order, taking the following steps:

1   In response to (4) above, we estimated the number of positive and negative mood tags, by counting occurrences of the sequence 'comma + Finite operator + personal pronoun + question mark', for example, *won't they?* The figure for positive tags was deducted from the total for positive, that for negative tags was deducted from negative. (We only remembered afterwards that we should have included *there* in the set of personal pronouns.) In the event, there were very few instances of mood tags at all, no doubt reflecting the fact that the corpus being used consisted of written English only.

In fact, many tags are not netted by this procedure; for example the following, all taken from the corpus:

He's an odd bird, isn't he.

She's really kissing it now, isn't she!

That's the whole point of it, isn't it, darling?

It's much worse, isn't it, like you, to have stayed?

Probably a more effective tactic would be to count 'comma + Finite operator + personal pronoun + (any) punctuation mark'.

2   Second, in response to (3) above, we counted all occurrences of the abbreviated forms *'ll, 'd, 'm, 's, 're, 've,* and labelled these "positive". We estimated the number of *'s* occurrences that were possessive, and deducted this total from the count for *'s.* (Of a total of 104,301 *'s,* 71,606 were estimated to be possessive, leaving 32,695 as Finite operator, either *is* or *has.*) Where an abbreviated form corresponds to more than one operator, as *'ll* to both *will* and *shall,* or *'s* to both *is* and *has,* the figures were assigned proportionately: thus, the 10,050 occurrences of *'ll* were assigned to *will* and *shall* according to the ratio in which these two forms themselves occurred (34,817 : 3,787). This is not necessary for calculating the overall figures involved but it makes them easier to tabulate.

3   In response to (2) on page 105, we estimated the number of negative clauses where the negative polarity was realized by *not* or another negative word. The problem here was that not all occurrences of *not* were to be treated as negative clauses. On the one hand, non-finite clauses are typically negated with *not* (for example, *so as not to be disturbed, with Jim not getting that job*); and we were not including non-finites in the count. On the other hand, *not* frequently occurs as part of a nominal group; and although in many such instances there is a case for considering as negative the clause in which that nominal group is functioning – the fact that such clauses tend to take a positive tag, as in *Not all your friends agree with that, do they?* – there are also many where this is not appropriate, including a common type where *not* is part of a Submodifier, for example *A not inconsiderable number of voters stayed away* (tag *didn't they?*). We decided, therefore, to count just those having the form "Finite operator + *not*", allowing up to one word to come in between: thus *will not, 'll not, will you not, will have not, 're certainly not* and so on.

As the software we used is set up, we could only easily retrieve word combinations up to a maximum of 4,000 occurrences of the **first** word; thus, for example, out of 4,000 occurrences of *will,* the figure for *will* + (... +) *not* was 241. We therefore extrapolated from this figure: there were altogether 34,817 occurrences of *will* – note that this had to be the original figure, not that adjusted for disqualified instances; then, multiplying 241 by 34,817/4,000, we

Table 6.2 (a) Tags, abbreviations, negatives with not

		Mood tags				Abbreviations (Finite operator)		Negatives with not				
	Positive	No. of tag questions in 10,000 citations	Extrapolated total no.	Negative	Total no. of tags	Positive (total)	Distribution	Full	No. with not in 4,000	Extrapolated (total)	Abbreviation (total)	Distribution
Modal and future temporal	can	26	86	can't	17							
	could	9	29	couldn't	20			could	462	3,715		·30
	may	1	2	mayn't	0			may	227	1,005		·35
	might	0	0	mightn't	4			might	166	519		·12
	will	50	174	won't	76	'll (10,050)	9,055	will	241	2,098	'll (42)	
	would	25	122	wouldn't	56	'd (10,886)	4,099	would	246	3,006	'd (94)	
	shall	3	28	shan't	3	'll	·995	shall		185	'll	
	should	3	5	shouldn't	5	'd	·1,344	should	264	1,059	'd	·12
	must	3	5	mustn't	11			must	146	566		
	ought		0	oughtn't	3			ought		92		
Present temporal	am	3	6	ain't	24	'm	9,812	am	432	713	'm	1,630
	is		75	isn't	420	's (32,695)	27,464	is	233	8,709	's (2,005)	1,684
	are		64	aren't	169	're	9,358	are	185	3,280	're	946
	have	4	30	haven't	55	've	9,028	have	42	800	've	62
	has	8	27	hasn't	20	's	·5,231	has	92	802	's	·321
	do	93	298	don't	172			do	561	4,490		
	does		43	doesn't	73			does	1,597	2,949		
Past temporal	was		36	wasn't	87			was	163	7,665		
	were		6	weren't	25			were		2,456		
	had	0	0	hadn't	16	'd	·5,443	had	119	3,268	'd	·47
	did	43	83	didn't	154			did	1,370	6,618		
Totals		Total pos.	Total 1,119	Total neg.	Total pos: 1,408	Total present: 60,893	Total 81,829			Total 53,995		Total 4,779

Total no. of tags subtotals: Total present: 1,476; Total past: 407. Abbreviations distribution subtotals: Total present: 60,893; Total past: 5,443.

Table 6.2 (a) *continued*

Result:

1 *Polarity* – add/deduct as follows:
   (a) add to 'positive' the total of abbreviations for Finite operators (81,829);
   (b) deduct from 'positive' positive tags, Finite operators + *not* and abbreviations for Finite operators + *not* (1,119 + 53,995 + 4,779 = 59,893);
   (c) add to 'negative' Finite operators + *not*, and abbreviations for Finite operators + *not* (53,995 + 4,779 = 58,774);
   (d) deduct from 'negative' the negative tags (1,408).

2 *Primary Tense* – add/deduct as follows:
   (a) add to 'present' the abbreviations for Finite operators (60,893);
   (b) deduct from 'present' the present tag questions (1,476);
   (c) add to 'past' the abbreviations for Finite operators (5,443);
   (d) deduct from 'past' the past tag questions (407).

Note: Figures with · were obtained by proportional distribution. For example, there were 10,050 instances of *'ll*. In Table 6.1, the proportion of occurrences of *will* to *shall* was 33,076 : 3,787. The figure of 10,050 was therefore distributed between 'will' and 'shall' in this same proportion, that is 9055 : 995. Likewise with *'d* and *'s*; and with all three abbreviations + *not*.

reached an estimate of 2,098 for *will* + (...+) *not*. Out of a total of 84,898 occurrences of *not*, 58,830 were netted by this procedure.

As far as other negative clauses were concerned, we inspected 200 instances of each word that can realize the clause feature "negative": *no, never, nothing, little, without* and so on, down to the least frequent *no one* (318 occurrences). Using the 'tag test', we established how many of the 200 should be counted as negative finite clauses; for example, the unmarked tag for *there was no chance* would be *was there?*, that for *very few people know about it* would be *do they?* The figure was then extrapolated as a proportion of the total number of occurrences of the word, and the combined figure was then deducted from the positive count and added to that for negative.

The results of the investigation up to this point are given in Table 6.2 (a, b).

4   This left the question raised under 1 on page 103, that of lexical verbs in simple past and simple present tense: *took, take(s)*, all of which are to be added to the "positive" score. This is a major topic and needs a section to itself.

3 Counting simple past and present tense of common verbs

3.1 Deciding which verbs to consider

We decided to proceed by counting the simple past and simple present tense occurrences of the most frequently occurring verbs (after *be, have* and *do* as already discussed), taking in about fifty verbs in all. Of course, to carry out a complete count we would have had to consider all verbs. We therefore decided to cut the sample into two parts, beginning with the most frequent set of about twenty-five and then proceeding to the next most frequent set. This would enable us to see whether the overall proportions of past and present remained constant as more verbs were included.

3.2 Functions of verb forms

Prototypically the English verb has five forms: the base form, for example, *take*; the third person singular present form *takes*; the past tense form *took*; the "present/active participle" *taking*; and the "past/passive participle" *taken*. We shall refer to these by the usual symbols v-0, v-s, v-d, v-ng and v-n. Most verbs in the language distinguish

Table 6.2 (b) Clauses with other negative words

	Number of instances	Spurious instances out of 200	Corrected count
not[i]	84,898		–
no	41,563	59	29,302
never	15,336	4	15,029
nothing	8,757	19	7,925
little	16,426	170	2,546
nor	3,038	51	2,263
hardly	2,130	14	1,981
unless	2,006	11	1,896
none	2,080	29	1,778
nobody	1,570	10	1,492
neither	1,881	43	1,477
few	9,956	180	996
rarely	707	20	636
seldom	580	20	522
scarcely	557	14	518
barely	518	14	482
nowhere	521	67	346
no(-)one	318	–	318
without[ii]	9,980	200	0
Total			69,507

Results:
Polarity: all 69,507 to be added to 'negative' and deducted from 'positive'.
Primary tense: no effect.

Notes:
i All instances of *not* in the proximity of a Finite operator had already been counted (Table 6.2 (a)). No further estimate was made of other possible negative clauses with *not*.
ii Predictably, all negative clauses with *without* were found to be non-finite (for example, *without telling anybody*). There were no instances in the 200 sample of the rarer type such as *without you knew* ('if you didn't know').

only four forms, because v-d and v-n are the same; this applies to all "weak" verbs (those that add -d / -ed for the past) and to some others as well; for example, *ask*, v-d and v-n both *asked*; *sit*, v-d and v-n both *sat*. Some distinguish only three forms, for example *put, set, cut* (and in writing also *read*, where v-0 and v-d are in fact different but are spelt alike). In some verbs (*come, become*), v-n is identical with v-0 but not with v-d. The one maverick verb is *be* which has eight forms: *be, am, is, are, was, were, being, been*.

The problems with identifying simple past and simple present forms are the following:

(a) The v–0, or base, form of the verb:
1. It functions as simple present tense, for example *say*.
2. It occurs as the "infinitive" form of the verb, which has four functions:
    (i) as Head (Event) of the verbal group following a modal operator, and following the tense/polarity operator *do* (*do, does, did* and their negatives), for example *can't say, did say*;
    (ii) as verb alone (that is, as Head of a verbal group with no other elements present) in a non-finite clause, typically following *to*, for example *to say the truth*;
    (iii) as verb alone in a "phased" verbal-group complex, also typically following *to*, for example *started to say*;
    (iv) as verb alone in imperative clause, for example *say what you mean!* Only the verb *be* distinguishes between functions (1) and (2), with *am, is, are* in (1) but *be* in (2).

    Only the occurrences in function (1) are relevant in the present context; those in (2) have to be disqualified. (Except that (2iv) remains in the polarity count, since imperative clauses are finite and were included in the count for negative. They are excluded, however, from primary tense. Note that the v–s form occurs only as simple present tense, so all occurrences of it are to be counted.)

(b) The v–d, or past tense, form of the verb:
    The v–d form of the verb functions only as simple past tense, for example *I said*. However, for most verbs the v–d and v–n forms are identical; and the v–n form, the "past / passive participle", functions as:
1. Head (Event) of the verbal group following the temporal operator *have* (*have, has, had*), for example *hasn't said*;
2. Head (Event) of the verbal group following the voice operator *be* (*am, is,* etc.), for example *was said, hadn't been said*;
3. verb alone in a non-finite clause, for example *that said, said in good faith*.

Only the occurrences of the v–d form are relevant in the present context.

To summarize our treatment of verb forms up to this point:

v-0   some instances to be counted (positive; present); all others to be disqualified (subject to the note on imperative above);

v-s   all instances to be counted (positive; present);

v-d   all instances to be counted (positive; past) (but see v–n below);

v-ng no instances to be counted;

v-n   no instances to be counted (but is usually identical with v–d, sometimes with v–0, sometimes with both).

All three relevant forms of the verb pose the additional problem that they may occur also in some nominal function. The picture is very varied; here are some typical examples:

Lexeme	Finite verb form	Other potential Word class	Other potential use: function in Nominal group	Example
work	v–0	noun	Head (Thing)	out of work
			Premodifier (Classifier)	work station
looks	v–s	noun	Head (Thing)	encouraging looks
thought	v–d	noun	Head (Thing)	the thought of packing
			Premodifier (Classifier)	thought processes
used	v–d	adjective	Premodifier (Classifier)	used cars
		verb (v–n)	(part of) Premodifier (Epithet)	an often used excuse
set	v–0/v–d	adjective	Premodifier (Classifier)	set lunch
		noun	Head (Thing)	television set
left	v–d	verb (v–n)	(part of) Postmodifier (Qualifier)	the only one left
called	v–d	verb (v–n)	(part of) Postmodifier (Qualifier)	a character called Hugo

These examples are all cases of polysemy (different meanings of the same lexeme); if we also take account of homonymy, or rather homography (as we have to do here), the examples will be extended to include unwanted instances of items like *means* (*unfair means, by all means*), *left* (*left wing*), *leaves* (*tea leaves*) and so forth. Such instances obviously have to be disqualified from the count of finite verb forms.

Interestingly, there were far more ambiguous forms of this kind in the second swath of verbs than in the first. We return to this below.

3.3 Steps taken to count the most common verbs

The first swath of 25 verbs was as follows:

say	make	take	find	feel	keep	use
know	go	want	ask	become	turn	
get	come	look	give	begin	call	
see	think	tell	seem	leave	put	

These were the ones of which (after we had deducted the estimated number of disqualified instances) there were at least 4,900 occurrences of **either** the v-0 form **or** the v-d form. (The cut-off point of 4,900 was adopted simply in order to end up with a set of 25 verbs.)

In order to establish figures of occurrence for past and present primary tense forms of these verbs, we proceeded as follows.

1 We counted the instances of all v-0, v-s and v-d forms of these verbs.

2 We inspected 200 instances of each of the forms which we knew also occurred in other guises (as Head or Modifier in a nominal group). We counted the number of verbal and nominal occurrences, and in this way estimated what proportion of the total should be disqualified in each case. For example, out of 200 occurrences of *looks*, 40 were found to be nouns; so 20 per cent of the total figure of 1,863 occurrences was subtracted.

Table 6.3 (a) shows the total number of occurrences for these verbs. These are assigned as follows:

(a) polarity: all v-0, v-s and v-d are positive;
(b) primary tense: v-0, v-s are present; v-d are past.

3 We counted the number of occurrences of all the v-0 forms which were preceded by a Finite operator, either immediately or at a distance of one word: "Finite operator + (... +) v-0"; for example *might say, didn't you say*. All such instances had been counted already, in the count of Finite operators, and were therefore disqualified.

4 Likewise, we counted the occurrences of v-d forms, when these were identical with v-n, preceded by a Finite operator, again either

immediately or with one word in between: "Finite operator + (. . . +) v–n"; for example *hasn't said, could have said, was never said*. Such instances, again, had already been counted, and therefore were disqualifiable. This was an approximation; it would not net instances with more than one word in between, such as *had never been said*, which would therefore get counted twice over, once as *had* and once as *said*; on the other hand, it would net, and therefore exclude, some instances which should have been left in, such as *whoever that was just said* . . . However, concordance lines showed that the error incurred was negligible. (Note that the **structured** sequence "Finite operator + v–d" cannot occur, so in those verbs where v–n was not identical with v–d this figure was not calculated. As a check, we conjured up "op + (. . . +) *became*"; out of 1,723 instances of *became*, only one displayed this sequence.)

5 We counted all occurrences of *to* + v–0, for example *to say*. These were disqualifiable because non–finite, for reasons given above. But all those of the form "op. + *to* + v–0" had already been netted by the previous procedure in (3); so those were counted separately and the figure deducted from the total of *to* + v–0. The resulting total was the number of instances to be disqualified under the present heading.

6 We estimated the number of instances of v–0 which were imperative, for example *say what you mean, don't say it*. In order to do this, we first inspected all the occurrences of *let's*, the only word in English which is always imperative. (One could, of course, construct counter-examples such as *to put the house up to let's the best idea;* but in fact there were none.) The word *let's* occurred 1,281 times, including 61 *let's not* and 19 *don't let's*. (Note that *let us, let us not* and *do not let us* are excluded from this count; these are not necessarily imperative.)

Of this total, 840 instances, or just under two-thirds, either had a capital letter, *Let's* (779), or, if lower case, followed directly after one of four punctuation marks: inverted commas, dash, suspension or opening parenthesis, *"let's, – let's, . . . let's,* or *(let's* (61). A further 142 directly followed either a capitalized paratactic conjunction, *And, But, So, Then* (64), or a capitalized continuative, *Now, Oh, Well, No, Yes* (78); and another 12, a capitalized *Do* (4) or *Don't* (8). In other words, 994 instances, or 77.6 per cent, of *let's* were shown orthographically to be either initial in the clause or following only a one-word marker of textual cohesion.

Our purpose was to establish what environments could be used to identify occurrences of the v-0 forms that were likely to be imperative. After inspecting 200 instances each of 10 of the 25 most frequent verbs, we decided to count, with every verb, those where

(a) v-0 itself was capitalized, for example *Say*;
(b) v-0 followed capitalized *Do* or *Don't*, for example *Do say*;
(c) v-0 followed a capitalized conjunction, *But say*;
(d) v-0 followed a capitalized continuative, for example *Well(,) say*.

These figures were taken as an estimate of the number of v-0 instances that were imperative, and hence to be disqualified from the count for primary tense.

7   We then added together the figures of all those instances rejected as disqualifiable, and subtracted the totals from the figures under (1) above, as follows:

(a) polarity: total of (2), (3), (4), (5) and (6) subtracted from positive;
(b) primary tense:
(i) figures for (2), (3), (5) and (6) subtracted from present;
(ii) figure for (4) subtracted from past.

The resulting totals are presented in Table 6.3 (b).

4 Summary

4.1 Omissions

In the way outlined in the previous sections we arrived at a quantitative profile of the two systems under investigation, polarity and primary tense, based on an assessment of the population of finite clauses in an 18 million word corpus. Those clauses included in the survey are:

1   for both systems
(a) clauses with temporal Finite operators,
(b) clauses in simple past and present tense having the verbs *be,*

Table 6.3 (a) Verbs other than *be*, *have* and *do*: first swath, v–0, v–s and v–d forms

v–0	Number of instances	Spurious instances out of 200	Corrected count	v–s	Number of instances	Spurious instances out of 200	Corrected count	v–d	Numbers of instances	Spurious instances out of 200	Corrected count
say	12,668	1	12,605	says	6,725		6,725	said	47,153		47,153
know	19,245		19,245	knows	2,121		2,121	knew	8,016		8,016
get	18,127		18,127	gets	1,554		1,554	got	11,939		11,939
see	17,968		17,968	sees	690		690	saw	6,705	2	6,638
make	14,424	0	14,424	makes	2,986	1	2,971	made	17,093		17,093
go	16,401	3	16,155	goes	2,377	0	2,377	went	11,677		11,677
come	14,266		14,266	comes	2,909		2,909	came	11,928		11,928
think	13,541		13,541	thinks	865		865	thought	11,875	27	10,272
take	12,517		12,517	takes	1,946		1,946	took	8,207		8,207
want	10,287	3	10,133	wants	1,751	2	1,733	wanted	5,734		5,734
look	9,433	30	8,018	looks	1,863	40	1,490	looked	9,083		9,083
tell	7,661		7,661	tells	680		680	told	8,589		8,589
find	8,181	1	8,140	finds	595	9	568	found	8,212		8,212
ask	3,745		3,745	asks	747		747	asked	8,090		8,090
give	7,876		7,876	gives	1,434		1,434	gave	4,969		4,969
seem	3,582		3,582	seems	3,791		3,791	seemed	7,415		7,415
feel	6,052		6,052	feels	838		838	felt	7,111	2	7,040
become	6,539		6,539	becomes	1,723		1,723	became	4,735		4,735
begin	2,025		2,025	begins	860		860	began	6,489		6,489
leave	4,069	12	3,825	leaves	1,554	143	443	left	9,493	64	6,455
keep	5,897	2	5,838	keeps	536		536	kept	3,660		3,660
turn	3,952	61	2,747	turns	801	36	657	turned	5,741		5,741
call	3,817	51	2,844	calls	849	79	514	called	7,012	39	5,645
put	11,057	100	★5,432	puts	587		587	put			★5,625
use	7,821		3,911	uses	598	70	389	used	8,481	84	4,921
	Total		227,216			Total	39,148			Total	235,326

Results: For *polarity*, all are to be added to 'positive' (227,216 + 39,148 + 235,326 = 501,690). For *primary tense*, v–0 and v–s are to be added to 'present' (227,216 + 39,148 = 266,364), and v–d are to be added to 'past' (235,326).

'Corrected' scores were derived from 'number of instances' scores by the same procedure as in Table 6.1.

★ *Note: put* is both v–0 and v–d. The totals without *put* were: 221,784 for v–0 and 229,701 for v–d, totalling 451,485. This is a ratio of 0.491 : 0.509. The 11,057 occurrences of *put* were therefore distributed into v–0 and v–d in this same proportion, that is, 5,432 : 5,625.

117

Table 6.3 (b) Verbs other than *be, have* and *do*: first swath, v-0, v-d (= v-n) following Finite operator, v-0 = 'imperative'

v-0	*Finite operator +v-0*	*to + v-0 (other than preceding)*	*v-0 = 'imperative'*	*v-d*	*Finite operator + (v-d = v-n)*
say	3,963	3,292	223	said	3,065
know	7,756	2,577	41		
get	4,932	6,419	487	got	1,985
see	5,128	6,032	332		
make	4,024	6,008	357	made	6,131
go	4,849	4,497	732		
come	6,534	2,290	864		
think	3,999	1,808	206	thought	1,748
take	3,776	3,980	716		
want	4,027	202	88	wanted	502
look	1,893	1,974	1,226	looked	685
tell	2,278	1,834	824	told	2,193
find	2,629	2,760	90	found	2,493
ask	1,106	1,073	309	asked	1,195
give	2,436	2,608	475		
seem	1,637	124	9	seemed	514
feel	1,773	917	62	felt	865
become	3,755	1,057	10		
begin	660	468	103		
leave	1,073	1,167	268	left	1,424
keep	1,164	2,603	492	kept	1,019
turn	983	699	108	turned	1,037
call	839	619	115	called	2,048
put	1,333★	1,653	399	put	1,381★
use	1,408	1,532	281	used	2,926
Totals	73,955	58,193	8,817		31,211

Results: For polarity, all are to be deducted from "positive" except for the "imperative" counts (73,955 + 58,193 + 31,211 = 163,359). For primary tense, all are to be deducted from "present" except for Finite operator + (v-d = v-n), which are to be deducted from past (from present: 73,955 + 58,193 + 8,817 = 140,965; from past: 31,211)

★ *Note*: The instances of *put* were distributed between v-0 and v-d in the same proportion as in Table 6.2 (a).

> *have, do* or one of the 25 most frequent verbs next to these three;
>
> 2 for polarity only, clauses with modal Finite operators (such clauses do not select for primary tense).

The results are presented in summary form in Tables 6.4 and 6.5. These tables show total figures and percentages for each of the two systems, as follows:

polarity:	positive 1,252,406 (86.75%)	negative 191,264 (13.25%)
primary tense:	past 598,065 (50.02%)	present 597,645 (49.98%)

There are two sources of inaccuracy in these figures. One is the inaccuracy in the counting that has been done: some of the figures are extrapolations from samples (for example, the proportion of occurrences disqualified as "nominal" being based on the inspection of 200 instances; the estimate for numbers of word sequences being based on the number turning up in 4,000 occurrences of the first word in the string); and there are inaccuracies on a minor scale arising from the way the texts were entered and indexed in the first place (as well as from errors in the transcription). The other, more serious source of inaccuracy is in the counting that has not been done.

Clauses which are elliptical, with ellipsis of the Subject and Finite operator (called "Mood ellipsis" in Halliday and Hasan 1976), will not have been netted wherever the verb was in v-ng form, or in v-n form when this was not identical with v-d; for example, [*was*] *waiting*, [*will be*] *given*, in:

I was watching everything with extreme care and waiting for something to happen.

The recovered animals will be released or given to zoos.

This will distort the figure for the total number of finite clauses. It will probably not significantly affect the proportions either for polarity or for primary tense, because such elliptical clauses maintain the primary tense of the clause to which they are 'phorically' related – the only way a clause can select independently for primary tense is by **not** ellipting the Finite operator; and they almost always maintain the polarity (for the same reason – that it typically requires a Finite operator to switch it, although here there are other strategies, for example *they weren't watching the game but simply taking a day off work*). We have not done anything more to bring elliptical clauses into the picture.

Table 6.4 Polarity

Positive			Negative		
Finite ops:			**Finite ops:**		
modal, and future temporal	213,573		modal/future	20,843	
present temporal	376,194		present	26,513	
past temporal	371,879	961,646	past	17,035	64,391
Abbr. Finite ops:			Finite op. + *not:*	53,995	
modal/future	15,493		Abbr. Finite op. + *not:*	4,779	58,774
present	60,893		Other negative clauses:	69,507	69,507
past	5,443	81,829			**192,672**
Verbs, swath 1 (first 25):					
v–0	227,216				
v–s	39,148				
v–d	235,326	501,690			
		1,545,165			
Subtract:			**Subtract:**		
Positive tag:	1,119		Negative tag:	1,408	
Finite op. + *not:*	53,995				
Abbr. Finite op. + *not:*	4,779	59,893			
Other negative clauses					
Verbs:					
Finite op. +v–0	73,955				
other *to* + v–0	58,193				
Finite op. + v–d	31,211	163,359			
Total positive	1,545,165		**Total negative**	192,672	
	−292,759			−1,408	
	1,252,406			191,264	

Results: Out of a total of 1,443,670 clauses, 1,252,406 were counted as positive and 191,264 were counted as negative. The ratio of positive : negative is therefore 86.75 : 13.25 per cent.

Table 6.5 Primary tense

Present				Past			
Finite ops:	positive	376,194		Finite ops:	positive	371,879	
	negative	26,513			negative	17,035	
		402,707				388,914	
Finite ops:		402,707		Finite ops:		388,914	
		60,893				5,443	
Abbr. Finite ops:				Abbr. Finite ops:			
Verbs, swath 1:	v-0	227,216		Verbs, swath 1:	v-d	235,326	
	v-s	39,148					
		266,364				629,683	
		266,364					
		729,964					
Subtract:				Subtract:			
Tag:		1,476		Tag:		407	
Finite op. + v-0:		73,955		Finite op. + v-d:		31,211	
other to + v-0:		58,193				31,618	
imperative:		8,817					
		140,965					
		142,441					
		729,964				629,683	
		−142,441				−31,618	
		587,523				598,065	
	Total present				Total past		

Results: Out of a total of 1,195,710 clauses, 587,523 were counted as present and 598,065 were counted as past. The ratio of present : past is therefore 49.55 : 50.45 per cent.

4.2 The second group of verbs considered

A more important omission is that **all** clauses having a verb other than *be, have* or *do* or one of the first swath of 25 verbs have been omitted altogether if they are in positive, active, simple past or simple present tense. So we took the next 25 verbs, which are those where one of the two forms v-0 or v-d occurs at least 2,400 times in the corpus (again with the figure corrected to exclude occurrences disqualified because nominal instead of verbal in function). These verbs are:

need	believe	bring	hold	let	lose	read
hear	work	try	live	understand	move	
mean	sit	stand	talk	run	show	
help	remember	change	start	happen	set	

The verbs in the second swath differ from those of the first in that nearly all of them occur significantly often in nominal function as well: in v-0 form, this includes all except *sit, remember, lose, understand* and *happen*. All the remaining v-0 forms also occur as nouns (that is, noun substantive or noun adjective), in differing proportions ranging from *try* (under 5 per cent as noun) to *work* (67.5 per cent as noun). (There were, of course, words of this type having a still higher percentage of nominal occurrences, for example, *act, love, mind, control, miss, close, rest* and *view*; but these disappeared from this swath altogether when only their verbal occurrences were taken into account.) In most cases these nouns also occur frequently in the plural, and so coincide with the v-s forms. The ones that did not were *helps, holds, starts* and *pays*: not that these never occur in the plural (for example *no holds barred, by fits and starts*), but their frequency is less than 0.5 per cent of the total.

(It should be stressed here, perhaps, to avoid misunderstanding, that there is no sense in which 'being a noun or being a verb' could ever represent a systemic choice: there is no environment in which you **choose** between *work* as noun and *work* as verb (and hence no such system anywhere in the grammar). We cannot expect to find any general pattern in the proportion of nominal and verbal occurrences: each form enters into different paradigmatic contexts. The relative frequency of, say, *set* noun and *set* verb is obviously affected by the fact that *set* verb is both v-0 and v-d /v-n; that of *pay* noun and *pay* verb by the fact that *pay* is a mass noun; the noun *show* has a very different collocational spread from the verb *show*, whereas the collocations of noun *help* and verb *help* are much more alike; and so on. If nouns were written with an initial capital letter, as was the practice for a time in the early modern period (and is today in German), the idea of noun and verb being 'the same word' would seem very different.)

The strategy used in investigating the verbs in the second swath was the same as that adopted for the first swath, as outlined in Section 3, (1)–(7) on pages 110–116. The results are shown in Table 6.6.

4.3 Conclusions

The final figures in both counts are shown in Table 6.7.

4.3.1 Polarity

Adding the second swath of 25 verbs increases the total number of "polarity" occurrences by 97,941. The count of negative is unaffected, at 191,264; that for positive is increased from 1,252,411 to 1,350,352. The proportion of positive to negative is now 87.6 : 12.4 per cent.

In considering the 50 most frequent verbs, we had included all the verbs occurring in the first part of the frequency list – that which accounts for half the tokens in the corpus. Within that set, the 25 verbs in the second swath covered a part of the frequency list that represents one-tenth of the tokens in the corpus. The difference in the polarity count that is introduced by including this second swath is less than 1 per cent.

We would have liked to be able to give a reasonable estimate of the number that would be added to the "positive" count if we could take in the v-0, v-s and v-d forms of all the other verbs occurring in the corpus – those with fewer than 2,400 occurrences of their most frequent form. But having worked out the steps that we should have to take in order to do this, we decided it was not worth trying: we faced the familiar pattern of massively diminishing returns. A best guess would be somewhere between 100,000 and 150,000. If 100,000 were added to the positive score, the proportion would become 88.35 : 11.65 per cent; if 150,000, then 88.69 : 11.31 per cent; hardly more than 1 per cent difference, even at this higher level.

One problematic feature is that of negative clauses (Table 6.3 (b)). We took the view that a significant number of clauses containing

Table 6.6 (a) Verbs other than *be*, *have* and *do*: second swath, v–0, v–s and v–d forms

v–0	Count	Spurious instances out of 200	Corrected count	v–s	Count	Spurious instances out of 200	Corrected count	v–d	Count	Spurious instances out of 200	Corrected count
need	7,690	74	4,845	needs	2,726	95	1,431	needed	2,667	24	2,347
hear	3,118	7	3,118	hears	164		164	heard	4,823		4,823
mean	4,968	60	4,794	means	4,279	97	2,204	meant	2,448		2,448
help	6,396		4,477	helps	545		545	helped	1,349		1,349
believe	4,444	135	4,444	believes	429		429	believed	1,646		1,646
work	13,630		4,430	works	1,498	101	742	worked	2,448		2,448
sit	1,991		1,991	sits	297		297	sat	4,094		4,094
remember	4,088		4,088	remembers	188		188	remembered	1,417		1,417
bring	3,049	9	3,049	brings	530		530	brought	4,266	5	4,053
try	4,222	30	4,032	tries	385	17	352	tried	3,615	3	3,561
stand	2,401		2,041	stands	700	24	616	stood	3,837		3,837
change	4,428	122	1,727	changes	1,863	163	345	changed	3,792	2	3,754
hold	2,616	40	2,093	holds	508		508	held	3,692		3,692
live	3,892	13	3,639	lives	2,189	149	558	lived	2,396		2,396
talk	4,168	37	3,397	talks	444	120	178	talked	1,537		1,537
start	3,334	51	2,484	starts	456		456	started	3,396	3	3,345
let	6,628	15	3,257	lets	161		161	let			*2,874
understand	3,193		3,193	understands	135		135	understood	1,247		1,247
run	3,795	33	3,169	runs	779	46	600	ran	1,957		1,957
happen	1,768		1,768	happens	1,131		1,131	happened	3,153		3,153
lose	1,361	56	1,361	loses	182		182	lost	3,610	30	3,069
move	3,011	57	2,168	moves	513	82	303	moved	3,032	4	2,971
show	3,847		2,751	shows	1,114	21	997	showed	1,784		1,784
set	6,246	40	*2,655	sets	620	114	267	set			*2,342
read	4,750	5	*2,460	reads	231		231	read			*2,171
		Total v–0	77,431			Total v–s	13,550			Total v–d	68,315

Results: For polarity, all are to be added to "positive" (77,431 + 13,550 + 68,315 = 159,296). For primary tense, v–0 and v–s are to be added to "present" (77,431 + 13,550 = 90,981), and v–d are to be added to "past" (68,315).

*'Corrected' scores were derived from 'number of instances' scores by the same procedure as in Table 6.1.

* *Note:* let, set and read are all both v–0 and v–d. The totals without these three verbs were: v–0, 69,059; v–d, 60,928, which is a ratio of 0.531 : 0.469. The occurrences of let, set and read were therefore distributed into v–0 and v–d in the same proportion, that is, (*let*) 6,131–3,257, 2,874; (*set*) 4,997–2,655, 2,342; (*read*) 4,631–2,460, 2,171.

Table 6.6 (b) Verbs other than *be, have* and *do*: second swath, v-0, v-d (= v-n) following Finite operator; v-0 = 'imperative'

v-0	Finite operator + v-0	to + v-0 (other than preceding)	v-0 = imperative	v-d	Finite operator + (v-d = v-n)
need	778	123	38	needed	778
hear	1,145	1,039	29	heard	1,639
mean	1,969	99	15	meant	606
help	1,910	1,634	157	helped	454
believe	1,190	853	93	believed	414
work	1,831	1,826	204	worked	717
sit	443	605	162	sat	72
remember	1,057	508	526	remembered	152
bring	923	1,099	183	brought	1,645
try	1,092	974	468	tried	716
stand	616	523	89	stood	211
change	654	750	103	changed	890
hold	534	743	168	held	937
live	787	1,269	46	lived	565
talk	776	1,376	154	talked	350
start	658	733	112	started	642
let	*707	833	1,378	let	*624
understand	1,197	901	23	understood	342
run	1,055	768	78		
happen	955	358	11	happened	1,248
lose	419	474	11	lost	1,495
move	588	890	79	moved	708
show	704	1,264	171		
set	*837	552	152	set	*738
read	*650	*1,170	169	read	*573
Totals	23,475	21,364	4,619	Total	16,516

Results: For *polarity*, all except imperative are to be deducted from 'positive' (23,475 + 21,364 + 16,516 = 61,355). For *primary tense*, the first three columns are to be deducted from 'present' (23,475 + 21,364 + 4,619 = 49,458), and the fourth column is to be deducted from 'past' (16,516).
* *Note*: *let, set* and *read* were distributed into v-0 and v-d by the same procedure as in Table 6.6 (a).

negative words, such as *never, nobody, hardly*, should be interpreted as negative clauses – that is, those where the most plausible form of the tag was the positive one, for example *he hardly ever takes his hat off, does he?* (Compare the northern English pattern with postposed Subject, where the repeated Finite operator is negative: *he hardly ever takes his hat off doesn't that inspector.*) There were 69,507 of these

Table 6.7 Final totals and percentages

Polarity			Primary tense		
	Positive	*Negative*		*Present*	*Past*
Table 6.4	1,252,406	191,264	Table 6.5	587,523	598,065
Table 6.6 (a)	159,296		Table 6.6 (a)	90,981	68,315
Table 6.6 (b)	−61,355		Table 6.6 (b)	−49,458	−16,516
Totals:	1,350,347	191,264		629,046	649,864
Results:					
Positive	1,350,347	= 87.6%	Present	629,046	= 49.18%
Negative	191,264	= 12.4%	Past	649,864	= 50.82%
Total	1,541,611		Total	1,278,910	

according to our estimate. An alternative interpretation would be to regard these clauses as being on the borderline of positive and negative and assign them to a special category of 'mixed' clauses, each scoring half negative and half positive. We would then take 34,753 away from the negative score and add that figure to positive. The percentages would then be as follows:

    (using original figures)   (+100,000)   (+150,000)
    89.85 : 10.15   90.47 : 9.53   90.75 : 9.25

This makes slightly more difference to the proportions because it affects the smaller negative count as well as the positive.

4.3.2 Primary tense

Adding the second swath of 25 verbs increases the total "primary tense" (past/present) count by 93,322 (97,941 minus the 4,619 imperatives). The count for present has increased proportionately rather less than that for past – present from 597,645 to 639,168, past from 598,065 to 649,864. But the overall proportion has changed only 0.4 per cent; it is now (past) 50.41 : (present) 49.59.

Intuitively, it seems likely that the proportion of positive : negative does not vary greatly from one genre, or functional variety of the language, to another. Whether spoken or written, formal or informal, monologue or dialogue, on whatever topic, it might remain roughly the same. This could be proved wrong, of course; there might be fewer negatives in narrative texts, for example, than was typical of other varieties. But for past : present there seems more room for variation, and it might well be that the figures here are affected by the relatively high proportion of narrative fiction in the

126

present corpus. It would be desirable to investigate a different corpus, perhaps one consisting entirely of spoken text, to match the figures against those we have presented here.

4.3.3 A note on modality and future tense

We are not pursuing the question of modality and future tense any further in this study; but a few observations may be of interest. The number of instances of Finite operators other than past and present temporal (that is, modal and future temporal taken together) was close to 250,000 (249,909 minus 644 identified as tags = 249,265). Of these, about half were accounted for by *can, could, may, might, must, ought* (125,692), half by *will, would, shall, should* (123,573) – including their negatives and abbreviated forms, where applicable.

The first group are modals only. The second group, *will, would, shall, should*, are sometimes modal and sometimes future temporal; but in very different proportions. Inspecting 200 instances of each (positive and negative forms), we found the figures shown in Table 6.8.

Table 6.8 Modality and future tense

Operator	Total instances	Future: n/200	Extrapolated	Modal: n/200	Extrapolated
will	41,957	160	33,566	40	8,391
won't	2,742	132	1,810	68	932
would	52,859	140	37,001	60	15,858
wouldn't	3,038	153	2,324	47	714
shall	4,724	134	3,185	66	1,569
shan't	134	–	105	–	29
should	17,392	23	2,000	177	15,392
shouldn't	697	21	73	179	624
Total	123,543		80,064		43,509

If we round off these figures to the nearest 5,000, then out of 125,000 occurrences of *will, would, shall, should* (with their negatives), 45,000 were modal and 80,000 future tense. Combining the former figure with that for *can, could, may, might, must, ought* (with their negatives), we get a total for modal operators of 170,000.

We could then represent the system of verbal deixis, using the precise figures obtained and converting them into percentages shown as probabilities:

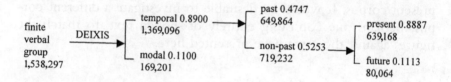

This postulates the following:

1. a system of verbal deixis, for the finite verbal group, whose terms are temporal (primary tense) and modal, with temporal unmarked;
2. within primary tense, a system whose terms are past and non-past, with neither being unmarked;
3. within non-past, a system whose terms are present and future, with present as the unmarked term.

We include this note to illustrate what it means to suggest that the probability profiles are not simply appendages to an existing network, but may play a part in the construction of the network as a theory of how the grammar works. But we have not incorporated it into the present investigation, because the distinction between modal and future temporal needs to be made much more precise and explicit.

Up to this point, however, the hypothesis of "equi" and "skew" systems may be retained, with the values lying within the limits predicted. We should acknowledge, in saying this, that it is not at all obvious how to define such "limits" in the case of a semiotic system (such as a language). Semiotic systems are different in crucial respects from systems of other kinds, whether physical, biological or social; and while we can measure standard deviations in general statistical terms, we would not know how to interpret the difference between, say, a frequency distribution of 50 : 50 and one of 60 : 40. But we will only come to understand these issues by learning a great deal more about the probability profiles of the most general systems in the grammars of different languages – something that with the advent of corpus linguistics we can at last hope to achieve.

Notes

1. This investigation forms part of the COBUILD (Collins–Birmingham University) project for Modern English Language Research. M. A. K.

Halliday's contribution was made possible by a grant from Harper-Collins, whose support is gratefully acknowledged.

2   We are aware that *ain't* is not usually the negative of *am*. But there is a convenient hole for it in the table at that location.

Chapter Seven

QUANTITATIVE STUDIES AND PROBABILITIES IN GRAMMAR (1993)

Part I

At a recent conference devoted to modern developments in corpus studies, I was struck by the way that a number of speakers at the conference were setting up an opposition between "corpus linguists" and "theoretical linguists" – not a conflict, I mean, but a distinction, as if these were members of two distinct species. I commented on this at the time, saying that I found it strange because corpus linguistics seemed to me to be, potentially at least, a highly theoretical pursuit. Work based on corpus studies has already begun to modify our thinking about lexis, about patterns in the vocabulary of languages; and it is now beginning to impact on our ideas about grammar. In my view, this impact is likely to be entirely beneficial. Corpus linguistics brings a powerful new resource into our theoretical investigations of language.

One consequence of the development of the modern corpus is that we can now for the first time undertake serious **quantitative** work in the field of grammar. Quantitative studies require very large populations to work with. This is obvious in lexis, where the underlying principles of the frequency distribution of lexical items have been known for quite some time (since the groundbreaking studies by Zipf (1935), in fact): if we want to investigate any words other than those of highest frequency in a language, we need text data running at least into millions of words, and preferably into hundreds of millions. Even to study the most frequent words, once we start investigating their collocational patterns, we need very large samples of text. It might be argued that grammatical patterns do not demand text data on that scale, because they will typically occur more often. That is true of the broadest, primary categories, like singular and plural in the English noun, or positive and negative in the verb. But the finer, more delicate our categories become the less frequently each instance will occur; and even with the broader categories, since many of the ones we are likely to be most concerned with are categories of the clause and above, it will require a rather large sample (if we are thinking in terms of the number of words) to yield a sufficiently large number of occurrences. Consider for example the clause nexus, a structure of two clauses related by expansion or projection: Nesbitt and Plum were able to retrieve 2,733 instances from a corpus of 100,000 words. If we want to compare the grammar of different registers, the functional varieties of a language, in quantitative terms (for example, the different proportions of active and passive in different registers of Modern English), then it is clearly going to require a very large corpus of data to produce reliable results.

I myself first became interested in grammatical frequencies in a crude and simplistic fashion many years ago in the course of my work as a language teacher – although, if I pursue this even further, the reason for my interest in such information as a teacher was that I had felt the need for it in the first place as a learner. Faced with the task of learning, from scratch, as a young adult, a language very distant from my own, or from any language I had had experience of before, I was constantly wanting to know what people actually said in this language. When I had to master very basic systems of mood, aspect, phase and so on that were unlike anything in English, I wanted to know which of a set of alternatives was the most likely – I did not know the term "unmarked" at that time, but what I was looking for was some guidance about which, if any, was the unmarked term. A few years later, when I started to teach that same language, although I had by then acquired some feeling for its patterns of discourse, I found it frustrating that I could not offer the students reliable information of the kind that I myself would have liked to have.

In other words, I wanted to know the probabilities that were associated with these grammatical choices. Given, for example, a particular grammatical system, say that of **aspect**, with terms **perfective / imperfective**, what was the relative probability of choosing one or the other in a Chinese clause (Chinese was the language I was teaching)? This is a considerable problem for a speaker of a western European language, for two reasons. On the one hand, the aspect system itself is unfamiliar; there is some form of grammatical aspect in English – its exact nature is disputed; but on any interpretation it is not the dominant temporal system in the clause, which is tense, whereas in Chinese the dominant temporal system is that of aspect. On the other hand, there is the problem of the nature of the unmarked term. Grammatical systems in Chinese typically embody an alternative which is "unmarked", not in the sense of being the default or most frequent choice (it often will be that too), but in the sense that it is a way of opting out – of not choosing either of the terms. So the aspect system is not simply "either perfective or imperfective" but "perfective, imperfective or **neither**". Speakers of European languages are much less accustomed to systems of this kind; and again, it would be helpful to know the relative probability of choosing one way or another.

Of course, every learner will carry over into the new language some predictions based on the experience of his or her mother tongue, and maybe also of other languages that he or she knows. Some of these predictions will hold good: I would imagine that the ratio of positive to negative clauses is substantially the same in all languages – although it would be nice to know. But some of them will not hold good; and there will be some cases where the learner has no idea what to predict at all. And this is often where one begins to reflect on these matters; as long as the predictions work, they tend to remain unconscious. But there was another question which kept arising in my work as a teacher, especially in preparing for con-versation classes; and this was something I found quite impossible to predict: was the probability of a choice in one system affected by a choice in another? Could I combine freely, say, negative polarity with perfective aspect; or different voice-like options (the Chinese *bǎ* construction, for example) with interrogative as well as with declarative mood?

When I wrote my first sketch of a grammar of Chinese (1956), I attached probabilities to most of the primary systems. These were, obviously, in a very crude form: I used the values 0+, ½−, ½, ½+ and 1−. The values were derived mainly from my own knowledge of the language, backed up from two sources: a small amount of counting of grammatical options in modern Chinese dramatic texts; and the work that I had subsequently been doing on a text in early Mandarin, the fourteenth-century Chinese version of the *Secret History of the Mongols*, in which I had counted every instance of those grammatical categories that I had been able to resolve into systems. One reason for doing all this counting had been to try to establish the extent of the association between different systems: to find out, for example, whether it was possible to predict the number of instances of negative interrogative by intersecting the probabilities of negative (versus positive) with those of interrogative (vs declarative). On the basis of this quantitative work, although obviously I was able to access only very minute samples from the modern language, I adopted the principle that frequency in text instantiated probability in the system.

Any concern with grammatical probabilities makes sense only in the context of a paradigmatic model of grammar, one that incorporates the category of **system** in its technical sense as defined by Firth.[1] The system, in Firth's system-structure theory, is the category which models paradigmatic relations: just as a **structure**, in Firth's specialized use of the term, is a deep syntagm, so to speak, so a system is a deep paradigm. The system, as Firth put it, "gives value to the elements of structure": it specifies the oppositions, or sets of alternatives, to which a defined place in structure provides the condition of entry. Firth's own application of these concepts was largely confined to phonology; but, if we want to give a brief illustration from grammar, using modern terms, we could say that the element "Finite operator" in the structure of the English verb (verbal group) is given value by the systems of **verbal deixis** (temporal / modal) and **polarity** (positive / negative) which originate there. This concept of the system enables us to show that, under given conditions, the speaker is selecting one, and only one, from among a small closed set of possibilities; and therefore it makes sense to talk about the probability of choosing one or the other. What I hoped to do was to model each system not just as "choose *a* or *b* or *c*", but as "choose *a* or *b* or *c* with a certain probability attached to each". In other words, I was positing that an inherent property of any linguistics system is the relative probability of its terms.

I have often encountered considerable resistance to this idea. People have become quite accustomed to lexical probabilities, and find no difficulty in accepting that they are going to use *go* more often than *grow*, and *grow* more often than *glow* (or, if you prefer a semantically related set of words, that they will say *go* more often than *walk* and *walk* more often than *stroll*). They do not feel that this constitutes any threat to their individual freedom. But when faced with the very similar observation that they are going to use active

133

more often than passive, or positive more often than negative, many people object very strongly, and protest that they have a perfect right to choose to do otherwise if they wish. And of course they have; that is exactly the point that is being made. They could choose to use negative more often than positive, just as they could choose to use *stroll* more often than *walk* – but they won't. The resistance seems to arise because grammar is buried more deeply below the level of our conscious awareness and control; hence it is more threatening to be told that your grammatical choices are governed by overall patterns of probability.

Before being able to pursue these studies any further with Chinese, however, I changed the focus of my work and found myself professionally involved with English. So again I started counting things, this time using an early version of a system-based grammar of the language worked out first in collaboration with Jeffrey Ellis and Denis Berg, and subsequently elaborated together with John Sinclair, Angus McIntosh and others at the University of Edinburgh in the early 1960s. I collected a small sample of four different registers of English, just big enough to yield a total of 2,000 occurrences of whatever category provided the entry condition to the systems I wanted to study. For example, in order to count instances of indicative / imperative mood, I had to have 2,000 independent clauses, because it is here that the choice is made: each independent clause selects one or the other. But to compare declarative with interrogative I had to count 2,000 indicative clauses, because it is the indicative clause that is either declarative or interrogative. The reason for settling on a figure of 2,000 occurrences was the following: first, I estimated it needed about 200 occurrences of the less frequent term to ensure a reasonable degree of accuracy; and second, that the less frequent term in a binary system seemed to occur about 10 per cent of the time. So if I restricted the counting to binary systems, 2,000 instances tended to yield around 200 occurrences of the less frequent term in the system.

The systems that I was interested in were mainly clause systems, although this did not imply that every clause would select in the system in question: each system would have its origin in some specific class of the clause (but a very large class, like the "indicative" referred to above). So from each of four registers (a science magazine, a novel, a conversation and a play) I took samples that would be large enough to yield 500 instances of whatever category was required. The systems I investigated were nine in all. The first eight were: (1) voice (active / passive); (2) transitivity (transitive / intransitive), (3) tense (simple / complex), (4) theme (unmarked / marked), (5,6) mood (indicative / imperative, and, within indicative, declarative / interrogative), (7) polarity (positive / negative), (8) nominal deixis (specific / non-specific). The ninth was the system of tone, one of the systems of intonation in English; here there is a separate unit as point of origin of the system, namely the tone group, and five terms (falling / rising / level (low rising) / fall-rise / rise-fall). For this I used a recorded conversation containing about 1,500 tone groups.

Such samples were of course extremely small, much too small for serious quantitative work; and in any case I was far from confident in the grammatical categories I was using as the basis, because these had not yet been put to the test – indeed one of my main reasons for doing this kind of close analysis of the data was to test the validity of the categories themselves when applied to natural, including spoken, texts. At this time a very sharp distinction was being drawn in linguistics between the system and the instance (the text), or between competence and performance; and quantitative effects were dismissed as "merely performance features", so very few people were interested in this sort of study (and there was certainly no question of anyone publishing the results!). However it seemed to me that these were important issues, very relevant to our overall understanding of language itself; and that some interesting patterns seemed to emerge. One which I reported on at the time was this. There seemed to be certain systems where the frequency of the terms was more or less equal: given a binary system (and as already noted I had confined the counting to systems that could be represented as binary, apart from the system of tone), this meant a ratio of about fifty : fifty, or (in terms of probabilities) of 0.5 : 0.5. There were then other systems where the frequency was unequal. But these latter were not distributed across the whole range of possible values. They seemed to tend – again, very roughly – towards a skewing by about one order of magnitude, a "ten to one" ratio. This I represented as 0.9 : 0.1. The former type were those where, from the point of view of frequency, there was no unmarked term; the latter were those in which one of the terms was unmarked.

I did not attach much weight to this observation, for obvious reasons: the whole procedure was far too unreliable. But I did wonder about whether such a pattern would make sense. We can imagine two possible alternatives: one, that the probability profiles of different systems might be randomly distributed across all possible values, from equiprobable to highly skew; the other where the skew systems might cluster around a particular value, but not at 0.9 : 0.1 – say at 99 to 1, or 3 to 1. It seemed easy to suggest that, in some vague sense, 99 to 1 would be too much skewed to be useful in the grammar of a language, while 3 to 1 would not be clearly enough distinguishable from even probabilities; but such an explanation would hardly stand up by itself. At the time, I was just beginning to investigate child language development, as a result of working with primary school teachers on an educational programme concerned with initial literacy; and since I had first faced up to the issue as a language learner, it seemed natural to try to look at it in developmental terms. I had not yet begun to make any direct observations of my own on how children learn their mother tongue; but later when I came to do this, I was struck by the way they respond to the more frequent options in the grammar and use these first, bringing in the less frequent ones by a later step. In other words, children seem to learn language as a probabilistic system; they are surrounded by large quantities of data, probably at least a hundred thousand clauses a year, and they are sensitive to relative frequency as a resource for ordering what they learn to say. (I am not suggesting they do any of this consciously, of course!) From this point of view, one could hypothesize that a semiotic in which the probabilities associated with various sets of options, or systems, were distributed randomly all the way from 0.5 : 0.5 to 0.99 : 0.01 would be virtually impossible to learn. One in which there was some kind of bimodal distribution, on the other hand, would be much more accessible to a learner. This did not in itself favour one particular profile over another, for systems of the type which were skew; but it did suggest that they might very well tend to cluster around just one set of values.

Among the systems I had counted at the beginning was tense. What I was counting here was not the opposition of past and present, or past and non-past; it was that of "simple tense" versus "complex tense". This was based on analysis of the English tense system different from that favoured by the structuralist linguists, which had only past and present tense (rejecting the traditional notion of future) and combined these with "continuous" (or "progressive") and "perfect" as forms of aspect. My own analysis was more in harmony with the traditional concept of tense, and as interpreted in semantic terms by Reichenbach (1947). In this view, tense (past / present / future) is a potentially iterative system, construing a "serial time", in which there is a primary tense choice of past, present or future relative to the moment of speaking, and also the option of then making a further choice, where the time frame of the primary tense is taken as the reference point for another tense selection of past, present or future – a secondary time system that is relative to the primary one. So as well as simple past *took*, simple present *takes* and simple future *will take*, there is the possibility of **past** in past, *had taken*, **present** in past, *was taking*, and **future** in past, *was going to take*; likewise past in **present** *has taken*, **present** in present *is taking*, **future** in present *is going to take*; and past in **future** *will have taken*, **present** in future *will be taking*, **future** in future *will be going to take*. This second time choice can then serve as reference point for a third, and so on. In this analysis, a verb form such as that in *I hadn't been going to tell you* is "future in past in past"; that in *he was going to have been looking after things for us all this time* is "present in past in future in past". In all, sequences of up to five tense choices have been observed to occur (see Matthiessen 1983, 1996).

Both this and the structuralist form of analysis can be used to throw light on the English tense system, and each will illuminate a different facet of it. The reasons for using the iterative form of analysis would take too long to go into here, particularly as they require illustration from discourse – this analysis treats tense more as a discourse feature. The relevance to the present discussion is that, when interpreted in this way, tense becomes an instance of a very general kind of system found in language: the kind of system that embodies an iterative option, a choice of "going round again". Another example of this would be projection (direct and indirect speech and thought), where we can say not only *Henry said that the day would be fine* but also *Mary reported that Henry had said that the day would be fine*, *Peter forgot that Mary had reported that Henry had said that the day would be fine*, and so on. Such systems obviously require very large samples for counting the relative frequency of sequences of different lengths; the only one I had tried to count was tense, which is less demanding because it is a system of the verb (verbal group) and so each tense form, however complex, remains within the limits of one clause. Comparing simple tense forms (primary tense only) with complex tense forms (primary plus secondary), I found that there was the same general pattern of skew distribution: simple tenses were about ten times as frequent as complex ones. In other words, having made one choice of tense, you can go round and choose again; but you are much more likely not to – and roughly in the same proportion as you are more likely to choose positive than negative or active than passive. This kind of iterative system is something that would appear highly prominent to a child learning the language; and it seems to provide a kind of prototype or model of a skew system, as being a system having one option that is highly marked (much less frequent than the other).

So while my original interest in the quantitative aspect of grammatical systems had been an educational one – its importance for learning and teaching languages – in the course of working on texts, first in Chinese and then in English, I had become aware of the different information loading that different systems can carry. Now, in the late 1950s I had had the privilege of working alongside Margaret Braithwaite, together with A. F. Parker-Rhodes and R. H. Richens, in the pioneering Cambridge Language Research Unit, one of the early projects concerned with machine translation (see Léon 2000). In this context it became necessary to represent grammatical features in explicit, computable terms. I wanted to formalize paradigmatic relations, those of the system; but I did not know how to do it – and I totally failed to persuade anyone else of this! The emphasis at that time – and for many years to come – was on formalizing syntagmatic relations, those of structure, which seemed to me less central to the task. One of the lines of approach that I tried to explore was through Shannon and Weaver's (1963 [1949]) information theory. This had already been rejected by linguists as being of no interest; partly because Shannon and Weaver's own incursions into language had been purely at the orthographic level (what they meant by the "redundancy of English" was the redundancy of the system consisting of twenty-six letters and a space), but partly also because of the current obsession with structure. Information theory has nothing to say about constituent structure; information and redundancy are properties of systems. But it does provide a very valuable measure of the information content of any one system.

A binary system whose terms are equiprobable (0.5 : 0.5) has an information value of 1 ($H=1$); redundancy is $1-H$, so it had a redundancy of 1-1, which is zero. Redundancy is therefore a measure of the skewness of a system; the greater the skewness (departure from equiprobability), the lower the value of H (information) and consequently the higher the redundancy. (This is, of course, "information" and "redundancy" in these specific mathematical senses, without any implication that one or other is to be avoided!) The original Shannon and Weaver formula for measuring information was

$$- \Sigma \; p_i \cdot \log_n p_i$$

where n is the number of terms in the system (so $\log_2$ if the system is binary) and p_i is the probability of each. I used a table of the values of $p_i \log_2 p_i$ for p = 0.01 to p = 0.99, in order to calculate the information of grammatical systems with different degrees of skewness. But when I reported on this it aroused no kind of interest; and when I came to count the frequencies of the systems referred to above, in texts in English, I did not have enough confidence in the figures (or in my own interpretation of them) to pursue the question of information and redundancy any further.

Meanwhile in the 1960s the foundations were being laid for an eventual breakthrough in our understanding of linguistic systems, both qualitatively and quantitatively: namely the beginning of corpus-based linguistics. The "corpus" had been the brainchild of two leading specialists in English linguistics: Randolph Quirk, in Britain, and Freeman Twaddell in the United States. By the middle of the decade the "Brown Corpus", at Brown University in Providence, and the Survey of English Usage at University College London were making available bodies of text data that were sufficiently large to allow valid quantitative studies to be carried out. A groundbreaking piece of work was Jan Svartvik's *On Voice in the English Verb*, in which Svartvik used the text resources of the Survey of English Usage to investigate the use and significance of the passive in written English. Since that time a steady output of research has come from these corpus projects, the high point of this achievement being the "Quirk grammar". At the same time other corpus studies were being undertaken; for example in lexis, by John Sinclair and his colleagues in Birmingham, and in grammar by Rodney Huddleston and the members of the "scientific English" project in my own department at University College London. Work of this kind clearly demonstrated the value of this general approach to the study of language.[2] By the 1970s the corpus was well established as a research resource, and was being extended into the domain of language education, both as a resource for foreign-language learning (for example the "Leuven Drama Corpus" compiled by Leopold Engels at the Catholic University of Leuven), and as a theoretical basis for work in initial literacy (e.g. the "Mount Gravatt Corpus" developed by Norman Hart and R. H. Walker at Mount Gravatt College of Advanced Education in Brisbane).

As far as quantitative studies were concerned, the corpus entirely transformed the scene. On the one hand, samples of text were becoming available that were large enough for reliable statistical investigation into features both of vocabulary and of grammar. On the other hand, these texts were now in machine-readable form, so that step by step, as appropriate software was developed, it was becoming possible to handle such large bodies of data in a way that would have been impossible with any form of manual processing. Meanwhile one critical contribution to these studies came from the sophisticated methodology for quantitative analysis developed by William Labov, together with Gillian Sankoff and David Sankoff, in their investigation of socially conditioned variation in the phonology and morphology of urban speech. This has been adapted to systemic-functional corpus studies in syntactic and semantic variation, where (unlike Labov's work) what is being investigated is systematic variation in patterns of meaning, on the plane of content rather than the plane of expression.

These studies are well known, and I have discussed them in a similar context elsewhere (Chapters 3, 5). What follows is a very brief summary. Plum and Cowling used the corpus of interviews from Barbara Horvath's *Sydney Social Dialect Survey* to study variation in the system of temporal and modal deixis in the English verbal group, and within temporal deixis the system of past / present / future primary tense. They examined 4,436 finite clauses, and found that 75 per cent selected temporal deixis and 25 per cent modal; while of those selecting temporal deixis, leaving out a very small proportion of futures, they found 57 per cent selecting past and 43 per cent selecting present. These were from texts in one particular register: spoken interviews in which the respondents were asked to recall their childhood experiences in primary school, especially the games they used to play. Examining the data for systematic variation within the population, Plum and Cowling found no significant variation in the choice of tense versus modality; but, within tense, they found significant variation among three social groups: relatively, the middle class favoured past tense in their narratives (70 per cent : 30 per cent), the lower working class favoured present tense (65 per cent : 35 per cent), while the upper working class fell in between, but closer to the middle-class figures (60 per cent of clauses past).

Using a different corpus, spoken interviews with dog fanciers discussing the breeding and showing of dogs, Nesbitt and Plum examined a sample of 2,733 clause nexuses to investigate the internal relationship between two systems within the grammar: inter-dependency (parataxis / hypotaxis) and logical-semantic relations (expansion / projection, and their sub-types). Here the question concerned the intersection (mutual conditioning) of the two sets of probabilities: were the two systems independent, or were they associated in some way? It would take too long to summarize their findings here (cf. Chapters 3, 4 and 5 of this volume); but let me mention one of them. In the intersection of interdependency with projection (the combination of "parataxis / hypotaxis" with "locution / idea" which defines the four categories traditionally referred to as "direct and indirect speech and thought"), they found that there was a strong association of parataxis with locution ("direct speech") and of hypotaxis with idea ("indirect thought"); both "indirect speech" and "direct thought" were highly marked com-binations. In other words, there was a strong conditioning of the probabilities within the grammar itself; and it remained constant whichever system was taken as the environment of the other.

On a considerably larger scale, since the mid-1980s Ruqaiya Hasan has been conducting research into conversation between mothers and children, where the children were just below school age (3½–4 years). Her aim has been to investigate how children's patterns of learning are developed through ordinary everyday interaction in the home, and to explore the consequences of this early semantic experience for their subsequent learning in school. Using a population of 24 mother-child dyads, structured by social class (12 "higher autonomy professions", 12 "lower autonomy professions") and sex of child (12 boys, 12 girls), Hasan and her colleagues collected over 60,000 clauses of natural conversation of which they analysed over one-third in terms of a detailed network of semantic features. Subjecting the results to a cluster analysis brought out some highly significant correlations between the social factors of class and sex on the one hand and the orientation towards certain patterns of semantic choice on the other. For example, while all mothers used a great deal of reasoning, middle-class and working-class mothers tended to favour different kinds of grounding for their explanations; while mothers of boys differed from mothers of girls in the ways in which they elaborated on their answers to their children's questions (Plum and Cowling 1987; Nesbitt and Plum 1988; Hasan and Cloran 1990; Hasan 1992).

Let me take up one final point before moving to the second part of the chapter. In 1980 William Mann, director of the "Penman" artificial intelligence project at the University of Southern California Information Sciences Institute, asked me to write a grammar for use in text generation by computer. I constructed a network, on systemic principles, for the grammar of the English clause, based on the work I had been doing since the mid-1960s; there were 81 systems in the network (Appendix, p. 268 ff. this volume). Whenever possible I represented these as binary systems and added probabilities to them, using just the two values of 0.5 : 0.5 and 0.9 : 0.1 that I had arrived at earlier. This network was then implemented computationally by their programmer Mark James. The network was of course designed to be used under the control of some higher-level system, a "knowledge representation system" of some kind; but for testing it was operated randomly. When let loose in this way it produced garbage, as such grammars always will until sufficiently constrained. But when it was operated still randomly but with the probabilities taken into account, Mann's comment was that, while it still produced garbage, the garbage now looked as if it might bear some distant resemblance to English. That may not sound to you very encouraging! – but that remark did more than anything else to persuade me to reactivate my interest in probabilities (see Mann 1985; Matthiessen 1985; Bateman and Matthiessen 1991).

I thought again about this bimodal effect, of probabilities tending towards either 0.5 : 0.5 or 0.9 : 0.1, and formulated it as a hypothesis about the typology of grammatical systems: that they fall into one or other of these two types, the "equi" and the "skew", with the "skew" having a value of very roughly nine to one, or one order of magnitude in our decimal scheme of things. Then, wondering again about this nine to one, I looked once more into the Shannon and Weaver formula for calculating information. We saw that, at $0.5 : 0.5$, $H = 1$, $R = 0$. What, I wondered, was the point at which information and redundancy exactly balance out ($H = 0.5$, $R = 0.5$)? – the property of 50 per cent redundancy that Shannon and Weaver had originally assigned to "English" (meaning by that the English writing system, based on the relative frequencies of the twenty-six letters of the alphabet and the space). It turns out that, in a binary system, the probability profile where information and redundancy match one another, at 50 per cent each, is almost exactly 0.9 : 0.1.

To give the exact probabilities to two places of decimals: at probabilities of 0.89 : 0.11, H (information) = 0.4999. In other words, the particular distribution of probabilities to which these skew systems seemed to conform was that where there is 50 per cent redundancy in the system. This could perhaps begin to suggest an explanation for this kind of phenomenon in the grammar – if it turned out to survive under adequate large-scale scrutiny. To investigate it properly, it was necessary to have access to a sufficiently large corpus of modern English.

Part II

During the 1980s John Sinclair launched the COBUILD Project in Lexical Computing at the University of Birmingham in England. COBUILD stands for "Collins Birmingham University International Language Database". The task of this project was to assemble a large corpus of modern English text and to develop a range of software that would make this text available for lexicographical purposes – specifically, for research into English lexis that would lead to the production of a dictionary, or a series of dictionaries. At the same time, the corpus would provide a database for various other purposes such as the production of reference grammars and teaching materials.

Sinclair and his colleagues compiled a corpus of twenty million words of contemporary English: British English, largely written, but including two million words of speech (mainly speech of a median level of formality such as interviews on BBC radio). The selection of texts was determined by various factors; but one guiding principle was that it should be in some sense "typical" – the sort of English that a learner would want to understand. In this way any material based on the corpus would be useful for students of English as a second or foreign language.

The output of the project in its first phase is now well known. It included a series of English teaching materials and a reference grammar; but above all it included the COBUILD series of dictionaries, recognized around the world for their highly innovative approach to defining, classifying and contextualizing English words. The fundamental feature of all these various publications is that they are corpus-based: not only in that all cited instances are taken from the corpus, but also in that the overall profile that is presented of each word is that which is revealed by studying how the word is actually used. The project has now entered its second phase, in which the dictionaries will be revised and updated, and other publications such as a dictionary of collocations will be put in hand. For this purpose, the original corpus of 20 million words has now been supplanted by one of two hundred million, covering a wider and more structured repertory of registers and dialects of English and including a more substantial component of texts in spoken language. The 200-million-word corpus is known as the "Bank of English".

In 1991 I was able to spend four months at the University of Birmingham, working with the COBUILD project; and in particular, during that time I was fortunate in being able to collaborate with one of their research staff, Zoe James, on problems of quantitative grammar: the quantitative analysis of grammatical systems through investigation of frequencies in the corpus. We decided to work with the original COBUILD corpus; the larger, new corpus was not yet fully accessible, and in any case 20 million words seemed enough for what we were trying to achieve. In the event we decided to use just the 18 million words of written text, so that later on, if we wanted, we could compare the results with an equivalent quantity of spoken. So the findings that I shall be presenting in the rest of this chapter are derived from a corpus of eighteen million words of modern written English. The results are set out in an article by Zoe James and myself (1993) entitled 'A quantitative study of polarity and primary tense in the English finite clause' (Chapter 6 of this volume).

The first question that we had to decide, obviously, was what to count. What grammatical systems should we use as our field of investigation? Here there were a number of factors that had to be kept in view.

1   The systems to be counted had to be very general ones, not those of a more "delicate" kind; they should be systems that apply to a large number of instances. This is partly to ensure that each term occurs with sufficient frequency; but there is a more significant factor, which is this – that any general hypothesis about probabilities ceases to apply when one moves to more specific sets of options, because these tend to have complex entry conditions. A system network is not a strict taxonomy. For example, we can make a prediction about "polarity: positive / negative" because this system is a very general one, entered by every member of the class of major clauses. But if we were interested in the system of "negative transfer" (the contrast between a pair of expressions such as *I think it's not*

fair and *I don't think it's fair*, or *you're required not to smoke* and *you're not allowed to smoke*, or *you mustn't smoke here* and *you can't smoke here*), not only would the population be hard to find but there is no prediction to be made about the relative frequency, because only clauses which are both negative and modalized enter into this system, and there is no way of knowing how far these two factors condition one another.

2   The features to be counted must, obviously, be systemic: that is to say, they must be such that, given some population *x*, we can ask how many have the feature *a* and how many have the feature *b*. That sounds very simple. But suppose there exists another population *y* that has feature *a* by default? Are these to be counted as instances of *a* or not? This is actually a very common phenomenon: for example, in English, a transitive verb (verbal group) can select either active or passive; but an intransitive one is active by default – so are intransitive to be included in the category of "active", or not? A countable noun (nominal group) is either singular or plural; but a mass one, which is uncountable, is singular by default. A strict version of the hypothesis would reject instances of *y, a* (intransitive active, or mass singular) because in system–structure theory (as formulated by Firth) what we are calling feature "*a*" cannot, in fact, be the same feature under those two different circumstances – it must have a different value in a context where it is in contrast with feature *b*, as opposed to a context where it is not. Eventually, of course, we would want to count such patterns both ways; but there is no point in doing this until the hypothesis has been tested in the simpler cases, those where this problem does not arise.

3   The systems should be ones that are highly loaded semantically: that do a large amount of work in the grammar. In fact this follows from 1. above, because systems which are very general in application will *ipso facto* be highly loaded. But this also suggests that they should be systems of higher rank (systems of the clause, rather than systems of the group or the word), because clause systems occupy a larger semantic domain. For example, positive / negative characterize a whole process, whereas singular / plural characterize only one participant in a process.

4   The systems should be such that we could formulate and test the hypothesis already outlined: that is to say, to start with there should

be one system which was predicted to be "equi" and one which was predicted to be "skew". And both should be binary systems, because for a system with any greater number of terms the notion of "skew" becomes more complex: if there were three terms, these might be conceived of as 0.9 : 0.05 : 0.05, or as 0.45 : 0.45 : 0.1, as well as other more convoluted profiles. With a binary system there was only one interpretation for "skew".

5 And finally, the system must be recognizable: that is, it must be such that instances of each term could be clearly identified in the corpus. This requirement overshadows all the rest.

Anyone who has tried to write a grammar, or a part of one, in computable form (and that means more or less any grammarian, these days, because thanks to Chomsky we have a much stronger sense of commitment to making our grammars explicit) is aware of the triviality trap: that the easier a thing is to recognize, the less it is worthwhile recognizing it. Any system that plays an important part in the grammar is likely to be more or less *cryptotypic*, construed through a complex string of realizations and/or field of reactances. This is not simply Murphy's law at work; on the contrary, it is precisely because fundamental contrasts like that between, say, material, mental and relational processes have such complex realizations and reactances that they can exert such a powerful role in the construction of meaning. But whereas in my small–scale counting in the 1960s I had been able to count by inspecting every instance myself ("manually", as they say!), now we had to be able to get the program to do the counting. Each instance had to be recognizable by the computer ("mechanically"). The text was entered in the machine in ordinary orthography, exactly as printed; and it was indexed by the orthographic form of each word. There were no clause boundaries or other grammatical boundary markers, and no grammatical analysis had been carried out on the text. So the systems had to be such that we could formulate some strategy for recognizing every instance in the corpus and assigning it to one feature or the other, with a reasonable chance of getting it right. We could only ever approximate to the true picture; but we wanted to be able to approximate to it with an acceptably low margin of error.

With these considerations in mind, we decided to tackle two systems, as follows:

1   Polarity: positive / negative

2   Primary (deictic) tense: past / present [see (2) below]

The hypothesis was that polarity would be skew, with 0.9 positive :
0.1 negative; while primary tense would be equi, with each term
around 0.5.

What was the relevant population for these systems, as represented
in a systemic grammar of English? In principle: all **major** clauses
choose for polarity, whether finite or non-finite; whereas only *finite*
clauses have primary tense, and not all of those because some finite
clauses select modal and not temporal deixis. Furthermore, of those
that select temporal deixis there are some which select neither past
nor present but future. So our two systems did not have the same
conditions of entry.

This does not matter. There is no reason why the two systems
being investigated should have identical populations. But certain
decisions had to be taken.

1   We decided to eliminate non-finite clauses from the polarity
    count as well. This was because non-finites are hard to
    identify: for every occurrence of an *-ing* form of verb it would
    have to be determined whether it was functioning as Pre-
    dicator in the clause or not.

2   We decided to eliminate "future" from the count for primary
    tense. This was because we wanted to treat tense also as a
    binary system. (In fact instances of primary future were also
    included in the count; we discuss the possible relevance of this
    at the end of our published paper.)

3   Imperatives are anomalous: they are non-finite verbal groups
    (and hence have no primary tense), but realizing finite clauses
    (as is shown by the possibility of adding a mod tag, as in *Keep
    quiet, will you!*). This means that they would belong in the
    polarity count but not in the primary tense count. We de-
    cided, in fact, to treat them where they belonged.

So our populations were:

polarity: all finite major clauses **including** imperatives, futures and modals
primary tense: ,,   ,,   ,,   ,,   **excluding**   ,,   ,,   ,,   ,,

[It turned out that the exclusion of these three categories reduced the
population by about 16 per cent.]

What we needed to do, then, could be summed up briefly as
follows:

A. Polarity:

1. identify and count all finite clauses;
2. within this set, identify and count all those that are negative;
3. subtract the negative from the total and label the remainder "positive";
4. calculate the percentage of positive and negative within the total set of finite clauses.

B. Primary tense:

1. [as A] identify and count all finite clauses;
2. within this set, identify all those that
   (i) are non-indicative (= imperative),
   (ii) have modal deixis (i.e. Finite operator is a modal), or
   (iii) have future tense deixis (i.e. Finite operator is temporal: future), and eliminate from the set;
3. within this reduced set, identify and count all those that are past;
4. subtract the past from the total and label the remainder "present";
5. calculate the percentage of past and present within the reduced set of finite clauses.

This could be considered as an idealized research strategy for the investigation. But that, of course, was the point: it was idealized, and quite remote from anything resembling reality. It depends on operations like "identify a clause", "identify a finite clause", "identify a negative clause" and so on; and these things cannot be done automatically. There are of course parsers in existence, including two or three systemic parsers in different stages of development; but even if any of them turned out to be **accurate** enough, they are nowhere near to being **fast** enough. After all, we are talking about a population of 18 million words, which we would expect to yield between one and two million finite clauses.

What is needed is a system for recognizing patterns: some kind of pattern specifier, or pattern matcher, which is specifically designed for the purpose, and which works on the principles of the existing battery of software. So we set out to design this together, with me saying what I thought needed to be done and Zoe working out how to do it – or else saying it couldn't be done and we'd have to think of something else. Now there were two possible approaches here. One would have been to try and work out all the steps in advance and then implement them all at once, counting the results at the end. The other was to proceed step by step, by progressive approximation, counting up as we went along. We decided on the latter course, so that we could monitor the problems encountered and the results obtained at each successive step.

As a first step, we began by listing all the finite verbal operators in English. These form a closed class, and one which is reasonably small: 43 members, when we restricted them to single word forms (that is, including *can't, couldn't* and *cannot*, but excluding *can not* and *could not* – all such forms are regarded by the program as two separate words and would therefore have to be retrieved in a separate operation). We took the decision to exclude the words *need* and *dare*, although these do occur as Finite operators; *dare* is fairly rare in the corpus overall, while *need*, though common, occurs mainly as "full" verb (that is, it is construed lexically not grammatically). The 43 Finite operators are shown in Table 6.1 (see p. 104, present volume). They are set out in two columns by 21 rows; but the rows fall into three blocks, so the Table is structured as two columns by three blocks. The **columns** show polarity: positive on the left, negative on the right. The **blocks** show the operators organized by categories of verbal deixis: at the top, modal, and future temporal; in the middle, present temporal; and at the bottom, past temporal. Those in the top block are those eliminated from the count of primary tense.

Table 6.1 also shows the results of this initial counting. The total number of instances of positive polarity come out at somewhere under a million, those of negative at between 60 and 70 thousand. Let me make one or two observations regarding this Table.

(1) Some occurrences of the **positive** forms will have been instances of a lexical verb, not an operator: namely some occurrences of all forms of *be, have* and *do* (for example, *does* in *he does his homework after tea*, of which the negative is *doesn't do*, not just *doesn't* as it would have been if *does* had been an operator). We shall see below that this does not in fact matter, **provided that such forms do not get counted twice**.

(2) The wordings *is to / was to, has to / had to* (e.g. in *who is to know?, he had to be told*) express modality; so it might seem as if they should not be counted as present and past temporals. But their *deixis* is, in fact, temporal not modal; that is to say, **as Finite operators** they do express primary tense, so they are in their appropriate place.

(3) The system cannot distinguish, in counting occurrences of a word, between pairs of homographs, for example *can* as modal and *can* meaning 'sealed metal container'. Since this problem was going to crop up all the time, we considered various possible solutions. One was to use a tagger; there are two taggers available in the COBUILD repertory, as well as others that have been developed elsewhere, e.g. by Geoffrey Leech at the University of Lancaster. But we reasoned that, even with the fastest tagger, tagging 33,000 instances of *can* is a lengthy business; and we were not convinced of the level of accuracy that could be attained. We adopted an alternative strategy: that of inspecting a random sample of 200 instances, one by one, counting the number that were "spurious" (not instances of the form we were looking for) and then extrapolating from this figure to arrive at a proportion of the total which was to be discarded. The results of this procedure are shown in the column headed "spurious instances out of 200". This is obviously a source of inaccuracy; there were no tin cans in the 200 instances of *can*, for example, whereas no doubt there would have been some in the total of 33,000 or so. On the other hand, 1.5 per cent of occurrences of *am* were found to be 'a.m.' (morning), written without full stops; and this was probably slightly above the average figure. But we reckoned that the margin of error was tolerably small.

If these figures were then taken as a first approximation to the picture for polarity and primary tense, what were the main errors and omissions that were involved? We identified four major sources of inaccuracy, as follows.

1.   Mood tags (e.g. *haven't you?*, in *You've seen it, haven't you?*) have been counted as separate instances. The fact that they do not form separate **clauses** does not matter – we are not counting clauses; so since they (typically) retain the tense of the clause, including them will not distort the proportions of past and present. But they do not retain the polarity – in fact they typically reverse it. The polarity system in mood tags is not an opposition of "positive / negative"; it is an opposition of "polarity reversed / polarity constant", with "polarity reversed" as the unmarked option. Hence, since the majority of clauses are positive, counting the tags separately will have **over**estimated the figure for **negative**.

2. All abbreviated Finite operators have been omitted. There are six of these: *'s 'd 've 're 'm 'll*. This may have affected the figures for primary tense, since only *'d* is past, whereas *'s 've 're* and *'m* are all present. It has certainly distorted the figures for polarity, since all those omitted are positive. This therefore has **under**estimated the figure for **positive**.

3. Clauses with negative **words**, such as *not, no, never, nothing* have been counted (if at all) as positive (for example *the idea was no good, nothing would have helped*). But at least some of these are negative clauses, as shown up by the tag: *the idea was no good, was it?* This has **both over**estimated the **positive** and **under**estimated the **negative** count.

4. But undoubtedly the major source of inaccuracy is the following: that not all English finite verbs have (distinct) Finite operators. Simple past and simple present tense, in positive declarative active form, have their finiteness fused with the lexical verb, as in *I think so, I thought so*; and these are likely to be the two most frequently occurring forms of the verb. They have been omitted altogether; they are all positive (except as under no. 3 above); so this had **under**estimated the total figure for **positive**.

We tried therefore to take steps to deal with each of these errors and omissions. The way we did this was as follows.

(1) We identified the mood tags by counting all occurrences of the sequence

comma + operator + personal pronoun + question mark

e.g., *won't they?* It turned out, when we checked this later, that it should have been "comma + operator + personal pronoun + any punctuation mark", since a tag may be followed, in written English, by full stop, exclamation mark or comma, as well as by a question mark. But the total number of tags was quite small (almost certainly under 3,000), no doubt because the corpus we were using was written English, so that they would tend to occur only in the dialogic passages of narrative fiction. So their effect on the total picture was negligible.

(2) We counted all the instances of the operators in their abbreviated form. The main problem here is the *'s*, since this can

also be possessive; by our estimate, about two-thirds of the occurrences of *'s* (about 70,000, out of just over 100,000) were possessive, leaving about 30,000 as abbreviation of *is* or *has*. The total number of abbreviated operators came to about 80,000. For polarity, these were all to be added to the positive count. For primary tense, about 60,000 were present and rather over 5,000 were past; the remainder were either future or modal, and so outside the population under study.

(3) For clauses with the words *not, no, never* and so on we adopted a rather complex strategy which I will not try to describe in detail; it took account of the distinction between *not*, as the usual form of the ordinary finite negative in writing (spoken *they didn't know*, written *they did not know*), and the remaining 18 negative words. Not every occurrence of *not* marks a negative clause, as can be shown by the tag; compare:

> Not all the eligible voters turned up to vote,
> did they?   [negative clause]

> A not inconsiderable number of voters stayed away,
> didn't they?   [positive clause]

So we devised a strategy for estimating those that were negative (all those where *not* followed a Finite operator, either directly or with one word in between); this yielded about 60,000, or around 70 per cent of all occurrences of *not*. (This was perhaps rather an underestimate.) With the other negative words, we inspected 200 occurrences of each and extrapolated; this had to be done separately for each word, because of the very different proportions involved: for example, whereas 98 per cent of all clauses with *never* turned out to be negative, the proportion was only 70 per cent of those with *no* and only 10 per cent of those with *few*. The total effect of this counting of the negative words was to deduct 70,000 instances from the positive total and add them on to the negative.

(4) We then faced the major problems of counting the instances of simple past and simple present tense forms of lexical verbs. It will be remembered that for the three most common verbs, *be, have* and *do*, these forms had already been counted, because they are the same as forms that occur as operators; and for our purposes we did not need to take account of the distinction between the two. So leaving out these three verbs we picked out from the overall frequency list the first fifty verbs, **as**

indicated by the ranking of their most frequent form. (Note that the system counts each form of a word separately, so there is a figure for occurrences of *say*, one for *says*, one for *said* and one for *saying*, but no overall frequency count, or frequency ranking, for the verb *say* taking all its variants together. English verbs typically have four forms, like *say*; some have five, like *take*; some have three, like *put*; and there is one exceptional verb *be*, which has eight.)

As a rule, the most frequent form of the verb was the base form, e.g. *take, put*; in a few cases it was the past form, e.g. *said*. [The figures are given in Chapter 6 of this volume, Table 6.3 (a).] By inspecting the frequency list we identified the fifty most frequent verbs after *be, have* and *do*; this included all verbs of which the most frequently occurring form occurred at least 2,400 times in the corpus of 18 million words. We then split this set of fifty verbs into two sets of 25 each, those above and those below the half-way line; we wanted to examine the two sub-sets separately so that we could see whether the various proportions we were concerned with stayed more or less the same in both halves. The top 25 – the "first swath" – were those whose most frequent form had occurred at least 4,900 times.

Now which forms were we counting? Not v–ng, the *-ing* form, because that never occurs as a finite form. Not v–n, the past participle, for the same reason; but here there is a complication, because for the majority of English verbs the v–n form is the same as the v–d form, that for the past tense, and this we did need to count. Of the other two forms, we wanted all occurrences of v–s, the 3rd person singular present, which is always finite; and of the v–0 or base form, we wanted those instances which are present tense but not those which are infinitive. So the problem of counting them was fairly complicated; and it was complicated still further by the fact that occurrences of some of these forms are often not verbs at all but something else, typically singular or plural forms of nouns. So with words like *look, looks, turn, leaves, calls* we have somehow to avoid including the spurious instances into our figures.

For these potentially ambiguous forms we adopted the same strategy as we had done elsewhere: that is, we inspected 200 instances chosen at random, counted all those that were to be discarded, and then extrapolated from this figure on to the total. So for example out of 200 occurrences of *looks*, 40 (i.e. 20 per cent) turned out to be nouns; so from the 1,863 occurrences of the form *looks* we deducted 20 per cent and estimated the total verbal (v-s) instances as 1490. This of course has the effect of changing the rank ordering of the verbs, and in some cases pushed the verb in question off the bottom of the list altogether (for example, *play* was in the list of first fifty verbs until it turned out that it had got there spuriously, by virtue of its frequency as a noun).

How did we then eliminate the other type of spurious instance, where the word in question was functioning as a verb but was non-finite (v-0 as infinitive, v-d = v-n as past participle)? For each v-0 form (base form), and for each v-d **where this is identical with v-n**, we counted all instances following a Finite operator, either directly or with one word in between (e.g. *might make, hadn't made, will certainly make, is being made*) and discarded them; likewise all **other** instances directly following *to* (*to make*) – that is, other than those that had been discarded already by the first procedure, such as *has to make*.

Finally, and again by a rather complicated procedure, we estimated the number of instances of v-0 that were **imperative**; these we eliminated from the primary tense count. (We left them in the polarity count because they do select independently between positive and negative.) [Table 6.3 (a) gives the figures for the first swath of 25 verbs, with the totals entered at the bottom. Tables 6.4 and 6.5 give the new revised totals for polarity and primary tense.] The results now read as follows: for polarity, 1,443,670 instances counted, of which 86.75 per cent were positive and 13.25 per cent were negative; for primary tense, 1,195,710 instances counted, of which 49.55 per cent were present and 50.45 per cent past.

We then used the same strategies over again to deal with the next swath of 25 verbs [see Table 6.6 (a)]. When we came to inspect these forms for "spurious" instances, an interesting difference appeared: very many more out of this second group had to be disqualified. In other words, within the 25 **most frequent** verbs, most of the forms occur **only** as verbs; whereas in the second swath, a large number of the forms occurring are words which function **both** as noun **and** as verb. Other than that, the excess of past over present was somewhat less marked in the second swath (56 per cent of past in swath 2, 62 per cent in swath 1, both figures corrected) – though the **totals** are of course very different: about 230,000 for swath 1, under 100,000 (c. 93,000) for swath 2. (Some of the difference is accounted for by the large number of occurrences of the past form *said*; but not all – if all forms of *say* are left out, swath 1 still shows 60 per cent as past.)

We have now taken into account the 53 most frequent verbs in the language: the two swaths of 25 each, plus *be, have* and *do*. This has now given us a total of just over 1½ million instances for polarity, just over 1¼ million for primary tense (because of the three categories omitted from the latter count). Note that the second swath of verbs accounted for only about 6 per cent of the total. We would have liked to know how many instances were still unaccounted for – the simple past and simple present instances of verbs having a frequency below about 5,000 (all forms taken together) in the corpus. It turned out that there was no satisfactory way of estimating this figure. I would make a rough guess of somewhere between 100,000 and 150,000; if this is right, then adding them in would not affect the total distribution by more than 1 per cent either way.

The final figures we obtained are given in Chapter 6, Table 6.7. They show positive at 87.6 per cent, as against negative at 12.4 per cent. They show past and present almost equal, within 1 per cent of 50 per cent each. Let us now look at these in the light of our original hypothesis, which was (polarity) positive 0.9, negative 0.1; (primary tense) past 0.5, present 0.5. There are perhaps three things that could be remarked on.

As I said in the first part of the chapter, the hypothesis was not plucked out of the air; it was based on various bits of counting that I had done, over the years, which although on a very small scale had been carried out carefully and, as far as I was able to do so, accurately and with the same general model of the grammar. So it seems to suggest that counting a sample of 2,000 instances may not be entirely without value for predicting a general pattern. But, of course, it needs to be done again and fully documented.

Secondly, on the other hand, we cannot easily gauge the accuracy of our own figures. We know of numerous places where errors will have been coming in, and there are no doubt other sources of error that we have not yet become aware of. We did our best to reduce the errors; and, when we could think of no way of reducing them further, to make them such as mutually to cancel out rather than to skew the findings in one direction or the other. Perhaps the most urgent task, at this stage, is to design pattern–matching software that will enable much more accurate estimates to be made.

However, I do not think the figures are so far out as to invalidate the general picture they present; and this leads me to the third point. Of course, it is a coincidence that they are so close to what was predicted; these were idealized modal values, and I am quite sure that such results will not turn up again in any future counting – this was just to encourage us to continue! Do not imagine, by the way, that we could possibly have influenced the results by our choice of strategy; we had no idea how they would develop, and would not have had the slightest notion how to steer them towards any particular outcome. (If one knew enough to do that, one would hardly need to count them.) The main significance of the result is that it suggests it would be worth while to count some more.

With the corpus of 200 million words, it would be possible to do this in a way which took account of variation in register, the systematic differences in grammar and lexis that distinguish one text type from another. In the smaller corpus, information about the source of each text is of course available; but the corpus is not organized on this principle. The larger corpus, the "Bank of English", on the other hand, is stored and indexed for access according to register; so it would be possible to keep an ongoing tally not only of the overall frequencies but of the frequencies displayed by each register that is represented. This would enable us to explore in accurate quantitative terms the notion of register variation defined as the resetting of probabilities in the lexis and in the grammar.[3]

As I said at the beginning, corpus linguists often modestly refer to themselves as the data gatherers in the linguistic profession. I do not think data gathering is anything there is reason to be modest about, certainly when it comes to data which are instances of semiotic systems. But in any case, data gathering and theorizing are no longer separate activities (I do not believe they ever were); and whether or not there is any significance in the particular quantitative study reported here, with the potential for quantitative research opened up by corpus linguistics our understanding of language, and hence of semiotic systems in general, seems likely to undergo a qualitative change.

Notes

1 For the discussion of "system" and "structure" as fundamental theoretical concepts see Firth 1957.
2 For a general perspective on corpus studies in English see Svartvik 1992. For examples of corpus-based lexicogrammatical studies in the 1960s, cf. Svartvik 1966; Sinclair *et al.* 1970; Huddleston *et al.* 1970.
3 For a detailed discussion of register, including register as a probabilistic concept, see Matthiessen 1993b.

Chapter Eight

THE SPOKEN LANGUAGE CORPUS: A FOUNDATION FOR GRAMMATICAL THEORY
(2002)

1 Introduction

I felt rather daunted when Professor Karin Aijmer invited me to talk at this Conference, because it is fifteen years since I retired from my academic appointment and, although I continue to follow new developments with interest, I would certainly not pretend to keep up to date – especially since I belong to that previous era when one could hope to be a generalist in the field of language study, something that is hardly any longer possible today. But I confess that I was also rather delighted, because if there is one topic that is particularly close to my heart it is that of the vast potential that resides in a corpus of spoken language. This is probably the main source from which new insights can now be expected to flow.

I have always had greater interest in the spoken language, because that in my view is that mainspring of semogenesis: where, proto-typically, meaning is made and the frontiers of meaning potential are extended. But until the coming of the tape recorder we had no means of capturing spoken language and pinning it down. Since my own career as a language teacher began before tape recorders were invented (or at least before the record companies could no longer stop them being produced), I worked hard to train myself in storing and writing down conversation as it occurred; but there are obviously severe limits on the size of corpus you can compile like that. Of course, to accumulate enough spoken language in a form in which it could be managed in very large quantities, we needed a second great technical innovation, the computer; but in celebrating the computerized corpus we should not forget that it was the tape recorder that broke through the sound barrier (the barrier to arresting speech sound, that is) and made the enterprise of spoken language research possible. It is ironical, I think, that now that the technology of speech recording is so good that we can eavesdrop on almost any occasion and kind of spoken discourse, we have ethics committees and privacy protection agencies denying us access, or preventing us from making use of what we record. (Hence my homage to Svartvik and Quirk (1980), which I still continue to plunder as a source of open-ended spontaneous dialogue.)

So my general question, in this chapter, is this: what can we actually learn about spoken language and, more significantly, about language, by using a computerized corpus on a scale such as can now be obtained? What I was suggesting by my title, of course (and the original title had the phrase "at the foundation of grammatics", which perhaps makes the point more forcefully), was that we can learn a great deal: that a spoken language corpus does lie at the foundation of grammatics, using "grammatics" to mean the theoretical study of lexicogrammar – this being located, in turn, in the context of a general theory of language. (I had found it necessary to introduce this term because of the confusion that constantly arose between "grammar" as one component of a language and "grammar" as the systematic description of that component.) In this sense, the spoken language corpus is a primary resource for enabling us to theorize about the lexicogrammatical stratum in language – and thereby about language as a whole.

I can see no place for an opposition between theory and data, in the sense of a clear boundary between "data-gathering" and theory construction. I remember wondering, when I was reading Issac Newton's *Opticks*, what would have happened to physics if Newton, observing light passing through different media and measuring the refraction, had said of himself "I'm just a data-gatherer; I leave the theorizing to others". What was new, of course, was that earlier physicists had not been able to observe and measure very much because the technology wasn't available; so they were forced to theorize without having adequate data. Galileo and Newton were able to observe experimentally; but this did not lead them to set up an opposition between observation and theory – between the different stages in a single enterprise of extending the boundaries of knowledge. Now, until the arrival of the tape recorder and the computer, linguists were in much the same state as pre-Renaissance physicists: they had to invent, to construct their database without access to the phenomena on which they most depended. Linguistics can now hope to advance beyond its pre-scientific age; but it will be greatly hindered if we think of data and theory as realms apart, or divide the world of scholarship into those who dig and those who spin.

It is not the case, of course, that linguists have had no data at all. They have always had plenty of written language text, starting with texts of high cultural value, the authors whose works survived from classical times. This already provoked disputation, in Europe, between text-based scholars and theoreticians; we find this satirized in the late medieval fable of the Battle of the Seven Arts, fought out between the Auctores and the Artes. But the "auctores" embodied the notion of the text as a model (author as authority); this was written language as object with value, rather than just as specimen to be used in evidence. And this in turn reflects the nature of written language: it is language produced under attention, discourse that is self-conscious and self-monitored. This does not, of course, invalidate it as data; it means merely that written texts tell us about written language, and we have to be cautious in arguing from this to the potentiality of language as a whole. After all, speech evolved first, in the species; speech develops first, in the individual; and, at least until the electronic age, people did far more talking than writing throughout their lives.

2 Spoken and written

Throughout most of the history of linguistics, therefore, there has been no choice. To study text, as data, meant studying written text; and written text had to serve as the window, not just into written language but into language. Now, thanks to the new technology, things have changed; we might want to say: well, now, we can study written texts, which will tell us about written language, and we can study spoken texts, which will tell us about spoken language.

But where, then, do we find out about language? One view might be: there's no such thing as language, only language as spoken and language as written; so we describe the two separately, with a different grammar for each, and the two descriptions together will tell us all we need to know. The issue of 'same or different grammars' has been much discussed, for example by David Brazil (1995), Geoffrey Leech (2000) and Michael Stubbs (1996); there is obviously no one "right answer" – it depends on the context and the purpose, on what you are writing the grammar for. The notion 'there is no such thing as language; there are only ...', whether 'only dialects', 'only registers', 'only individual speakers' or even 'only speech events' is a familiar one; it represents a backing away from theory, in the name of a resistance to "totalizing", but it is itself an ideological and indeed theoretical stance (cf. Martin's [1993] observations on ethnomethodology). And while of all such attempts to narrow down the ultimate domain of a linguistic theory the separation into spoken language and written language is the most plausible, it still leaves "language" out of account, and hence renders our conception of semantics particularly impoverished – it is the understanding of the meaning-making power of language that suffers most from such a move.

It was perhaps in the so-called "modern" era that the idea of spoken language and written language as distinct semiotic systems made most sense, because that was the age of print, when the two were relatively insulated one from the other – although the spoken "standard language" of the nation state was already a bit of a hybrid. Now, however, when text is written electronically, and is presented in temporal sequence on the screen (and, on the other hand, more and more of speech is prepared for being addressed to people unknown to the speaker), the two are tending to get mixed up, and the spoken / written distinction is increasingly blurred. But even without this mixing, there is enough reason for postulating a language, such as "English", as a more abstract entity encompassing both spoken and written varieties. There is nothing strange about the existence of such varieties; a language is an inherently variable system, and the spoken / written variable is simply one among many, unique only in that it involves distinct modalities. But it is just this difference of modality, between the visual-synoptic of writing and aural-dynamic of speech, that gives the spoken corpus its special value – not to mention, of course, its own very special problems!

I think it is not necessary, in the present context, to spend time and energy disposing of a myth, one that has done so much to impede, and then to distract, the study of spoken language: namely the myth that spoken language is lacking in structure. The spoken language is every bit as highly organized as the written – it couldn't function if it wasn't. But whereas in writing you can cross out all the mistakes and discard the preliminary drafts, leaving only the finished product to offer to the reader, in speaking you cannot do this; so those who first transcribed spoken dialogue triumphantly pointed to all the hesitations, the false starts and the backtrackings that they had included in their transcription (under the pretext of faithfulness to the data), and cited these as evidence for the inferiority of the spoken word – a view to which they were already ideologically committed. It was, in fact, a severe distortion of the essential nature of speech; a much more "faithful" transcription is a rendering in ordinary orthography, including ordinary punctuation. The kind of false exoticism which is imposed on speech in the act of reducing it to writing, under the illusion of being objective, still sometimes gets in the way, foregrounding all the trivia and preventing the serious study of language in its spoken form. (But not, I think, in the corridors of corpus linguistics!)

3 Spoken language and the corpus

Now what the corpus does for the spoken language is, in the first instance, the same as what it does for the written: it amasses large quantities of text and processes it to make it accessible for study. Some kinds of spoken language can be fairly easily obtained: radio and television interviews, for example, or proceedings in courts of law, and these figured already in the earliest COBUILD corpus of twenty million words (eighteen million written and two million spoken). The London–Lund corpus (alone, I think, at that time) included a considerable amount of spontaneous conversation, much of it being then transcribed in the *Corpus of English Conversation* I referred to earlier (see Svartvik and Quirk, 1980). Ronald Carter and Mike McCarthy, in their CANCODE corpus at Nottingham, work with five million words of natural speech; on a comparable scale is the UTS–Macquarie corpus in Sydney, which includes a component of "spoken language in the workplace" that formed the basis of Suzanne Eggins and Diana Slade's (1997) *Analysing Casual Conversation*. Already in the 1960s there was a valuable corpus of children's speech, some of it in the form of interview with an adult but some of children talking among themselves, at the Nuffield Foreign Language Teaching Materials Project under the direction of Sam Spicer in Leeds; and in the 1980s Robin Fawcett assembled a database of primary school children's language in the early years of his Computational Linguistics Unit at the (then) Polytechnic of Wales.

These are, I am well aware, just the exemplars that are known to me, in what is now a worldwide enterprise of spoken language corpus research, in English and no doubt in many other languages besides. What all these projects have in common, as far as I know, is that the spoken text, as well as being stored as speech, is also always transcribed into written form. There are numerous different conventions of transcribing spoken English; I remember a workshop on the grammar of casual conversation, about twenty years ago, in which we looked into eight systems then in current use (Hasan, ed., 1985), and there must be many more in circulation now. What I have not seen, though such a thing may exist, is any systematic discussion of what all these different systems imply about the nature of spoken language, what sort of order (or lack of order) they impose on it – or, in general terms, of what it means to transcribe spoken discourse into writing. And this is in fact an extraordinarily complex question.

In English we talk about "reducing" spoken language to writing, in a metaphor which suggests that something is lost; and so of course it is. We know that the melody and rhythm of speech, which are highly meaningful features of the spoken language, are largely absent; and it is ironical that many of the transcription systems – the majority at the time when I looked into them – abandoned the one feature of writing that gives some indication of those prosodies, namely punctuation. Of course punctuation is not a direct marker of prosody, because in the evolution of written language it has taken on a life of its own, and now usually (again referring to English) embodies a compromise between the prosodic and the compositional (constituent) dimensions of grammatical structure; but it does give a significant amount of prosodic information, as anyone is aware who reads aloud from a written text, and it is perverse to refuse to use it under the pretext of not imposing patterns on the data – rather as if one insisted on using only black-&-white reproductions of representational art, so as not to impose colours on the flowers, or on the clothing of the ladies at court. The absence of punctuation merely exaggerates the dog's-dinner image that is being projected on to spoken language.

There are transcriptions which include prosodic information; and these are of two kinds: those, like Svartvik and Quirk (deriving from the work of Quirk and Crystal in the 1960s [1964]), which give a detailed account of the prosodic movement in terms of pitch, loudness and tempo, and those (like my own) which mark just those systemic features of intonation and rhythm which have been shown to be functional in carrying meaning – as realization of selections in the grammar, in the same way that, in a tone language, they would be realizations of selections in vocabulary. I use this kind of transcription because I want to bring out how systems which occur only in the spoken language not only are regularly and predictably meaningful but also are integrated with other, recognized grammatical systems (those marked by morphology or ordering or class selection) in a manner no different from the way these latter are integrated with each other. [Texts 1–4 below illustrate some different conventions of transcription: Text 1 from a tape recording made and transcribed in about 1960; Text 2 from Svartvik and Quirk, 1980; Text 4 from Halliday 1994.]

Thus there is a gap in the information about spoken discourse that is embodied in our standard orthographies; and since one major function of a spoken language corpus is to show these prosodically realized systems at work, it seems to me that any mode of transcription used with such a corpus should at least incorporate prosodic features in some systematic way. They are not optional extras; in some languages at least, but probably in all, intonation and rhythm are meaningful in an entirely systematic fashion.

But while it is fairly obvious what an orthographic transcription leaves out, it is perhaps less obvious what it puts in. Orthographies impose their own kind of determinacy, of a kind that belongs to the written language: a constituent-like organization which is not really a feature of speech. Words are given clear boundaries, with beginnings and endings often somewhat arbitrarily assigned; and punctuation, while in origin marking patterns of prosodic movement, has been preempted to mark off larger grammatical units. (There is considerable variation in practice: some writers do still use it more as a prosodic device.) It is true that spoken language is also compositional: the written sentence, for example, is derived from the clause complex of natural speech; but its components are not so much constituents in a constituent hierarchy as movements in a choreographic sequence. The written sentence knows where it's going when it starts; the spoken clause complex does not. [Text 3 illustrates this second point.]

But writing imposes determinacy also on the paradigmatic axis, by its decisions about what are, or are not, tokens of the same type. Here the effect of "reducing speech to writing" depends largely on the nature of the script. There is already variation here on the syntagmatic axis, because different scripts impose different forms of constituency: in Chinese, and also in Vietnamese, the unit bounded by spaces is the morpheme; in European languages it is the word, though with room for considerable variation regarding what a word is; in Japanese it is a mixture of the morpheme and the syllable, though you can generally tell which morpheme begins a new word. On the paradigmatic axis, Chinese, as a morphemic script, is the most determinate: it leaves no room for doubt about what are and what are not regarded as tokens of the same type. But even English and French, though in principle having a phonological script, have strong morphemic tendencies; they have numerous homonyms at the morpho-syllabic interface, which the writing system typically keeps apart. Such writing systems mask the indeterminacy in the spoken language, so that (for example) pairs like *mysticism / misty schism*, or *icicle / eye sickle*, which in speech are separated only by minor rhythmic differences, come to be quite unrelated in their written forms – James Joyce made brilliant use of this as a semogenic resource (but as a resource for the written language). But even in languages with a more purely phonological script, such as Russian or Italian, the writing system enforces regularities, policing the text to protect it from all the forms of meaningful variation which contribute so much to the richness and potency of speech.

So transcribing spoken discourse – especially spontaneous conversation – into written form in order to observe it, and to use the observations as a basis for theorizing language, is a little bit problematic. Transcribing is translating, and translating is transforming; I think to compile and interpret an extensive spoken corpus inevitably raises questions about the real nature of this transformation.

4 Some features of the spoken language

I would like to refer briefly to a number of features which have been investigated in corpus studies, with reference to what they suggest about the properties of language as a whole. I will group these under seven headings; but they are not in any systematic order – just the order in which I found it easiest to move along from each one to the next.

4.1 Patterns in casual conversation

Eggins and Slade, in their book *Analysing Casual Conversation* (1997), studied patterns at four strata: lexicogrammatical, semantic, discoursal and generic. The first two showed up as highly patterned in the interpersonal domain (interpersonal metafunction), particularly in mood and modality. At the level of genre they recognized a cline from storytelling to chat, with opinion and gossip in between; of the ten genres of conversation that they ranged along this cline, they were able to assign generic structures to seven of them: these were narrative, anecdote, exemplum, recount, observation / comment, opinion and gossip. Of the other three, joke-telling they had not enough data to explore; the other two, sending up and chat, they said "cannot be characterized in generic terms". Their analysis, based on a spoken corpus, suggests that casual conversation is far from lacking in structural order.

4.2 Pattern forming and re-forming

Ronald Carter, in a recent study 'Language and creativity: the evidence from spoken English' (2002), was highlighting, as the title makes clear, the creative potential of the spoken language, especially casual speech. He referred to its "pattern forming and re-forming", emphasizing particularly the "re-forming" that takes place in the course of dialogue: one speaker sets up some kind of lexicogrammatical pattern, perhaps involving a regular collocation, an idiom or cliché, or some proverbial echo; the interlocutor builds on it – but then deflects, "re-forms" it into something new, with a different pattern of lexicogrammatical wording. This will usually not all happen in one dyadic exchange; it may be spread across long passages of dialogue, with several speakers involved; but it can happen very quickly, as illustrated in one or two of Carter's examples from the CANCODE corpus:

(i) [Two students are talking about the landlord of a mutual friend]
   A: Yes, he must have a bob or two.
   B: Whatever he does he makes money out of it just like that.
   A: Bob's your uncle.
   B: He's quite a lot of money, erm, tied up in property and things. He's got a finger in all kinds of pies and houses and stuff.

(ii) [Two colleagues, who are social workers, are discussing a third colleague who has a tendency to become too involved in individual cases]

A: I don't know but she seems to have picked up all kinds of lame ducks and traumas along the way.

B: That – that's her vocation.

A: Perhaps it is. She should have been a counsellor.

B: Yeah but the trouble with her is she puts all her socialist carts before the horses.

4.3 Patterns in words and phrases

There might seem to be some contradiction between this and Michael Stubbs' observation, in his *Words and Phrases: Corpus Studies of Lexical Semantics* (2001), that "a high proportion of language use is routinized, conventional and idiomatic", at least when this is applied to spoken language. Of course, one way in which both could be true would be if speech was found to consist largely of routinized stuff with occasional flashes of creativity in between; but I don't think this is how the two features are to be reconciled. Rather, it seems to me that it is often precisely in the use of "routinized, conventional and idiomatic" features that speakers' creativity is displayed. (I shall come back to this point later.) But, as Stubbs anticipated in his earlier work (1996), and has demonstrated in his more recent study (of "extended lexical units"), it is only through amassing a corpus of speech that we gain access to the essential regularities that must be present if they can be played with in this fashion. There can be no meaning in departing from a norm unless there is a norm already in place to be departed from.

4.4 Patterns in grammar

Michael Stubbs' book is subtitled "corpus studies of lexical semantics"; Susan Hunston and Gill Francis' (2000) is titled *Pattern Grammar: a Corpus-driven Approach to the Lexical Grammar of English*: one "lexical semantics", the other "lexical grammar". I have written about Hunston and Francis' book elsewhere (in 2001); what they are doing, in my view, is very successfully extending the grammar in greater detail (greater delicacy) across the middle ground where lexis and grammar meet. There is no conflict here with theoretical grammar, at least in my own understanding of the nature of theory; indeed they make considerable use of established grammatical categories. But this region of the grammar, with its highly complex network of microcategories, could not be penetrated without benefit of a corpus – and again, it has to include a spoken corpus, because it is in speech that these patterns are most likely to be evolving and being ongoingly renewed.

4.5 The grammar of appraisal

Eggins and Slade referred to, and also demonstrated in the course of their analysis, the centrality, in many types of casual conversation, of the interpersonal component in meaning. Our understanding of the interpersonal metafunction derives particularly from the work of Jim Martin: his book *English Text: System and Structure* (1992), several articles (e.g. 1998), and a new book co-authored with David Rose (2003). Martin focused especially on the area of "appraisal", comprising appreciation, affect, judgement and amplification – all those systems whereby speakers organize their personal opinions, their likes and dislikes, and their degree and kind of involvement in what they are saying. These features have always been difficult to investigate: partly for ideological reasons – they weren't recognized as a systematic component of meaning; but also because they are realized by a bewildering mixture of lexicogrammatical resources: morphology, prosody (intonation and rhythm), words of all classes, closed and open, and the ordering of elements in a structure. Martin has shown how these meanings are in fact grammaticalized – that is, they are systemic in their operation; but to demonstrate this you need access to a large amount of data, and this needs to be largely spoken discourse. Not that appraisal does not figure in written language – it does, even if often more disguised (see Hunston 1993); but it is in speech that its systemic potential is more richly exploited.

4.6 "Non-standard" patterns

There is a long tradition of stigmatizing grammatical patterns that do not conform to the canons of written language. This arose, naturally enough, because grammatics evolved mainly in the study of written language (non-written cultures often developed theories of rhetoric, but never theories of grammar), and then because grammarians, like lexicographers, were seen as guardians of a nation's linguistic morals. I don't think I need take up time arguing this point here. But, precisely because there are patterns which don't occur in writing, we need a corpus of spoken language to reveal them. I don't mean the highly publicized "grammatical errors" beloved of correspondents to the newspapers; these are easily manufactured, without benefit of a corpus, and I suspect that that kind of attention to linguistic table manners is a peculiarly English phenomenon – perhaps shared by the French, I've heard it said. I mean the more interesting and pro-ductive innovations which pass unnoticed in speech but have not (yet) found their way into the written language – and are often hard to construct with conscious thought; for example, from my own observations:

> It's been going to've been being taken out for a long time. [of a package left on the back seat of the car]

> All the system was somewhat disorganized, because of not being sitting in front of the screen. [cf. because I wasn't sitting ...]

> Drrr is the noise which when you say it to a horse the horse goes faster.

> Excuse me – is that one of those rubby-outy things? [pointing to an object on a high shelf in a shop]

> And then at the end I had one left over, which you're bound to have at least one that doesn't go.

> That's because I prefer small boats, which other people don't necessarily like them.

> This court won't serve. [cf. it's impossible to serve from this court]

4.7 Grammatical intricacy

Many years ago I started measuring lexical density, which I defined as the number of lexical items (content words) per ranking (non-embedded) clause. I found a significant difference between speech and writing: in my written language samples the mean value was around six lexical words per clause, while in the samples of spoken language it was around two. There was of course a great deal of variation among different registers, and Jean Ure (1971) showed that the values for a range of text types were located along a continuum. She, however, counted lexical words as a proportion of total running words, which gives a somewhat different result, because spoken language is more clausal (more and shorter clauses) whereas written language is more nominal (clauses longer and fewer). Michael Stubbs (1996), using a computerized corpus, followed Jean Ure's model, reasonably enough since mine makes it necessary to identify clauses, and hence requires a sophisticated parsing program. But the clause-based comparison is more meaningful in relation to the contrast between spoken and written discourse.

What turned out to be no less interesting was what I called "grammatical intricacy", quantified as the number of ranking clauses in the clause complex. A clause complex is any sequence of structurally related ranking clauses; it is the spoken language analogue of (and of course the underlying origin of) what we recognize in written language as a sentence. In spontaneous spoken language the clause complex often became extraordinarily long and intricate [see Texts 3 and 5]. If we analyse one of these in terms of its hypotactic and paratactic nexuses, we get a sense of its complexity. Now, it is very seldom that we find anything like these in writing. In speech, they tend to appear in the longer monologic turns that occur within a dialogue. (That is, they are triggered dialogically, but constructed by a single speaker, rather than across turns.) Since dialogue also usually has a lot of very short turns, of just one clause, which is often a minor clause which doesn't enter into complex structures in any case, there is no sense in calculating a mean value for this kind of intricacy. What one can say is, that the more intricate a given clause complex is, the more likely it is that it happened in speech rather than in writing. But the fuller picture will only emerge from more corpus studies of naturally occurring spoken language (cf. Matthiessen 2002: 295 ff.).

5 Some problems with a spoken corpus

So let me turn now to some of the problems faced by corpus linguists when they want to probe more deeply into the mysteries of spoken language. One problematic area I've mentioned already: that of representing spoken language in writing; I would like to add some more observations under this heading. As I remarked, there are many different conventions used in transcribing, and all of them distort in some way or other.

The lack of prosodic markers is an obvious – and serious – omission, but one that can be rectified in one way or another. In another few decades it may be possible to devise speech-recognition systems that can actually assign prosodic features – patterns of intonation and rhythm – at the phonological level (that is, identifying them as meaningful options); meanwhile we might explore the value of something which is technically possible already but less useful for lexicogrammar and semantics, namely annotation of speech at the phonetic level based on analysis of the fundamental parameters of frequency, amplitude and duration.

But, as I suggested, a more serious problem is that of over-transcribing, especially of a kind which brings with it a false flavour of the exotic: speech is made to look quaint, with all its repetitions, false starts, clearings of the throat and the like solemnly incorporated into the text. This practice, which is regrettably widespread, not only imparts a spurious quaintness to the discourse – one can perhaps teach oneself to disregard that – but, more worryingly, obscures, by burying them in the clutter, the really meaningful sleights of tongue on which spoken language often relies: swift changes of direction, structures which Eggins and Slade call "abandoned clauses", phonological and morphological play and other moments of semiotic inventiveness. Of course, the line between these and simple mistakes is hard to draw; but that doesn't mean we needn't try. Try getting yourself recorded surreptitiously, if you can, in some sustained but very casual encounter, and see which of the funny bits you would cut out and which you would leave in as a faithful record of your own discourse.

But even with the best will, and the best skill, in the world, a fundamental problem remains. Spoken language isn't meant to be written down, and any visual representation distorts it in some way or other. The problem is analogous, in a way, to that of choreographers trying to develop notations for the dance: they work as aids to memory, when you want to teach complex routines, or to preserve a particular choreographer's version of a ballet for future generations of dancers. But you wouldn't analyse a dance by working on its transcription into written symbols. Naturally, many of the patterns of spoken language are recognizable in orthographic form; but many others are not – types of continuity and discontinuity, variations in tempo, paralinguistic features of timbre (voice quality), degrees of (un)certainty and (dis)approval – and for these one needs to work directly with the spoken text. And we are still some way off from being able to deal with such things automatically.

The other major problem lies in the nature of language itself; it is a problem for all corpus research, although more acute with the spoken language: this is what we might call the lexicogrammatical bind. Looking along the lexicogrammatical continuum (and I shall assume this unified view, well set out by Michael Stubbs (1996) among the "principles" of Sinclair's and my approach, as opposed to the bricks-and-mortar view of a lexicon plus rules of syntax) – if we look along the continuum from grammar to lexis, it is the phenomena at the lexical end that are the most accessible; so the corpus has evolved to be organized lexically, accessed via the word, the written form of a lexicogrammatical item. Hence corpuses have been used primarily as tools for lexicologists rather than for grammarians.

In principle, as I think is generally accepted, the corpus is just as useful, and just as essential, for the study of grammar as it is for the study of lexis. Only, the grammar is very much harder to get at. In a language like English, where words may operate all the way along the continuum, there are grammatical items like *the* and *and* and *to* just as there are lexical items like *sun* and *moon* and *stars*, as well as those like *behind* and *already* and *therefore* which fall somewhere in the middle; occurrences of any of these are easily retrieved, counted, and contextualized. But whereas *sun* and *moon* and *stars* carry most of their meaning on their sleeves, as it were, *the* and *and* and *to* tell us very little about what is going on underneath; and what they do tell us, if we just observe them directly, tends to be comparatively trivial. It is an exasperating feature of patterns at the grammatical end of the continuum, that the easier they are to recognize the less they matter.

And it is here that the spoken language presents special problems for a word-based observation system: by comparison with written language, it tends to be more highly grammaticalized. In the way it organizes its meaning potential the spoken language, relative to the written, tends to favour grammatical systems. We have seen this already in the contrast between lexical density and grammatical intricacy as complementary ways of managing semantic complexity: the written language tends to put more of its information in the lexis, and hence it is easier to retrieve by means of lexical searching. Consider pairs of examples such as the following (and cf. those cited as Text 6):

Sydney's latitudinal position of 33° south ensures warm summer temperatures.

Sydney is at latitude 33° south, so it is warm in summer.

The goal of evolution is to optimize the mutual adaption of species.

Species evolve in order to adapt to each other as well as possible.

If you are researching the forms of expression of the meaning "cause", you can identify a set of verbs which commonly lexify this meaning in written English – verbs like *cause, lead to, bring about, ensure, effect, result in, provoke* – and retrieve occurrences of these together with the (typically nominalized) cause and effect on either side; likewise the related nouns and adjectives in *be the cause of, be responsible for, be due to* and so on. It takes much more corpus energy to retrieve the (mainly spoken) instances where this relationship is realized as a clause nexus, with 'cause' realized as a paratactic or hypotactic conjunction like *so, because* or *as*, for at least three reasons: (i) these items tend to be polysemous (and to collocate freely with everything in the language); (ii) the cause and effect are now clauses, and therefore much more diffuse; (iii) in the spoken language not only semantic relations but participants also are more often grammaticalized, in the form of cohesive reference items like *it, them, this, that*, and you may have to search a long way to find their sources. Thus it will take rather longer to derive a corpus grammar of causal relations from spoken discourse than from written; and likewise with many other semantic categories. Note that this is not because they are not present in speech; on the contrary, there is usually more explicit rendering of semantic relationships in the spoken variants: you discover how relatively ambiguous the written versions are when you come to transpose them into spoken language. It is the form of their realization – more grammaticalized, and so more covert – that causes most of the problems.

Another aspect of the same phenomenon, but one that is specific to English, is the way that material processes tend to be delexicalized: this is the effect whereby *gash slash hew chop pare slice fell sever mow cleave shear* and so on all get replaced by *cut*. This is related to the preference for phrasal verbs, which has gained momentum over a similar period and is also a move towards the grammaticalizing of the process element in the clause. Ogden and Richards, when they devised their Basic English in the 1930s, were able to dispense with all but eighteen verbs, by relying on the phrasal verb constructions (they would have required me to say "... were able to *do away with* all but eighteen verbs"); they were able to support their case by rewording a variety of different texts, including biblical texts, using just the high-frequency verbs they had selected. These are, as I said, particular features of English; but I suspect there is a general tendency for the written varieties of a language to favour a more lexicalized construal of meaning.

So I feel that, in corpus linguistics in general but more especially in relation to a spoken language corpus, there is work to be done to discover ways of designing a corpus for the use of grammarians – or rather, since none of us is confined to a single role, for use in the study of phenomena towards the grammatical end of the continuum. Hunston and Francis, in their work on "pattern grammar" (2000), have shown beyond doubt that the corpus is an essential resource for extending our knowledge of the grammar. But a corpus-driven grammar needs a grammar-driven corpus; and that is something I think we have not yet got.

6 Corpus-based and corpus-driven

Elena Tognini-Bonelli, in her book *Corpus Linguistics at Work* (2001), defines corpus linguistics as a "pre-application methodology", comprising an empirical approach to the description of language use, within a contextual-functional theory of meaning, and making use of new technologies. Within this framework, she sees new facts leading to new methodologies leading to new theories. Given that she has such a forward-looking vision, I find it strange that she finds it strange that "more data and better counting can trigger philosophical repositioning"; after all, that's what it did in physics, where more data and better measuring transformed the whole conception of knowledge and understanding. How much the more might we expect this to be the case in linguistics, since knowing and understanding are themselves processes of meaning. The spoken corpus might well lead to some repositioning on issues of this kind.

Like Hunston and Francis, Tognini-Bonelli stresses the difference between "corpus-based" and "corpus-driven" descriptions; I accept this distinction in principle, though with two reservations, or perhaps caveats. One, that the distinction itself is fuzzy; there are various ways of using a corpus in grammatical research that I would not be able to locate squarely on either side of the boundary – where, for example, one starts out with a grammatical category as a heuristic device but then uses the results of the corpus analysis to refine it further or replace it by something else. (If I may refer here to my own work, I would locate both my study of the grammar of pain, and the quantitative study of polarity and primary tense carried out by Zoe James and myself, somewhere along that rather fuzzy borderline (1998; 1993/this volume, Chapter 6).) And that leads to the second caveat: a corpus-driven grammar is not one that is theory-free (cf. Matthiessen and Nesbitt's 'On the idea of theory-neutral descriptions' (1996)). As I have remarked elsewhere (2002), there is considerable recourse to grammatical theory in Hunston and Francis' book. I am not suggesting that they deny this – they are not at all anti-theoretical; but it is important, I think, to remove any such implication from the notion of "corpus-driven" – which is itself a notably theoretical concept.

I don't think Tognini-Bonelli believes this either, though there is perhaps a slight flavour in one of her formulations (p.184): "If the paradigm is not excluded from this [corpus-driven] view of language, it is seen as secondary with respect to the syntagm. Corpus-driven linguistics is thus above all a linguistics of parole". I wonder. Paradigm and syntagm are the two axes of description, for both of which we have underlying theoretical categories: structure as theory of the syntagm, system as theory of the paradigm. It is true that, in systemic theory, we set up the most abstract theoretical representations on the paradigmatic axis; there were specific reasons for doing this (critically, it is easier to map into the semantics by that route, since your view of regularity is not limited by structural constraints), but that is not to imply that structure is not a theoretical construct. (Firth, who first developed system-structure theory, did not assign any theoretical priority to the system; but he developed it in the context of phonology, where considerations are rather different.) So I don't think corpus-driven linguistics is a linguistics of parole – but in any case, isn't that notion rather self-contradictory? Once you are 'doing linguistics', you have already moved above the instantial realm.

I can see a possible interpretation for a linguistics of parole: it would be a theory about why some instances – some *actes de parole* – are more highly valued than others: in other words, a stylistics. But the principle behind corpus linguistics is that every instance carries equal weight. The instance is valued as a window on to the system: the potential that is being manifested in the text. What the corpus does is to enable us to see more closely, and more accurately, into that underlying system – into the *langue*, if you like. The "corpus-driven grammar" is a form of, and so also a major contributor to, grammatics.

7 Aspects of speech: a final note

I am assuming that the spoken language corpus includes a significant amount of "authentic" data: unsolicited, spontaneous, natural speech – which is likely to mean dialogue, though there may be lengthy passages of monologue embodied within it. Not because there is anything intrinsically superior about such discourse as text – if anything, it tends to carry a rather low value in the culture; but because the essential nature of language, its semogenic or meaning-creating potential, is most clearly revealed in the unselfconscious activity of speaking. This is where systemic patterns are established and maintained; where new, instantial patterns are all the time being created; and where the instantial can become systemic, not (as is more typical of written language) by way of single instances that carry exceptional value (what I have called the Hamlet factor) but through the quantitative effects of large numbers of unnoticed and unremembered sayings.

For this reason, I would put a high priority on quantitative research into spoken language, establishing the large-scale frequency patterns that give a language its characteristic profile – its "characterology", as the Prague linguists used to call it. This is significant in that it provides the scaffolding whereby children come to learn their mother tongue, and sets the parameters for systematic variation in register: what speakers recognize as functional varieties of their language are re-settings of the probabilities in lexicogrammatical choice. The classic study here was Jan Svartvik's study of variation in the English voice system (1966). It also brings out the important feature of partial association between systems, as demonstrated in their quantitative study of the English clause complex by Nesbitt and Plum (1988; cf. my discussion in Chapters 3 and 4 of this volume). My own hypothesis is that the very general grammatical systems of a language tend towards one or other of two probability profiles: either roughly equal, or else skew to a value of about one order of magnitude; and I have suggested why I think that this would make good sense (cf. Chapter 7). But it can only be put to the test by large-scale quantitative studies of naturally occurring speech. Let me say clearly that I do not think this kind of analysis replaces qualitative studies of patterns of wording in individual texts. But it does add further insight into how those patterns work.

It is usually said that human language, as it evolved and as it is developed by children, is essentially dialogic. I see no reason to question this; the fact that other primates (like ourselves!) send out warnings or braggings or other emotional signals, without expecting a response, is not an objection that need be taken seriously. Dialogue, in turn, provides the setting for monologic acts; and this is true not only instantially but also systemically: monologue occurs as extended turns in the course of dialogic interaction, as a good-sized corpus of casual conversation will show. Clearly monologue is also the default condition of many systemic varieties: people give sermons, make speeches, write books, broadcast talks and so on; but they do so, even if it is largely for their own satisfaction, only because there are others who listen to them (or at least hear them) and who read them.

Any piece of spoken monologue can be thought of as an extended turn: either given to the speaker by the (contextual) system, as it were, like a conference paper, or else having to be established, and perhaps struggled for, as happens in casual conversation. Speakers have many techniques for holding the floor, prolonging their speaking turn. Some of these techniques are, in Eggins and Slade's terms, generic: you switch into telling a joke, or embark on a personal narrative. But one very effective strategy is grammatical: the clause complex. The trick is to make the listeners aware another clause is coming.

How you do this, of course, varies according to the language; but the two main resources, in many languages, are intonation and conjunction. These are, in effect, two mechanisms for construing logical-semantic relationships in lexicogrammatical form – in wording. The highly intricate clause complexes that I referred to earlier as a phenomenon of informal speech embroil the listener in a shifting pattern of phono-syntactic connections. This is not to suggest that their only function is to hold the floor; but they help, because listeners do, in general, wait for the end of a sequence – it takes positive energy to interrupt.

What the clause complex really does, or allows the speaker to do, is to navigate through and around the multidimensional semantic space that defines the meaning potential of a language, often with what seem bewildering changes of direction, for example (Text 3) from the doctor's expectations to corridors lined with washing to the danger of knocking out expectant mothers, all the while keeping up an unbroken logical relationship with whatever has gone before. It is grammatical logic, not formal logic; formal logic is the designed offspring of grammatical logic, just as the written sentence is the designed offspring of the clause complex of speech. This kind of spontaneous semantic choreography is something we seldom find other than in unselfmonitored spoken discourse, typically in those monological interludes in a dialogue; but it represents a significant aspect of the power of language as such.

I have been trying to suggest, in this chapter, why I think that the spoken language corpus is a crucial resource for theoretical research: research not just into the spoken language, but into language in general. Because the gap between what we can recover by introspection and what people actually say is greatest of all in sustained, unselfmonitored speaking, the spoken language corpus adds a new dimension to our understanding of language as semiotic system-&-process. That there is such a gap is not only because spontaneous speech is the mode of discourse that is processed at furthest remove from conscious attention, but also because it is the most complexly intertwined with the ongoing socio-semiotic context. Tognini-Bonelli's observation that all corpus studies imply a contextual theory of meaning is nowhere more cogent than in the contexts of informal conversation. Hasan and Cloran's work on their corpus of naturally occurring dialogue between mothers and their three-to-four-year-old children showed how necessary it was not merely to note the situations in which meanings were exchanged but to develop the theoretical model of the contextual stratum as a component in the overall descriptive strategy (Hasan and Cloran 1990; Hasan 1991, 1992, 1999; Cloran 1994). People's meaning potential is activated – and hence ongoingly modified and extended – when the semogenic energy of their lexicogrammar is brought to bear on the material and semiotic environment, construing it, and reconstruing it, into meaning. In this process, written language, being the more designed, tends to be relatively more focused in its demands on the meaning-making powers of the lexicogrammar; whereas spoken language is typically more diffuse, roaming widelier around the different regions of the network. So spoken language is likely to reveal more evidence for the kind of middle range "grammar patterns" and "extended lexical units" that corpus studies are now bringing into relief; and this in turn should enrich the analysis of discourse by overcoming the present disjunction between the lexical and the grammatical approaches to the study of text.

Already in 1935 Firth had recognized the value of investigating conversation, remarking "it is here we shall find the key to a better understanding of what language really is and how it works" (1957:

32). He was particularly interested in its interaction with the context of situation, the way each moment both narrows down and opens up the options available at the next. My own analysis of English conversation began in 1959, when I first recorded spoken dialogue in order to study rhythm and intonation. But it was Sinclair, taking up another of Firth's suggestions – the study of collocation (see Sinclair 1966) – who first set about compiling a spoken corpus. Much later, looking back from the experience with COBUILD, Sinclair wrote (1991: 16) "... a decision I took in 1961 to assemble a corpus of conversation is one of the luckiest I ever made". It would be hard now to justify leaving out conversation from any corpus designed for general lexicogrammatical description of a language. Christian Matthiessen (1999; 2002), using a corpus of both spoken and written varieties, has developed "text-based profiles": quantitative studies of different features in the grammar which show up the shifts in probabilities that characterize variation in register. One part of his strategy is to compile a sub-corpus of partially analysed texts, which serve as a basis for comparison and also as a test site for the analysis, allowing it to be modified in the light of ongoing observation and interpretation. I have always felt that such grammatical probabilities, both global and local, are an essential aspect of "what language really is and how it works". For these, above all, we depend on spoken language as the foundation.

Text 1

A. Transcript of Recorded Conversation

Key:

Indented lines represent the contributions of the interviewer, the
asterisks in the informant's speech indicating the points at which
such contributions began, or during which they lasted.

The hyphens (-, --, ---) indicate relative lengths of pauses. Proper
names are fictitious substitutes for those actually used.

The informant is a graduate, speaking RP with a normal delivery.

```
       i is this true I heard on the radio last night that
         er pay has gone net pay but er -- retirement age has
         gone up - *for you chaps*
       *yes but er*
5        to seventy*
       *yes I think that's scandalous*
         *but is it right is it true*
       *yes it is true yes it is true*
         *well it's a good thing*
10   yes *but the thing is that er -* everybody wants more money --
         *I mean you you've got your future secure*
       but er the thing is you know -- er I mean of course er the
       whole thing is absolutely an absolute farce because -- really with
       this grammar school business it's perfectly true that -
15   that you're drawing all your your brains of the country are
       going to come increasingly from those schools - therefore
       you've got to have able men - and women to teach in them -
       but you want fewer and better ** - that's the thing they want
         *hm*
20   - fewer grammar schools and better ones --- *because at the
         *Mrs Johnson was saying*
       moment* it's no good having I mean we've got some very good
       men where I am which is a bit of a glory hole -- but er there's
       some there's some good men there there's one or two
25   millionaires nearly there's Ramsden who cornered the - English
       text book market -- *and er* - yes he's got a net income of
         *hm*
       about two thousand five hundred a year and er there's some
       good chaps there I mean you know first class men but it's no
30   good having first class men - dealing with the tripe that we
       get *-- you see that's the trouble that you're wasting it's
         *hm*
```

179

a waste of energy -- um an absolute waste of energy - your -
your er method of selection there is all wrong -- *um
35   *but do you think it's better to have -- er teachers who've
had a lot of experience - having an extra five years to
help solve this - problem of of fewer teachers -- er or
would you say - well no cut them off at at sixty-five
and let's get younger*
40   *it's no good having I would if I were a head I'd and you
know and I knew well I'd chuck everyone out who taught more
than ten years on principle *--
      ha ha ha why
*because after that time as a boy said they either become
45   too strict or too laxative* --
      ha ha ha ha ha ha - hm
*yes - but ha ha ha no they get absolutely stuck you know
after ten years ** -- they just go absolutely dead - we all
      hm
50   do - bound to you know you you churn out the same old stuff
you see - but um - the thing is I mean it's no good having
frightfully - well anyway they they if they paid fifteen
hundred a year I mean - if you could expect to get that
within -- ten years er er for graduates er you you still
55   wouldn't get the first class honours - scientists - they'd
still go into industry because it's a present er a pleasanter
sort of life ** you're living in an adult-world and you're
      yes
living in a world which is in the main stream -- I mean school
60   mastering is bound to be a backwater you're bound to you want
some sort of sacrifice sacrificial type of people you know **
      yes
no matter what you pay them you've got to pay them more but
you've got to give -- there's got to be some reason you know
65   some - you're always giving out and you get nothing back **
      hm
and --- I mean they don't particularly want to learn even the
bright ones they'd much rather -- fire paper pellets out of
the window or something or -- no they don't do that but they
70   they -- you know you've got to drive them all the time ---
they've got to have some sort of exterior reason apart from
your own - personal satisfaction in doing it you know

Text 2

A   938 +‖YÈS■ · 939 ‖that's – ‖that's △very GÒOD■ · + 940 I ‖wouldn't be
△ÀBLE■ 941 to ‖HÂVE 'that one■ 942 for ‖some 'reason you see · ‖THÌS■ ·
943 the ‖CHÈCKER board effect■ – 944 [ə:m] I re‖coil ‛△BÀDLY from THÍS■
945 I ‖find I △hadn't LÒOKED at it■ 946 and I ‖think it's △probably be'cause
[ə:] · ‖probably re'minds me you 'know of △nursing △{WÀLTER} 'through his
‛△THRÒAT■ – 947 ‖when you △PLÀY■ 948 ‖CHÈCKER boards {or
‖SÒMETHING■} 949 I ‖think it's [rə] it re‖minds me of the △LÙDO 'board that
{‖we HÀD■}■ · 950 and I ‖just RE△CÒILED■ 951 ‖straight ☆AWÀY■ 952 《and
thought》

C   953 ☆(– laughs) · ‖[m̀]■☆

> A   952 《not》 ‖not THÀT one■☆ · 954 and I ‖didn't ▷look IN△SÌDE■ 955 but
‖that's +△very △FÌNE■+

C   956 +‖[m̄]■ – + 957 ‖[m̀]■

> A   958 ‖ÌSN'T it■ – 959 ‖VÈRY 'fine■ – – – 960 ‖YÈS■

C   961 it's ‖very ÌNTERESTING■ 962 to ‖try and △△ANALYSE■ 963 ‖why one LÌKES■
964 ‖abstract PÀINTINGS■ 965 cos ‖I ‛△LÌKE 'those CHÈCKS■ · 966 ‖just the
△{FÀCT} that they're ‛△NÒT■ · 967 ‖all [ə:] · △at RÌGHT 'angles■ ·
968 ‖means that my △eyes △don't go out of △FÒCUS■ 969 ‖chasing the △LÌNES■

A   970 ‖YÈS■

C   971 ‖they △actually △can △FÒLLOW the 'lines■ · 972 [əm] with‖out – [?ə:] sort
of ‖getting out of △FÒCUS■

A   973 ‖yes I've △GÒT it NÒW■ 974 ‖it's ‖it's [i] △those ex'act two CÒLOURS you
SÉE · {TO‖GÉTHER■}■ · 975 he ‖had [ə:m] – he ‖had a △blue and orange
CRÀNE■ – 976 I re‖member it △very WÈLL■ – · 977 ‖and you know ‖one of
those 'things that △wind ÙP■ – 978 ‖ÀND [ə]■ – 979 ‖that's ÌT■ ·

C   980 it ‖does re△mind MÈ■ 981 of MEC‖CÀNO 'boxes■ ·

A   982 ‖YÈS■ 983 + well +

C   984 + the ‖box + that CON△TÀINS ☆Mec'cano 《ÀCTUALLY》■☆

A   985 ☆‖YÈS■ 986 ‖well we☆ △had a ‛△bad 'DÒ you 'know■ 987 we ‖had a – ·
‖《oh》 we △had ▷six or △eight WÈEKS■ 988 when ‖he 'had [ə:m] – a ‛THRÒAT■
989 +‖which + was [ə] – well at

C   990 +‖[m̀hm]■+

> A   989 the be‖ginning it was △LÈTHAL■ 991 if ‖anybody 'else CÀUGHT it■

C   992 ‖YÈAH■

> A   993 it was ‖lethal to ex△pectant 'mothers with △small CHÌLDREN■ – 994 ‖ÀND
[ə]■ – 995 I ‖had to do △barrier △NÙRSING■ – 996 it was ‖pretty HÒRRIBLE■
· 997 and the ‖whole [ə] △CÒRRIDOR■ · 998 ‖was☆ ‖full of △pails of
DISINFÈCTANT■ 999 you ‖KNÒW■

C 1000 ☆‖[m̄]∎☆

A 1001 and you ‖went ÍN∎ · 1002 ‖AND ⟪of ‖course 2 to 3 sylls⟫ ₐbarrier 'nursing
I ₐdidn't go 'in in a MÁSK∎ 1003 I ‖CÒULDN'T with a 'child that SMÁLL∎ ·
1004 and I ‖didn't 'care if I CÁUGHT it∎ 1005 ‖but I ▷mean it was [i?] ‖⟪ours
ₐemptied⟫ OUTSÍDE you SÉE∎

C 1006 ‖[m̄]∎

>A 1007 ‖and you ₐhad to · ₐcome ÓUT∎ 1008 ‖and you · ₐbrought ₐall these
ₐTHÌNGS∎ 1009 ‖on to a preₐpared ☆'surgical BÓARD∎☆

C 1010 ☆‖[m̄]∎ -☆ 1011 ‖[m̄]∎

>A 1012 and you ‖stripped your GLÒVES off∎ 1013 be‖fore you ₐTÒUCHED
'anything∎

C 1014 ‖[m̄]∎

>A 1015 and you ‖DISINFÈCTED ‖oh it was ₐreally APPÀLLING∎

C 1016 ‖[m̄]∎

>A 1017 ‖AND [əm]∎ - - - 1018 ‖I don't think the 'doctor had EXₐPÈCTED∎
1019 that I 'WÒULD do 'barrier 'nursing ☆you SÉE∎☆

C 1020 ☆‖[m̄]∎∎☆

>A 1021 ⟪I ‖think⟫ she said 'something a'bout [i ? ɑ:] she ‖wished that ₐeverybody
would 'take · [ə:] the 'thing 'ₐSÈRIOUSLY∎ 1022 you ‖KNÓW∎ 1023 when they
were ‖TÒLD {as ‖I did∎}∎ 1024 cos she ‖came in and the ₐwhole CÒRRIDOR∎
· 1025 was '‖LÌNED∎ ·

C 1026 ☆‖[m̄]∎∎☆

>A 1027 ☆with☆ ‖various FÒRMS of∎ · 1028 ‖WÀSHING · and só on∎ ·1029 ‖BUT
[ə]∎ · 1030 ‖after ÀLL∎ 1031 I mean you ‖CÀN'T go 'down and SHÓP∎ 1032 if
you ‖know that you're 'going to ₐknock 'out an exₐpectant MÓTHER∎ - 1033 it
was ‖some ▷⟪violent⟫ ▷STREPTOCÒCCUS {that he'd ‖GÒT∎}∎ - 1034 ‖AND∎
1035 he ‖could have gone to an ₐiso'lation HÓSPITAL∎ 1036 but I ‖think she just
ₐDÈEMED {that he was ☆‖too SMÀLL -

C 1037 ☆‖YÈS∎ 1038 ‖[m̄]∎ 1039 ‖[m̄]∎ ·☆

>A 1036 {for the EXₐPÈRIENCE∎} ∎}∎☆ - 1040 ‖and then ₐafter we'd ₐHX̌D him∎
1041 [ə:] you ‖know ₐHX̌D him for a 'few days at HÓME∎ 1042 this ‖couldn't be
ₐDÒNE∎

C 1043 ‖[m̄hm]∎

A 1044 ‖she 'made the DEₐ{CÌSION} 'ₐFÒR me RÉALLY∎ · 1045 ‖which at the
ₐtime I 'thought was 'very IMₐPRÈSSIVE∎ 1046 but she ‖didn't ₐknow me 'very
WÈLL∎

C 1047 (- laughs)

A   ¹⁰⁴⁸ I ‖think she 'thought I was a ca∆reer ∆WÒMAN■ · ¹⁰⁴⁹ who would be
‖only too ∆GLÀD■ ¹⁰⁵⁰ or ‖would say oh well he's ∆GÒT to 'go into a
HÓSPITAL■ ¹⁰⁵¹ ‖YÓU 'know■ · ¹⁰⁵² so she ‖made the de'cision ∆FÒR me■
¹⁰⁵³ and ‖THÈN said■ ¹⁰⁵⁴ it's ‖too ∆LÀTE now■ ¹⁰⁵⁵ to ‖put him 'into a · an
∆iso'lation HÓSPITAL■ ¹⁰⁵⁶ ‖I would have 'had to do 'that a ∆few ∆DÀYS a'go■
¹⁰⁵⁷ «which» ‖I thought «I 'didn't WĂNT her to 'do■» ¹⁰⁵⁸ (– laughs)

C   ¹⁰⁵⁹ ‖«this 'one 'man» [ə:] – ‖do 'nurses ∆TÈND to be ag'gressive■ · ¹⁰⁶⁰ or
‖does one just ∆THÌNK that 'nurses are ag'gressive■

A   ¹⁰⁶¹ well ‖that was my ∆DÒCTOR■

C   ¹⁰⁶² ☆‖ÒH■☆

> A   ¹⁰⁶³ ☆‖ĀND☆ [əm]■ – ¹⁰⁶⁴ she ‖didn't at that 'time UNDER∆STÀND me 'very
'well I THÍNK■ ¹⁰⁶⁵ ☆she ‖DÒES NÓW■☆

183

Text 3

(1) A: Yes; that's very good. .... I wouldn't be able to have that one for some reason you see: this checker board effect—I recoil badly from this. I find I hadn't looked at it, and I think it's probably because it probably reminds me you know of nursing Walter through his throat, when you play checker boards or something. I think it's—it reminds me of the ludo board that we had, and I just recoiled straight away and thought [mm] not—not that one, and I didn't look inside; but that's very fine, [mm mm] isn't it?— very fine, yes.

B: It's very interesting to try and analyse why one likes abstract paintings, 'cause I like those checks; just the very fact that they're not all at right angles means that my eyes don't go out of focus chasing the lines [yes]—they can actually follow the lines without sort of getting out of focus.

A: Yes I've got it now: it's those exact two colours you see, to- gether. He had—he had a blue and orange crane, I remember it very well, and you know one of those things that wind up, and— that's it.

B: It does remind me of meccano boxes [yes well]—the box that contains meccano, actually.

A: Yes. Well, we had a bad do you know; we had—oh we had six or eight weeks when he had a throat which was—[mhm] well at the beginning it was lethal if anyone else caught it. [yeah] It was lethal to expectant mothers with small children, and I had to do barrier nursing; it was pretty horrible, and the whole corridor was full of pails of disinfectant you know [mm], and you went in, and of course with barrier nursing I didn't go in in a mask—I couldn't with a child that small, and I didn't care if I caught it, but I mean it was—ours emptied outside you see [mm] and you had to come out and you brought all these things on to a pre- pared surgical board [mm mm] and you stripped your gloves off before you touched anything [mm] and you disinfected—oh it was really appalling [mm]. I don't think the doctor had expected that I would do barrier nursing you see [mm]—I think she said something about she wished that everybody would take the thing seriously you know, when they were told, as I did, 'cause she came in and the whole corridor was lined [mm] with various forms of washing and so on, but after all I mean you can't go down and shop if you know that you're going to knock out an expectant mother. It was some violent streptococcus that he'd got and he could have gone to an isolation hospital but I think she just deemed that he was too small [yes mm mm] for the experience, and then after we'd had him, you know, had him for a few days at home this couldn't be done. [mhm] She made the decision for me really, which at the time I thought was very impressive, but she didn't know me very well: I think she thought I was a career woman who would be only too glad and would say 'oh well he's got to go into a hospital', you know, so she made the decision for me and then said 'it's too late now to put him into an isolation hospital; I would have had to do that a few days ago'—which, I thought, I didn't want her to do!

B: Do nurses tend to be aggressive, or does one just think that nurses are aggressive?

A: Well, that was my doctor [oh], and she didn't at that time understand me very well. I think she does now.

(Svartvik and Quirk 1980: 215–18)

Text 4 [from Allen D. Grimshaw (ed.), *What's Going on Here: Complementary Studies of Professional Talk*, Norwood NJ: Ablex, 1994]

   . . . ˄ and I / think she's / a/<u>ware</u> of this and I / think you / know she —— . . . // 4 ˄ I / think one / thing that'll / <u>happen</u> I / think that . . . // 1 ˄ that / Mike may en/<u>courage</u> her // 1 ˄ and I / think   that'll be / all to the / <u>good</u> //

P.   // 4 ˄ to / what ex/tent are / these / ˄ the / three / theories that she se/<u>lected</u> // 1 truly repre/<u>sentative</u> of / theories in this / area //

A.   // 1 that's / <u>it</u> / ˄ // 1 that's / <u>it</u> //

P.   // 1 ˄ they / are in/<u>deed</u> //

S.   // 1 <u>yeah</u> //

P.   // 1 <u>oh</u> // 2 they are / <u>the</u> / theories //

A.   // 1 that's about / <u>it</u> //

P.   // 1 they are / not / <u>really</u> repre/sentative / then //

S.   // 1 <u>well</u> there are // 1 ˄ there are / vari/<u>ations</u> // 1 ˄ there are / vari/<u>ations</u> // 1 on / <u>themes</u> but . . . // 4 ˄ but / I don't / know of any / <u>major</u> con/tender ˄ there / may be // 1 ˄ well / I don't / know of / anything that / looks much / <u>different</u> from the / things she's . . . ˄ she has / looked at in the spe/cific / time //

A.   // 4 ˄ ex/cept for the / sense that ——

P.   // 1 ˄ so / nobody / nobody would at/tack her on / <u>that</u> ground / then if she —— //

A.   // 1 oh no / I don't / <u>think</u> so // 4 ˄ I think the / only / thing that would be sub/<u>stantially</u> / different would be a /˄ real / social / <u>structuralist</u> who would / say // 4 ˄ you / don't have to / worry about cog/<u>nitions</u> // 1 what you have to / do is / find the lo/cation of these / people in the / social / <u>structure</u> // 1- ˄ and / then you'll / find out how they're / going to be/have with/out having to / get into their / heads at / <u>all</u> // 4 ˄ and / <u>that</u> // 1 hasn't been / <u>tested</u> // 1- ˄ ex/cept in / very / gross / kinds of / <u>ways</u> with // 1 macro / data which has / generally / not been / very satis/<u>factory</u> // 1 yeah / ˄ // 1 ˄ so I can / tell her that —— // 3 ˄ you / <u>know</u> I ——

S.   // 1 ˄ she's / <u>won</u> //

Text 5 [clause complex from Text 3 above]. Choreographic notation for the clause complex of spoken language (cf. forms of notation in Martin, *English Text: System and Structure*)

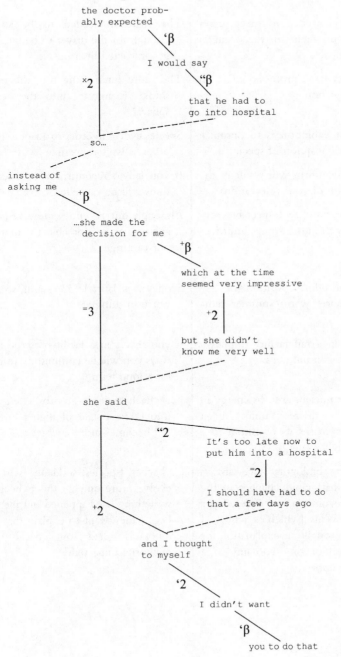

187

Text 6 [spoken "translations" of some sentences of written English]

Metaphorical original	*More congruent version*
Set 1	
Strength was needed to meet driver safety requirements in the event of missile impact.	The material needed to be strong enough for the driver to be safe if it got impacted by a missile.
Fire intensity has a profound effect on smoke injection.	The more intense the fire, the more smoke it injects (into the atmosphere).
The goal of evolution is to optimize the mutual adaption of species.	Species evolve in order to adapt to each other as well as possible
Failure to reconfirm will result in the cancellation of your reservations.	If you fail to reconfirm your reservations will be cancelled.
We did not translate respectable revenue growth into earnings improvement.	Although our revenues grew respectably we were not able to improve our earnings.
Set 2	
Sydney's latitudinal position of 33° south ensures warm summer temperatures.	Sydney is at latitude 33° south, so it is warm in summer.
Investment in a rail facility implies a long-term commitment.	If you invest in a facility for the railways you will be committing [funds] for a long term.
[The atomic nucleus absorbs energy in quanta, or discrete units.] Each absorption marks its transition to a state of higher energy.	[...] Each time it absorbs energy it (moves to a state of higher energy **) becomes more energetic.
[Evolutionary biologists have always assumed that] rapid changes in the rate of evolution are caused by external events [which is why ...] they have sought an explanation for the demise of the dinosaurs in a meteorite impact.	[...] when [species] suddenly [start to] evolve more quickly this is because something has happened outside [...] they want to explain that the dinosaurs died out because a meteorite impacted.

[It will be seen ... that] a successful blending of asset replacement with remanufacture is possible. Careful studies are to be undertaken to ensure that viability exists.

[...] it is possible both to replace assets and to remanufacture [current equipment] successfully. We must study [the matter] carefully to ensure that ([the plan] is viable =) we will be able to do what we plan.

The theoretical program of devising models of atomic nuclei has been complemented by experimental investigations.

As well as working theoretically by devising models of atomic nuclei we have also investigated [the topic] by experimenting.

Increased responsiveness may be reflected in feeding behaviour.

[The child] is becoming more responsive, so s/he may feed better.

Equation (3) provided a satisfactory explanation of the observed variation in seepage rates.

When we used equation (3) we could explain satisfactorily (the different rates at which we have observed that seepage occurs =) why, as we have observed, [water] seeps out more quickly or more slowly.

The growth of attachment between infant and mother signals the first step in the child's capacity to discriminate among people.

Because / if / when
   the mother and her infant grow /
     more/ attached to one another //
   the infant grows / is growing /
     more/ attached to its mother
   we know that / she knows that /
     [what is happening is that]
   the child has begun / is beginning /
     is going to begin
   to be able to tell one person from
     another / prefer one person over
     another

PART THREE

TOWARDS 'INTELLIGENT COMPUTING' (COMPUTING WITH MEANING)

EDITOR'S INTRODUCTION

The first two chapters in this section, *On language in relation to fuzzy logic and intelligent computing* and *Fuzzy grammatics: a systemic functional approach to fuzziness in natural language*, were presented at the Joint International Conference of the Fourth IEEE International Conference on Fuzzy Systems and the Second International Fuzzy Engineering Symposium held in Yokohama, Japan in 1995. The final chapter in this section, Chapter 11, *Computing meanings: some reflections on past experience and present prospects* (1995), was presented as a plenary at PACLING 95, and was subsequently translated for publication in Japanese and Chinese.

Professor Halliday derives this notion of "computing with meaning" from what Professor Michio Sugeno – a leading authority on fuzzy systems – refers to as "intelligent computing", i.e. computing based on natural language. In order for the computer to become truly intelligent, "we have to make it function, as people do, through the medium of language". If natural language is to become a metalanguage for intelligent computing, then we need a theory of language which models natural language *paradigmatically* – as a system network; *contextually* – in terms of field, tenor and mode; *functionally* – by reference to that "metafunctional diversity in the grammar that has enabled human language to evolve as the form of higher-order consciousness"; *fuzzily* – "in terms of categories that are typically indeterminate and fluid"; and *developmentally* – "taking account of how it is learnt by children ... [enabling] us to understand how, and why, language evolved as it did".

Not only is the linguistic system inherently probabilistic, as we

193

saw in the previous section, it is also inherently fuzzy, "both ideationally, in construing our experience, and interpersonally, in enacting our social relationships". The complexity and indeterminacy in language simply reflects the fact that "human experience, and human relationships, are much too complex and many-sided to be captured in categories that are well-formed, bounded and stable". The very features of natural language that may seem to some to be its flaws are in fact its assets. Elaborating further on this point in Chapter 9, Professor Halliday writes,

> all these features which make language seem disorderly and unmanageable (the indeterminacy of the categories, or the unpredictable dynamic of the discourse) are truly features of language **as a system**. They are essential properties of knowing, understanding, reasoning and planning – of the human ability to "mean". There is no distinction to be made between "system" and its "use": no Cartesian dichotomy to be made between an idealized "competence" and a hopelessly messy "performance". The task for **grammatics**, therefore, is to account for the disorder and the complexity, not as accidental and aberrant, but as systemic and necessary to the effective functioning of language.

Or as he puts it: "The only determinate language is a dead one (as my teacher Professor Firth used to say, rigour in a linguistic context could only mean *rigor mortis*)."

In Chapter 11, Professor Halliday summarizes those aspects of linguistic complexity that need to be taken into account if one is computing with natural language:

(1) **words** function by being organized into **wordings** (lexico-grammatical patterns);
(2) **wordings**, in turn, construct semantic patterns, or **meanings**;
(3) **meanings** relate systematically to features of the **context**;
(4) particular **instances** of wording/meaning derive their value from their place in the **system** (relationships within the system network, or **agnation**);
(5) the **system** accommodates **sub-systemic variation** (variation in **register**);
(6) the **system** is organized **metafunctionally** (into zones of semantic space, which determine both the form of the grammar and its relationship to the context);
(7) **meaning** involves three dimensions of history: **evolution** of the system, **unfolding** of the individual text, **development** of the

human infant into adulthood (phylogenesis, logogenesis, ontogenesis).

There is one system, language, with two levels of representation: lexicogrammatical and semantic; and one phenomenon, language, with two degrees or phases of instantiation: system and text. The boundary between grammar (wordings) and semantics (meanings) is a stratal one; while that between system (langue) and instance (parole) is an instantial one. The two dimensions of stratification and instantiation, Professor Halliday explains, "can be used to define a matrix for locating computational linguistic representations", thereby paving the way for truly intelligent computing, or computing with meaning.

Chapter Nine

ON LANGUAGE IN RELATION TO FUZZY LOGIC AND INTELLIGENT COMPUTING (1995)

I

I feel honoured and privileged to be invited here to address you at this 1995 Conference on Fuzzy Systems and Fuzzy Engineering. As I understand it, you would like me to talk about language as it relates to your concerns; especially, perhaps, to "intelligent computing" that is mediated by language, as envisaged by Professor Sugeno.

In thinking about how I might do this, I began by making three assumptions. First: that language is important in this context because it is central to human consciousness and to human actions. Second: that language can be studied as a domain of technical, theoretical knowledge (there is a "science of language", called linguistics). Third: that within the domain of language you are interested mainly in the functional, the semantic, and in everyday discourse as contextualized in real life – rather that in the formal, the syntactic, or in idealized sentences as concocted in the philosopher's den. In my written paper for the Conference, I made some observations about language that seemed to me to be relevant in this connection. Today in my talk I shall adopt a somewhat different approach, hoping to underpin those observations by making them on the one hand more general and on the other hand more concrete. But let me first contextualize myself, with a few words about my own professional background.

I was first a teacher of languages; through this experience, I was led to explore theoretical linguistics, and since then I have been mainly concerned with language as a field of systematic study. It is now almost half a century since I taught my first language class. Since

1955, I have worked from time to time in various branches of computational linguistics: different aspects of natural language processing such as machine translation and text generation. In all my work I have given priority to informal, unselfconscious, everyday spoken language – "natural language" in the true sense of the term; and so have been primarily engaged with language in the experiential and interpersonal contexts of daily life. This general approach to language has come to be known as **social semiotics**; while the technical, theoretical model that we have developed in attempting to explain how language works, from this point of view, is known as **systemics** or **systemic functional** theory. Since grammar is at the centre of this explanatory model we sometimes refer to it as systemic functional **grammatics**.

Some of you may ask – as I did myself – why bother with linguistics? Would it not be simpler to deal with language directly, just in commonsense terms? This is very tempting; but it does not really work. Let me recall to you an experience from the past. In the early days of machine translation, computer engineers thought that the task could be approached along those lines, representing language in commonsense terms without any systematic analysis. It seemed to them that machine translation was simply a problem in engineering, which did not need to involve linguistic theory. After about ten years, the attempt was given up. It had turned out to be necessary to take language more seriously; without engaging with language in systematic and theoretical terms it was impossible to manage its complexity. Furthermore, the computer specialists were in fact deceiving themselves. Literate, educated adults no longer have access to commonsense knowledge about language; what they bring to language are the ideas they learnt in primary school, which have neither the unconscious insights of everyday practical experience nor the theoretical power of designed systematic knowledge. One would not expect to design a robotic system on the basis of Year Six mathematics!

I would have liked to be able to assure you that informal colloquial language, as used in everyday situations, is very straightforward and simple, so that one could handle it without the apparatus of linguistics as a technical discipline. But it is not so. Language is complex – and the complexity of it is real; it is not something imposed upon it by linguists. Of course we do sometimes **make** things complicated, when we are struggling to understand some general principle that is still obscure. On the whole, however, linguists do the opposite: they tend to **oversimplify**, through excessive idealizing of the data. In its natural state, human adult language (HAL, we might call it) is perhaps the most complex phenomenon we know. One reason for this complexity is that all systematic knowledge, about anything at all, is construed and transmitted in language – including, of course, knowledge about language itself.

I do not mean that language **becomes** complex **because** it is being used technically, for systematic knowledge. On the contrary: the technical discourse of science is in many respects **less** complex (because it is partially designed) than the everyday discourse of commonsense, which has evolved without being regularized by design. (I shall return to this point later.) I mean that language is complex because it has to encompass everything that can be meant in any realm of human experience. We have to accept this complexity; and we need theory to help us to manage it.

The final point, in this introductory part of my talk, concerns language and cognition. Language is often presented as if it were the outward manifestation of some inner, so-called "cognitive" processes. This, as Matthiessen has shown (1993, 1998), is a commonsense view which has been transplanted into Western philosophy and some of our scientific thinking. But it brings serious problems. It imposes an artificial **dualism**: it suggests that there are two kinds of phenomena taking place, the cognitive, and the semantic. But cognitive processes **are** semantic; they are processes of meaning. And since they are construed in language (that is how we are able to apprehend them) it seems more helpful to interpret them in linguistic terms, using our theoretical understanding of grammar (our "grammatics") as the means of doing so. In other words, rather than explaining language by reference to cognition we explain cognition by reference to language. This helps us to avoid the trap of treating natural language as if it were an optional, simplified and imperfect outward form of idealized processes taking place in some inner mind. In fact we do not need the concept of "mind", or of "cognition", in our theoretical investigations of language.

II

The general term for referring to systems of meaning is *semiotic* systems. Note that the word "semiotic" here means 'having to do with meaning' rather than 'having to do with signs'; and that the term "system" always covers **both system and process** – both the potential and its output. Thus a semiotic system is a *meaning potential* together with its *instantiation* in acts of meaning.

One special kind of semiotic system is a *semantic* system; this is the meaning system of a natural language (HAL). What distinguishes a semantic system from semiotic systems of other types is that a semantic system is founded on a *grammar*, a system of *wordings* (words together with associated structural patterns); it is the presence of a grammar that gives language its unique potential for creating meaning.

In order to explore this further, let me first set up a simple evolutionary typology of systems:

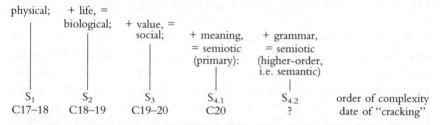

Semiotic systems are of a fourth order of complexity, in that they are at once semiotic **and** social **and** biological **and** physical. The bottom line of the figure shows the approximate date of "cracking the code" of these systems (bringing them within the domain of "scientific" inquiry).

Semiotic systems first evolve in the form of what Gerald Edelman calls "primary consciousness" (see e.g. his (1992) *Bright Air, Brilliant Fire*). They evolve as inventories of *signs*, in the classical sense of this term: that is, content/expression pairs. We find a system of this kind (a "primary semiotic", $S_{4.1}$) developed by human infants in the first year of their lives. (I have referred to this system as "protolanguage"; see Collected Works Vol. 4.) Such a system has no grammar. The more complex type of semiotic system is that which evolves in the form of what Edelman calls "higher order consciousness". This has a grammar; and it appears to be unique to adult (i.e. post-infancy) human beings, who learn it as "mother tongue" from early in the second year of life. It is this higher-order semiotic that we commonly refer to simply as "language", and we give names to its different varieties: "Japanese", "Chinese", "English" and so on.

Certain features of the protolanguage, the primary semiotic, persist into adult life, for example expressions of pain, anger, astonishment or fear ("interjections" like *ouch!, oy!, wow!*). On the other hand, human adults also develop numerous non-linguistic semiotic systems: forms of ritual, art forms etc.; these have no grammars of their own, but they are parasitic on natural language – their meaning potential derives from the fact that those who use them **also** have a grammar. Thus all human semiotic activity, making and exchanging meanings, from early childhood onwards, depends on natural language.

What, then, is a ***grammar***? And how does it reshape a semiotic system? A grammar is a purely abstract semiotic construct (that is, having no direct interface with material phenomena) that evolves as a distinct "stratum" **in between** the content and the expression. Hence a semiotic system with a grammar in it is said to be "stratified".

A system of this kind – that is, a higher-order semiotic organized around a grammar – has a unique property that is critical from our point of view in this present context: it has the potential for **creating** meaning. A primary semiotic (such as a human infant's protolanguage) "means" by a process of reflection: its meanings are **given**, from elsewhere. These are meanings such as 'here I am!', 'I'm in pain', 'let's be together', 'that's nice!'. By contrast, a stratified system – a language in the adult sense – can **constitute**: it does not **reflect** meaning, it **creates** meaning. It creates meaning in contexts of function; and because the meanings are non-randomly related to features of the context, it can also create the contexts themselves. For example: the grammar of English construes a particular class of phenomena as 'flash' + 'lightning', as in *there was a flash of lightning*, or *lightning flashed*. Now, if I say *there was a flash of lightning*, there may be a thunderstorm going on outside the building. On the other hand, I may just be telling you a story – or even presenting a paper about language.

The functional contexts of language fall into two major types; and the semiotic function that language is performing differs as between the two types. On the one hand, language constitutes human **experience**; and in this aspect, its function is to ***construe*** – language **imposes order on** the world that lies around us, and within our own bodies. On the other hand, language constitutes human **relationships**; and in this aspect, its function is not to construe but to ***enact*** – language **brings about** our ongoing social interaction. The grammar integrates these two modes of meaning into a single structure, such that every instance – everything we say or write, listen to or read – "means" in these two ways at once. (In the process of doing this, it creates a third functional context of its own; I will come back to this in a moment.) Thus, I cannot give you a command (interpersonal function) without tying that command to some domain of experience, such as driving a car; and I cannot talk about driving a car (experiential) unless combining it with some interpersonal act, such as giving a command. Even if the driving instructor shouts out one single word, such as *Brake!*, this carries a full grammatical load in both these functional contexts. We refer to these major functional types as ***metafunctions***; such a system is said to be metafunctionally ***diversified***.

This interdependence of the two metafunctions, the experiential (or ***ideational***, to give it its more inclusive name) and the interpersonal, is central to the evolution of language, and to its persistence through constant change in interaction with its environment. The ideational mode of meaning corresponds to what people usually think of as "meaning" in the ordinary sense: that is, 'content', especially 'referential content'. It is language as the categorization of human experience: language taking over the material processes and conditions of human existence and transforming them into meanings. We usually become aware of this ***semiotic transformation*** only when we think of systematic, scientific or technical knowledge, where we have a clear sense of the semiotic energy involved (for example in writing a theoretical paper); compare Lemke's (1984) observation that "a scientific theory is a system of related meanings". But all knowledge is like this. To "know" anything is to have transformed it into meaning; and what we call "understanding" is the process of that transformation.

But how does this transformation take place? The explanation lies in the metafunctional diversity. Experience is construed (understood, known) in the course of, and by means of, being acted out interpersonally; and in the same way, interpersonal relations are enacted in the course of, and by means of, being construed ideationally. And, as I noted a moment ago, the two are integrated together, and activated, by a third component of the grammar – a third metafunction, which we call the ***textual*** – which creates a flow of meaning, a semiotic current, that we know as ***discourse***. It is this metafunctional diversity in the grammar that has enabled human language to evolve as the form of higher-order consciousness. In commonsense terms, what makes it possible for humans to develop and use language, in the contexts of daily life, is that every linguistic act (every *act of meaning*) involves both talking about the world and acting upon those who are in it. Both these sets of phenomena may of course be purely imaginary; that in itself is the best demonstration of the constitutive power of language.

III

A primary semiotic system, such as an infant's protolanguage, or the communication system of a domestic pet such as a cat, is an inventory of simple signs: they are functionally related, and can be combined in a simple sequence, but they have very limited possibilities for expansion. By contrast, a higher-order semiotic, or HAL, being stratified and diversified, can be expanded almost indefinitely. If we ask how big a language is, the answer is: as big as it needs to be. The output of the system, text, is of course finite; but the system itself, as a potential, is indefinitely large – it is always capable of growing further, without any limits that we are aware of. (This is not to say that there are no limits; the capacity of the human brain, though very large, is undoubtedly finite. But we have no idea yet where those limits are.)

If we want to become aware of this potential, we model it in the form of a **system network**. The system network represents the language **paradigmatically**: that is, as abstract sets of possibilities, or choices. At each choice point, we ask: what is the environment, or **entry condition**, of the choice? what options are available? and how is each of these options made explicit? Here is a little network (Figure 9.1, p. 211) representing part of the grammar of the English verbal group (the verb together with its associated categories). The network describes, or "generates", something over 70,000 variants, different combinations of meanings that can be associated with a single verb. This takes us up to a certain depth of detail; we could go on and add many more. Once we start to consider the different possible clause types in a language, we soon have to be reckoning in terms of billions.

So, when the driving instructor says *Brake!*, or some other wording such as *Hadn't you better start braking?* (now we know that the situation is not dangerous; and the instructor is patient and mild-mannered – or perhaps sarcastic?), he or she is using one of (let us say) a million possible expressions that can be construed in the grammar of English around the lexical verb *to brake*. Each of these expressions would be the outcome of one particular pass through the network.

There is no doubt that all these variants make sense and could occur, even though many of them are very unlikely. A million possibilities implies, after all, only twenty independent binary choices. It is true that the different choices within a system network are not usually independent; they are at least partially associated. But there are far more than twenty of them in any typical network; and by no means all of them are binary. It has sometimes been objected that speakers, and listeners, could not possibly process a million possibilities every time they used a verb. I am not convinced that that is so impossible! – but it is beside the point, because this is not what the system network means. The network maps out, as accurately as we can make it, the total potential inhering in a given region of grammatical or semantic space. It does not attempt to characterize the neural processes involved in moving through that space. In any case, as already pointed out, the actual number of choice points that are traversed in any one pass is relatively small. (I shall not attempt here to explain the difference between the concepts of "grammatical space" and "semantic space"; see Martin and Matthiessen 1991.)

Let us note, at this point, that when we talk about the richness and complexity of language, we are not referring to the size of the vocabulary – the number of words. It is not very useful to try to count the words of a language, for at least three reasons. First, the "word" is too problematic a concept: we may not know where a word begins and ends (its *syntagmatic* boundaries are fuzzy), or when two words are tokens of the same type (its *paradigmatic* boundaries are fuzzy). Secondly, whatever a word may be, it differs markedly from one language to another (what would we take as the equivalent unit in Vietnamese, for example?). Thirdly, however you identify them, the words of a language do not constitute a fixed list: people are creating new words all the time. If you put all the current technical dictionaries of English together, how many words will you find? – one million? five million? ten million? But no single person uses more than a tiny fraction of these; whereas everybody takes up most of the options in the grammar. (In fact, words and grammar are not two different things. What we call "words" are one component of the total resource with which the grammar constructs meaning – an important component, of course! but not a separate entity. The technical name for this stratum is *lexicogrammar*.)

Let me try to summarize what I have been saying about the nature of **complexity** in language. The picture I have been trying to suggest to you, in this brief sketch, is one of **networks** of **grammatical systems** which together **construe** a **multidimensional semantic space**. Each such system, taken by itself, is just a choice among a small set of options, like 'positive or negative?', 'past, present or future?', 'possible, probable or certain?' and so on. What is important is how these systems relate to one another; and that is where the complexity arises. They are not fully independent; but nor do they form any kind of strict taxonomy. There are various degrees and kinds of partial association among them, and this makes the network extremely complex. But, by the same token, there is plenty of "play" (flexibility) in it, so that the system as a whole becomes manageable. It can be learnt, step by step, by children; it can be varied to suit the situation; and it can be modified as the discourse proceeds.

In other words, there is a great deal of indeterminacy, both in the systems themselves and in their relationship one to another. The overall picture is notably fuzzy. We do not normally use the term "fuzzy" – we refer to this property as "indeterminate"; and we try to model language in such a way as to capture the indeterminacy (a "fuzzy grammatics", as in the title of my pre-Conference written paper).

As Matthiessen has pointed out in his paper for Professor Ralescu's workshop (n.d.), when we talk about indeterminacy in language we are not referring to the explicit **formulation** of fuzziness in the lexicogrammar. All languages have ways of **referring to** different kinds of inexactness; for example, degrees of assignment to a property, like *rather, fairly, slightly*; expressions of uncertainty, like *perhaps, apparently, surely*; degrees of generality, like *on the whole, for the most part*; but these are quite marginal, in relation to language as a whole.

When we say that language is indeterminate, or fuzzy, we are talking about the whole set of categories that the lexicogrammar construes – the basic meanings of words and of grammatical features. Both ideationally, in construing our experience, and interpersonally, in enacting our social relationships, language is inherently fuzzy. It is always needing to **compromise**. This is because human experience, and human relationships, are much too complex and many-sided to be captured in categories that are well-formed, bounded and stable. Any system of rigid definitions and clear-cut boundaries would impose far too much constraint. The only determinate language is a dead one (as my teacher Professor Firth used to say, rigour in a linguistic context could only mean *rigor mortis*). Thus the indeterminacy is not an incidental feature, something added on to the grammar as a kind of optional extra; still less is it a pathological condition to be ignored or done away with. On the contrary: indeterminacy is an essential property on which the effective functioning of language depends.

IV

It has been recognized by neurobiologists for some time that the mammalian brain evolved in the context of the increasingly complex relationship of the organism to its environment. This explanation, however, focuses exclusively on the ***experiential***. For the human brain, at least – that is, for the evolution of higher-order consciousness – we need to add the ***interpersonal*** component of the picture: the brain has evolved also in the context of the increasingly complex relationship of organisms one to another. This then coincides closely with our functional interpretation of language. Language evolves in the course of managing these two complementary types of complexity.

To take the experiential aspect first. Ellis (1993) has pointed out that there are no "natural classes": all classes – the categories of human experience – have to be **construed** in language, by what I have called the transformation of experience into meaning. The grammar does not proceed by **recognizing** things that **are alike**. It proceeds by **treating as alike** things that are in fact **different**. Another way of looking at this is to say that things may be alike **in indefinitely many ways**; the grammar **picks out** just a few of these as **parameters** for its categorization. Then, rather than saying that there are no natural classes, we might say that there are far too many, and that transforming experience into meaning involves selecting the ones to be construed. Either way, it is obvious that this construal cannot be achieved by means of a single, flat, compartmentalized categorical schema. The construal of experience has to be multifaceted, multidimensional and fluid. Things have to be seen from many angles, be related along many vectors, and have boundaries that are indeterminate and may shift in the course of time. Hence the lexicogrammar of every HAL is based on the principle of **compromise**.

Turning to the interpersonal aspect of meaning, we find exactly the same is true. Social relationships in human cultures cannot be enacted in terms of simple 'yes' or 'no', 'this' or 'that' options. Negotiation and assignment of speech roles, forms of address and personal reference, maintenance of power and distance, and the like, all need to be modulated, cushioned, hedged around, coded and disguised in various ways. The management of interpersonal relationships, in other words, is also dependent on lexicogrammatical compromise, although the forms that this compromise takes will be different in the two metafunctions.

It is possible to enumerate some general forms of grammatical compromise, as follows:

1. Clines (gradations, continuities): categories as a continuous scale rather than as discrete classes.
2. Overlaps ("borderline cases"): categories lying across the border of two or more others, having some of the features of each.
3. Blends: categories arising from the mixing of the features of two or more others.
4. Neutralizations: categories whose difference disappears in certain environments.
5. Metaphors: categories created by metaphoric transfer ("reconstrual").
6. Complementarities: categories construed as multiple perspectives, competing and often contradictory.

Such "compromises" occur in all languages, but in different places and different mixes. I give a few brief examples from the grammar of English in the table at the end of this chapter.

The above are what we might call "categorization strategies", used by the grammar in construing our experience of processes (actions and events, and the participants and other elements involved), and in enacting our everyday *speech functions*, the small-scale semiotic roles of telling, asking, ordering and the like. Over and above the construction of particular categories, however, the grammar takes the further step of construing the relationship of one such category to another. An example would be the conditional relation, as in *Hold on to it, or it'll fall! . . . if it falls, it'll break.* There is a special component in the grammar which construes iterative relationships of this kind, which we refer to as the **logical** metafunction. (Note that this is "logical" in the grammatical sense, the logic of natural language, not the derived sense of formal or mathematical logic. Formal logic is often cited as a criterion for evaluating natural language; but formal logic is itself an idealization of natural language in the first place.) In effect, this logical component adds a further dimension of complexity into the meaning potential; this is a **dynamic** complexity, whereby "one thing leads on to another".

We sometimes tend to think of this feature in the grammar – relating phenomena to each other by time, cause, condition and so on – as a special property of the designed discourses of science and technology, or at least of the discourse of educational as distinct from commonsense knowledge. But it is not. Hasan's (1992) study of "Rationality in everyday talk", together with other studies based on her extensive corpus of natural interaction between mothers and their three-year-old children, shows how the semantic relations of cause and condition are well established in the discourse of children before they become literate or go into school. And among adults, the grammar reaches its highest level of *intricacy* (in constructing *clause complexes*, grammatically structured sequences of clauses) in informal casual conversation, where there is a rapid process of ongoing "recontextualization" – the logical significance of each clause is updated in the light of what has been said before, or in the light of changes in the context of situation. We find this happening both in monologue and in dialogue, as speakers build semantic sequences in their own discourse or in interplay with other people.

I want to make it clear that all these features which make language seem disorderly and unmanageable (the indeterminacy of the categories, or the unpredictable dynamic of the discourse) are truly features of language **as a system**. They are essential properties of knowing, understanding, reasoning and planning – of the human ability to "mean". There is no distinction to be made between "system" and its "use": no Cartesian dichotomy to be made between an idealized "competence" and a hopelessly messy "performance". The task for *grammatics*, therefore, is to account for the disorder and the complexity, not as accidental and aberrant, but as systemic and necessary to the effective functioning of language.

V

In this final section, I shall outline the basic principles we adopt in attempting to theorize about language, with a brief illustration of each. My aim is to suggest how this overall perspective on language might relate to your own concerns. (See p. 210.)

First, we model language *paradigmatically*: that is, as **choice**, with the system network as organizing concept. This enables us to represent the meaning potential of the *system*; but in a way which shows how any *instance* is related to it, and therefore to other possible instances. The fact that people can use language effectively in real-life contexts is because each **instance** is **systemic**: it derives its meaning from the overall semantic potential created by the resources of the grammar. The meaning of what **was said**, in any situation, depends on what **might have been said** but **was not**. The network also enables us to vary the *delicacy* (depth of detail) of the representation.

Secondly, we model language *contextually*: that is, as discourse **in social contexts**. The context is represented as *field* (what is going on, in what domain of social activity), as *tenor* (who are taking part, in what kind of social relationships) and as *mode* (what rhetorical function is assigned to the discourse, and in what medium). This shows up the systematic relationship between situation and language, and enables us to make predictions from the one to the other. We take as primary datum the language of everyday life, since this is most strongly contextualized and displays most effectively how new meanings are opened up as the discourse proceeds.

Third, we model language *functionally*: not just in the general sense of 'according to how it is used' but in the specific technical sense of 'by *metafunction*' – that is, according to the functional principles on which the grammars of all languages have evolved. These are the *ideational* (related to **field**), the *interpersonal* (related to **tenor**) and the *textual* (related to **mode**). This enables us to show the grammar "at work", in its *constitutive* roles (construing experience, enacting social processes), and to analyse the different strands of meaning that are present in every instance of language use.

Fourth, we model language *fuzzily*: that is, in terms of categories that are typically indeterminate and fluid. This allows us to explore the various ways in which language **compromises**, the various strategies of categorization that make it possible to accommodate differing and often conflicting aspects of reality. This in turn shows how the "fuzziness" is not a matter of "performance error" or "careless use of language"; nor is it a special feature of certain regions of the grammar, like modality; rather, it is an essential corollary of the **complexity** that language attains in its different functional capacities.

Fifth, we model language *developmentally*: that is, taking account of how it is learnt by children as a "mother tongue". In general terms, this enables us to understand how, and why, language evolved as it did – the origins of grammar, and of functional complementarity. More particularly, it provides a timeframe within which we can locate, and order, the different components that make up adult discourse. Linguistically, children progress from *generalization*, through *abstractness*, to *metaphor*; and these seem to correspond, in our cultures, with the development from commonsense knowledge, through literate knowledge, to technical knowledge (from home and neighbourbood, through primary school, to secondary school). Adult discourse contains all these layers simultaneously; and the tension set up among them, as the discourse shifts from one to another, gives an added dimension to the meaning.

Professor Sugeno has said: we cannot put language into the machine. And he is right: we cannot put the whole of a natural language, or even a significant fraction of it, into a computer. But we can put **some features** of language, some very important features, into the machine if we know what it is we want to achieve by doing so. Many models of grammar have been used in computational linguistic research; systemics has figured there prominently ever since the pioneering work of Henrici and of Winograd in the 1960s. Mann and Matthiessen, Bateman, Fawcett and their colleagues have all developed powerful representations of system networks, and applied them not only to English but also to Japanese, Chinese, German and French. What these scholars have in common, in their approach to language, is a concern with meaning, with discourse, and with the complex ways in which languages varies in resonance with the contexts in which it is used.

I am not a specialist in any of the fields of study represented at your Conference; and I recognize that what I have been presenting on this occasion may be far from your immediate concerns. But what I have wanted to suggest is that, if natural language has a significant role to play in any complex operation, such as intelligent computing, then we shall need to engage with it seriously and in appropriate theoretical terms. Just because you are foregrounding commonsense grammar and semantics – the kind of discourse that functions in the contexts of daily life – this does not mean that, in designing systems where such discourse has a place, you can operate with no more than commonsense **ideas about** language. You have to think about these systems grammatically, just as in dealing with physical systems you have to think mathematically – finding the appropriate logic, in each case. For us, as linguists, there is a great deal to be learnt from seeing language put into the context of your work; which is why I am especially grateful to be allowed to take part today.

Some examples illustrating the principles of "systemic" modelling

---

1. Why "paradigmatic"? – Meaning depends on **choice**
   You should have **braked**!   differs in ONE FEATURE from:

You should **brake**! [tense]	I should have **braked**! [person]
Should you have **braked**? [mood]	You shouldn't have **braked**! [polarity]
You could have **braked**! [modality]	You **should** have braked! [info. focus] &c.

   You should have **braked**!   differs in TWO FEATURES from:
   You **shouldn't** have braked! [polarity and information focus]
   You needn't have **braked**! [polarity and modality]   &c.&c.

---

2. Why "contextual"? – Meaning depends on **situation**
   You should have **braked**!   outline of FIELD, TENOR and MODE:
   Field: Learning, under instruction; a skill: (mechanical: driving car)
   [→ ideational meanings]
   Tenor: Instructor: professional (power = knowledge: can give orders) x
   learner: client (power = authority: can withdraw custom)
   [→ interpersonal meanings]
   Mode: Spoken; instructional: action-oriented; largely monologic
   [→ textual meanings]

---

3. Why "metafunctional"? – Meaning depends on **function** (in system)
   You should have **braked**! IDEATIONAL, INTERPERSONAL & TEXTUAL
   meanings:
   Ideational: material process: action: 'make + stop'; active participant:
   'the learner'; time: past ... unfulfilled ...
   Interpersonal: ... (statement of) obligation: high (strong); key:
   moderate; person responsible: 'the listener'
   Textual: message complete; theme: 'you (learner / listener)'; information
   focus: 'brake (action)'

---

4. Why "fuzzy"? – Meaning depends on **compromise** (indeterminacy)
   Examples of CLINE, BLEND, METAPHOR, COMPLEMENTARITY:
   Cline: force (tension): **Brake**! (mild: low falling) – **Brake**!!! (strong: high falling)
   [intonation as continuous variable]
   Blend: obligation / probability: The brake should have been on.
   should = 'ought to have been' x 'I thought it was'
   Metaphor: it's necessary to put full brakes on / total braking is a necessity
   ['obligation' transformed into predicate; 'action' transformed into nominal]
   Complementarity: the driver braked /   ⎫ [conflicting construals of
   the car braked / the driver   ⎬ reality]
   braked the car   ⎭

---

5. Why "developmental"? – Meaning depends on **history** (ontogenesis of language)
   Age (of learner; a rough guide to the language of driving instruction!)

   [1] Don't go too fast! You'll hit something.
   [2] You shouldn't go so fast. If you go too fast, you won't be able to stop.
   [5] You'd better slow down! The faster you go, the harder it is (the longer it takes) to
   stop.
   [9] It's important to keep at low speed. Faster speed makes stopping difficult.
   [13+] Low speed maintenance is essential. Braking distance increases more rapidly at
   high speeds.

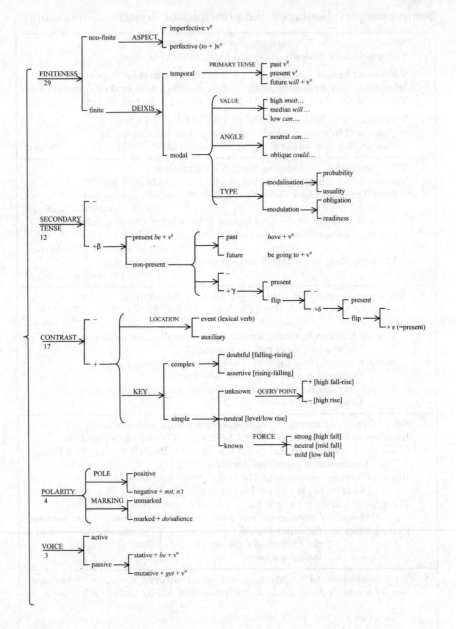

Figure 9.1 System network for the English verbal group

FUZZY GRAMMATICS: A SYSTEMIC FUNCTIONAL APPROACH TO FUZZINESS IN NATURAL LANGUAGE[1] (1995)

This chapter is concerned with theory of language, specifically of grammar, in the context of natural language as a metalanguage for intelligent computing (Sugeno 1993).

In part 1, I raise the question of whether we need to model the properties of texts in terms of a general theory of language; and if so, in what ways. In part 2 I consider the basic *functions* of natural language (known here as *metafunctions*) which have determined the general form taken by grammars. These are: (1) ideational (construing experience), (2) interpersonal (enacting social relationships), (3) textual (creating discourse).

In part 3, I refer to some *properties* of natural language which are relevant to its user as a metalanguage. Natural language is (a) comprehensive, (b) extravagant, (c) telescopic, (d) non–autonomous, (e) variable and (f) indeterminate. In part 4 I discuss systemic functional linguistics as possible source of a low-level metalanguage for representing natural language in this context ("fuzzy grammatics").

I shall distinguish *grammar* (Japanese: 文法) from the study of grammar, which I shall call *grammatics* (Japanese: 文法學). A *grammar* is part of a language, comprising its "syntax" (including the syntax of words, called "morphology") and its "vocabulary" (lexical stock). *Grammatics* is part of linguistics: specifically, it is that part of the theory of language that is concerned with theory of grammar.

Part 1 Natural language as metalanguage: some problems

Everyone knows that language can be used to lie, to deceive, to lead astray. I shall assume that an intelligent computer user is **not** playing this sort of game, and I shall say no more about it. But there are other discursive practices – typical features of language use – that speakers engage in all the time, which may be problematic when natural language is functioning as a metalanguage. Here are some general headings:

A. Rhetorical "toning" (undertones, overtones):
   tentativeness, obliqueness; exaggeration; claims of objectivity, certainty
B. Indistinctness (lack of clarity):
   ambiguities; indeterminate categories; unclear "phoricity" (reference to co-text or context)
C. Unexpectedness (disturbance of probabilities):
   redundancy, repetition; low-probability forms and meaning
D. "Logogenesis" (building up new meanings in the course of a text):
   technicalizing (creating technical terms); thematizing (creating and maintaining a discourse topic)
E. Complexity:
   grammatical intricacy (spoken); lexical density (written)
F. Irrelevance:
   following the "wrong" trail; answering the "wrong" question
G. Jocularity:
   irony, sarcasm; analogies of various kinds
H. Error:
   "slips of the tongue" (spoken); misprints (written)

Text 3 in Chapter 8 (see pp. 184–85), taken from a spontaneous dialogue, provides instances of a number of these features.

Two brief comments may be made at this stage, one concerning *instances* of language ("text"), the other concerning language as *system*.

(1) It was pointed out many years ago, in the early history of work on machine translation, that a text, rather than being envisaged as a Markov process with probabilities becoming steadily more constrained as it proceeded, should be seen as a complex wave with periodic alternation between more and less predictable states. This effect could be seen clearly in the grammar, where larger and smaller cycles corresponded to structural boundaries (between clauses, between groups, etc.). We should add here that texts are often characterized by an analogous kind of periodic movement at the

level of semantics: an alternation between *meanings* that are more, and less, expected by a listener or reader in the given context of situation.

(2) We are now familiar with the notion that a language imposes *categories* on the flux of human experience. But a category is typically something that is (i) bounded (has defined borders), (ii) distinct (differs from other categories), (iii) objective (has specific properties), (iv) stable (persists through time) and (v) "effable" (is capable of being described). Linguistic "categories", however, tend to be unbounded (admitting gradience, or "clines"), indistinct (not clearly opposed to others), non-objective (admitting hybrids, blends etc.), unstable (admitting tendencies and transitions) and ineffable (not capable of being described; hence admitting rhetorical "toning" of various kinds) (Halliday 1987/2002).

In order to be able to discuss such features in general and systematic terms, we need to work with some model of language that incorporates both the *system* and the *instance*, as well as the relation of one to the other (the "instantiation cline"). Formal models – those which foreground the *forms* of a language – tend to be mainly concerned with structures, and with what **cannot** be *formed* (with excluding the "ungrammatical"), and have little to say about text, actual instances of language in use. Functional models – those which foreground the *meanings* of language – are more centrally concerned with what **can** be *meant*. The problem is to relate "what can be" to "what is" (the system to the instance). Pragmatic analysis focuses on instances; but without relating them to any general theory of language as system. We need a model that is functional, and theoretical, but is able to operate at a median level of generality so as to encompass "what is and what can be": that is, to be able to explain particular instances by reference to a general interpretation of the system of a language as a whole.

The first point to stress, I think, is that the way the grammar of every language is organized closely models, or recapitulates, the *functional contexts* in which human language has evolved.

Part 2 Metafunctions of natural languages

2.1 Ideational, interpersonal and textual

The *grammar* of every natural language, such as Japanese, or English, has two primary functions:

(1) It *construes* human experience: making sense of what we perceive as "reality", both the world outside us and the world of our own inner consciousness.

(2) It *enacts* social and personal relationships: setting up both immediate and long-term interaction with other persons, and in this way establishing each one's identity and self-awareness.

In systemic functional theory these are called ***metafunctions***: (1) ***ideational*** and (2) ***interpersonal***. There is also a third metafunction, the ***textual***, whereby the grammar gives substance to the other two:

(3) It *creates* discourse: formulating a distinct "semiotic reality" in which (1) and (2) are combined into a single flow of meaning, as spoken or written text.

This flow of discourse is sometimes called "information flow"; we can use this term, provided we avoid any suggestion that language evolved as the communication of information.[2]

To put this in other terms: the grammar of a natural language is both (1) a way of thinking (a "theory" of human experience) and (2) a way of doing (a form of social "praxis"). Furthermore, neither of these can occur without the other; every grammatical construct embodies **both** ideational **and** interpersonal meanings. It is the intersection of these two that is (3) formed by the grammar into discourse.

As an example, consider a clause such as the following, from everyday spoken English:

Don't tease your baby sister!

(1) Ideationally, it construes a form of action, 'tease', verbal and/or non-verbal; with two human participants, one 'doing' the other 'done to'; the latter as 'young female sibling' to the former; ...

(2) Interpersonally, it enacts a negative command 'don't!', the speaker demanding compliance from the listener; peremptory, to take immediate effect; ...

(3) Textually, it creates a coherent message, with a discursive movement from the speaker-oriented theme 'I want you not to (tease)' to the listener-oriented focus of information on the 'other' (third party) [the last shown by the intonation, not marked in writing]; ...

These features are brought out in the grammatical analysis of the clause, as shown in Figure 10.1. (For the metafunctional analysis of the clause and other features of the grammar of English referred to in this chapter, see Halliday 1985/1994.)

	don't		tease		your baby sister
ideational	Process: material / verbal				Goal / Target
interpersonal	Mood: negative	Residue:			
		Predicator			Complement
textual: theme information	Theme:				Rheme
	interpersonal		topical		
	------------------------------➤				
	Focus				

Figure 10.1

2.2 Meaning and context; context of discourse, and context of situation

It is customary in natural language processing, especially in the context of text generation, to make a distinction between "meaning" as constructed in the grammar and "inference" from "knowledge of the world". Thus, in the case of the example above, it would be said that we assume the addressee must be not more than (say) 25 years old, because the third party is a baby and we know that siblings cannot normally be more than 25 years apart.

But there is no clear line between "meaning" and "knowing/ inferring". We might suggest, rather, that this "knowledge" is part of the **meaning** of *sister* and of *baby* – which must be taken together with the meaning of the grammatical relationship that is here constructed between the two (one of Classifier + Thing in the nominal group), as well as that between *baby sister* and *your*. There seems no need to postulate two separate realms of cognition, one semantic (within language), the other conceptual (outside language).

In any case, the third party in this instance may not be an infant; she might be middle-aged, the clause being addressed jokingly to an older sibling who still thought of her as a baby. She might even be the older of the two, being treated as if she were a baby; the possibilities are open. But they are open because we have taken the clause out of its context.

The "context" of an utterance, however, is an essential aspect of its meaning. Decontextualized words and clauses have a place in grammar books and dictionaries, but seldom in real life. (Of course, they are not really "decontextualized" – rather, citation is a very special type of context.) Our grammatics would engage with this clause in its **context of situation**, consisting of (say) a mother with two daughters, one aged about four years old and the other around one year; and in its **discursive context**, which might be something like the following:

Child: Do you want that balloon? Well you can't have it; it's mine!
Baby [*cries*]
Mother: Now look what you've done! Don't tease your baby sister; you make her cry.

Of course, we can also construct the context from the text. The grammatical analysis should show that it is part of the meaning of this clause that it enables us to construct a discursive and situational context such as the above. It should also show that other contextual possibilities exist – but under more closely specified conditions: the possibilities are clearly ordered, such that a type of situation like that illustrated above is the most likely, or "default" choice. (For the relation of text and context, see Hasan 1980; Halliday and Hasan 1985.)

2.3 Figure, proposition/proposal, message; sequences; elements

Let me now say a little more about the metafunctional components of the grammar; looking at them, this time, from a functional semantic viewpoint ("from above", instead of "from below").

(1) Ideational. The central organizing unit here is a **figure**. A figure construes a "quantum" of experience, categorizing it as (a) material, (b) mental, (c) verbal or (d) relational. (The experience may be purely fictitious or imaginary, of course!) Grammatically, this is formed as a **configuration** consisting typically of (i) a process, (ii) a small number of participating entities, and perhaps (iii) one or two circumstantial elements. For examples, see Figure 10.2.

Each component within the figure is an **element**. Prototypically, in English, the grammar construes the figure as a **clause** and the elements as (1) [process] verbal group, (ii) [participating entity]

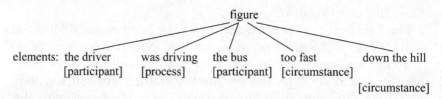

figure

elements: the driver   was driving   the bus   too fast   down the hill
           [participant]   [process]   [participant] [circumstance]
                                                            [circumstance]

Figure 10.2

nominal group, and (iii) [circumstance] adverbial group or pre-positional phrase.

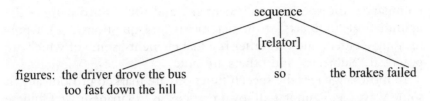

Figure 10.3

Two or more figures may combine to form a *sequence*, as in Figure 10.3. Prototypically, the grammar construes a sequence as a *clause complex*. [Note that it is important to stress the "proto-typically" throughout; the grammar always has alternative strategies for construing sequences, figures, and the various types of element within a figure. Cf. Figures 10.4 and 10.5.]

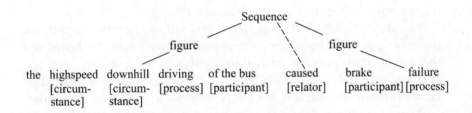

Figure 10.4

	the driver's	highspeed	downhill	driving	of the bus
nominal group:	Deictic	Epithet	Classifier	Thing	Qualifier

	the driver	was driving	the bus	too fast	down the hill
clause:	Actor	Process: material	Goal	Manner	Location

Figure 10.5

(2) Interpersonal. Here the central organizing unit is a *proposition* or a *proposal* (i.e. one move in an exchange). The proposition/proposal enacts a "speech function", either (a) statement or question [proposition], or (b) offer or command [proposal]. Grammatically,

this is formed as a ***predication***, which is something that can be argued over – confirmed, disputed, rejected etc.; containing (i) some element that is held responsible (typically, the addressee 'you' in commands, the speaker 'me' in offers, and some third party – the grammatical "Subjects" – in statements and questions); (ii) a predicating element and (iii) other residual elements, some of which are potential "Subjects" and others are not.

In most languages the speech functions are marked prosodically in some way: e.g. "annotated" by a particle, as in Japanese *ka*, Chinese *ma, ba*, etc.; "clustered" into two parts, as in English (Mood + Residue; see Figure 10.1); "re-predicated", as in English and Chinese (*it is . . ., isn't it?*; *shi bushi . . .?*); and/or realized by intonation contour. The different speech functions are often further accompanied by expressions of the speaker's attitude (judgements, emotions etc.), e.g. *for God's sake please don't . . .!*

Typically the grammar construes the proposition/proposal as a ***clause***, and the elements as (i) [predicator] verbal group, (ii) [subject, and potential subjects] nominal group, and (iii) [other residual elements] adverbial group or prepositional phrase.

The details given here are those of English. But the significant point is that, in all languages, the grammar constructs the ***figure*** and the ***proposition/proposal*** **simutaneously**, in such a way that the two are mapped on to each other as a single, unitary ***clause***. The clause is the main gateway between the grammar and the semantics.

If two (or more) clauses are combined in one ***clause complex***, so as to form a ***sequence***, then (1) each clause construes a ***figure***, but (2) depending on the type of sequence, not every clause may function as ***proposition/proposal***. A "paratactic" sequence is one in which each predication does achieve propositional status, e.g.

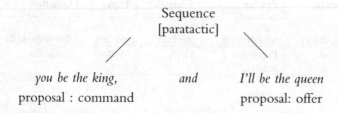

A "hypotactic" sequence is one in which only one predication achieves propositional status, e.g.

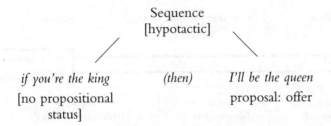

(3) Textual. The central organizing unit here is a **message**. This is a complex notion, with a great deal of variation among different languages; what is common to all, however, is that the message creates the discursive flow, turning the progression of figures/propositions into **text**. The account here relates specifically to English.

In English, the "flow" is a blend of two discursive currents, one **thematic**, the other **informational**; there are various ways of modelling this, in grammatical terms – my own preference is to model it as two separate movements with partial association between them. Let me use the analogy of a television camera. (a) The "thematic" movement is the **siting** of the camera, locating the **operator** of the camera at a particular angle. (b) The "informational" movement is the **focusing** of the lens, bringing some object into the **viewer's** focus. The "operator" of the camera corresponds to the speaker; the "viewer" corresponds to the listener. (It is of course the operator who **selects both** the thematic angle **and** the informational focus.) (On the grammatical category of "theme", see Hasan and Fries 1995, Matthiessen 1992).

Grammatically, in English, the thematic movement is construed as a **clause**, with the "theme" as the initial element; the informational movement is organized as a distinct unit, the **information unit**, which is formed as an **intonation contour** (technically, a "tone group") with the **focus** taking the form of **tonic prominence**. These two movements provide a complex periodicity to discourse; the typical phasing of the two yields a regular kind of "wave shape" with each clause moving from an initial theme (the "siting" or location of the message) to a final point of focus (the "news-point" of the message), as shown in Figure 10.1. But the association between "theme" and "focus" – between the ongoing siting of the camera and the ongoing focusing of the lens – is fluid, not fixed; so the resulting wave shape may be indefinitely varied.

A summary of the principal categories is given in Figure 10.6.

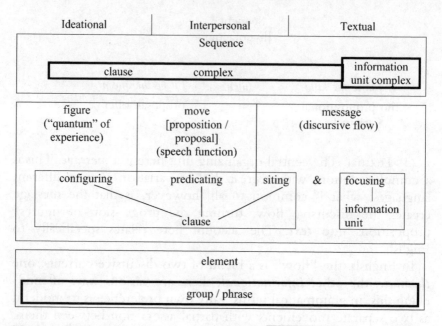

Figure 10.6 Note: categories enclosed in |inner boxes| are the typical realizations in grammar of the semantic categories shown above them.

Part 3 Some general properties of grammars

It seems reasonable to suggest that a theory of "grammatics" should be capable of representing all the systems and processes of meaning, not leaving out some arbitrary subset to be handled (by a separate domain of "pragmatics") as special features of the occasion. These too are, after all, construed in language. The grammar functions as a single whole, construing all human reportable subjective experiences (all our individual "qualia") and enacting all our intersubjective relationships. It does so, of course, in context; so we need to be able to model the context also. But it does not depend on outside reinforcements. (There are gestures, and facial expressions; but speakers can manage without these – as they have to do on the telephone, or as writers.)

The key question is: what is it that enables a grammar – the grammar of a natural language – to do these wonderful things? Let me try to identify some of the salient properties of grammars that seem to be crucial in this respect. (1) They are **comprehensive**: they can 'mean' anything we want. (2) They are **extravagant**: they always pack extra power. (3) They are *telescopic*: they carry their history with them. (4) They are *non-autonomous*: they interact with their environment. (5) They are *variable*: they change under differing conditions. (6) They are *indeterminate*: they work with approximations and tendencies. I shall discuss briefly each of these properties in turn. (For theory and method of discourse analysis in systemic functional terms see Martin 1992.)

(1) Comprehensive. There are few, if any, experiences that cannot be construed in language; even dreams, which offer the greatest challenge to a grammar. This is perhaps not surprising, since language evolved (in its ideational capacity) as the repository of human experience. Where "words fail us", it seems, is usually on the interpersonal wavelength; but here, if we are honest, we will admit that it is not, in fact, the grammar that is letting us down – it is our own inability to negotiate the reefs and shallows of our interactions with other people. There seems to be no relationship that cannot be enacted in language, from the most intimate to the most formal (with the baby sister, or the emperor), and from the most instantial to the most systemic (from the speech function of a single proposition to the lifetime role of teacher, parent or friend.)

Implications for grammatics. We model the *system*, as a whole, as a network of *meaning potential*. Each "text" (any actual *instance* of language in use) gets its meaning by reference to that potential; so we describe a *text* as (the product of) multiple choices, the repeated selection of "paths" traced through the network.

(2) Extravagant. The grammar offers multiple perspectives – different angles, or ways of looking at things. It often displays *complementarities*: different construals of experience (like tense and aspect as theories of time, or transitive and ergative as theories of agency and causality) which contradict each other, yet where the contradiction opens up new meanings in unpredictable ways. It has an unending reserve of *metaphor*, both ideational and interpersonal, constantly "de-coupling" itself from the semantics and re-coupling in other alignments, again in this way extending the overall meaning potential. Brief examples from English: (i) complementarity: conscious processes are grammaticized both as 'subject acting mentally, with object as scope' e.g. *I notice it, I believe it* and as 'object acting materially, with subject as goal' e.g. *it strikes me, it convinces me*; (ii) metaphor: event as 'process' [verb], e.g. *an electron moves in an orbit* is regrammaticized with event as 'entity' [noun], e.g. *the orbital motion of an electron*.

Implications for grammatics. In principle there is no unique grammatical representation for a piece of text. But the different representations are systemically related; e.g. (i) by **agnation** (systematic proportionality within the grammar; thus *I notice it : it strikes me :: I believe it : it convinces me*), (ii) by **semantic junction** ("re-entrant" analysis from the semantics, showing e.g. that *motion* is both process and entity).

(3) Telescopic. The grammar takes a long view; it carries its own history along with it, both systemically (in the evolving of the language) and instantially (in the unfolding of a text). Systemically, the elaborated grammar of an adult is built upon its origins as first developed by an infant learning its mother tongue, and carries the traces of these meanings as the child moves through adolescence to maturity (epigenetically recapitulating the evolutionary trajectory). Instantially, the grammar of each text retains its history, continuing to "bounce off" meanings from the past (by **anaphora**: e.g., from a conversation:

I thought it was half price for students?
– It is; but I'm not a student unfortunately.

Then, over 100 clauses later,

– I was a student *then*.

with *then* on the contrastive falling-rising tone); and building up new meanings instantially by a process of **distillation**. (This is how technical terms are formed, as new abstractions – virtual objects – created discursively in the course of a scientific text.) (On technicality in scientific discourse see Halliday and Martin 1993.)

Implications for grammatics. We model the **system** in historical terms, noting especially transitional features and changes which have flowed topologically through a region of the grammar (e.g. in English the "syndrome" of related changes that took place when it became a "standard" language, used in interaction among strangers). We try to model the **text** "logogenetically", as a meaning-creating process: its structure potential, its thematic development, its dialogic movement, methods of argumentation and so on.

(4) Non-autonomous. The grammar does not constitute an autonomous system. First, language itself is not autonomous: it is part of human history, having evolved (a) in the course of evolution of the brain, (b) in the context of emerging human cultures, (c) alongside other semiotic systems (particularly visual art, since writing

224

evolved from the conjunction of visual art with language), and (d) in the environment of the material world. Secondly, within language, grammar is not autonomous; it evolved from the deconstruing of the original "content plane" (as seen, for example, in the protolanguage of infants before they embark on the mother tongue; and in the "languages" of other species) into the two strata of *semantics* and *grammar*. In this process, far from detaching itself and becoming an "autonomous syntax", the grammar remained linked naturally to the semantics. Hence grammars are shaped by being held in tension both with other strata of language and with non-linguistic systems/processes of various kinds.

Likewise, a text does not constitute an autonomous process. Text – spoken and written discourse – is produced and understood in context. This is shown, e.g., by *deixis*, those features whereby the discourse is ongoingly related to the here-&-now of the speech situation (e.g. person: 'I, you, my, your' etc.; proximity: 'this, here, that, there'; tense: 'is, was, will be' etc.). By the same token the text can also refer to itself, so regulating the information flow and resetting the expectations of what is to follow. (For example, a series of instructions, like a cooking recipe: these (i) refer to the persons and objects on hand, and (ii) take each step in the sequence as the point of departure for the next.)

Implications for grammatics. We model the language as a social semiotic system; and the grammar in functional terms, relating externally to the context of culture and internally to the semantics. [Note that "functional" does not imply "instead of formal"; it means "as well as formal" – there has to be, also, an account of the words and structures by which the meaning is construed.] We analyse the text in relation to its context of situation, and in respect of each of the "metafunctions" referred to in Part 2.

(5) Variable. A language forms a multidimensional semiotic space, which accommodates a great deal of variation: "sub-languages" of various kinds which selectively exploit, or foreground, different regions of that space. (a) Most familiar, perhaps, is *dialectal* variation; this is typically variation in the *expression* space (the "lower" interface of the grammar, and the phonology), although dialects can also vary in content, particularly on the standard / non-standard dimension. (b) *Functional* variation, or *register*, on the other hand, is typically variation in the *content* (semantic) space; this is the variation that is associated with the different functions of a language in society – the different kinds of activities that people engage in. When new

activities come into being, as often happens with changes in technology, new registers evolve along with them, opening up further
regions of semantic space. (For discussion of register variation in
language, see Ghadessy 1994; Matthiessen 1993b.) (3) There is also
what is known as *idiolectal* variation, between one individual
speaker and another. People develop different habits of meaning,
individually and in small social groups.

Implications for grammatics. The variation has to be accounted
for, as a normal feature of language. The variants are not different
languages, or even different grammars; the differences are not
categorical, but matters of relative frequency – a resetting of probabilities from global to local norms. This means that the grammatics
has to accommodate probabilities [see Part 4].

(6) Indeterminate. A language is not an inventory of well-formed
structures. On the contrary; it is a highly indeterminate, open-ended
resource for making and exchanging meaning. It is indeterminate in
many ways (not the least being the indeterminacy among the different types of indeterminacy).

Most obvious (but perhaps least significant) are **ambiguities**, where a
distinction in meaning is obscured by identity of form. Some of
these, such as puns, are random and unpredictable; others arise out of
conflicts and neutralizations in the system of the grammar (e.g., in
English, *her training was highly effective*: was she the trainer, or the
trainee?). Less obvious, but more problematic, are indeterminacies
within the meaning itself: (a) **clines**, categories which shade one into
another without clear boundaries; (b) **overlaps**, categories which
display some features from each of two (or more) others; (c) **blends**,
categories which combine two (or more) features that are normally
contrastive. Examples from English: (a) grammatical systems realized
by intonation, such as **key**, ranging from "strong" [high falling tone]
to "mild" [low falling tone]; (b) in the system of **process type**, there
are "behavioural" processes like *sleep, chatter, laugh* which have some
features of "material" and some features of "mental" processes; (c)
modals, which are ambiguous in the "direct / immediate" form (e.g.
can), become blended in "oblique + remote" (e.g. *could have*): *she can
be happy* = **either** 'she is sometimes happy' **or** 'she is capable of being
happy', **but not both**; whereas in *she could have been happy* the
distinction seems to disappear.

Implications for grammatics. In formal linguistics indeterminacy was often seen as a pathological feature of language, something that needed to be excised by surgical idealization. In fact it is a positive characteristic, without which language would not be able to achieve its richness or its variety; so it needs to be given status in a theory. Of the types mentioned above, ambiguity is unproblematic, since it is simply the juxtaposition of two descriptions (the issue then being which, if either, is to be preferred). Perhaps the most problematic are blends, where we have to find the general conditions under which the ambiguity which "ought" to be present is somehow dissipated or neutralized. The overall challenge is to achieve significant generalizations about such indeterminacies without imposing on them an artificial exactitude. For a discussion of other, more general types of indeterminacy, see Halliday and Matthiessen 2000.

Part 4 Systemic functional linguistics as "fuzzy grammatics"

4.1 The relation of linguistic theory to natural language

A theory of any kind, whatever it is theorizing about, is itself a **semiotic system**: it is "a system of related meanings". In that respect, a scientific theory is no different from the "commonsense" accounts of experience that are embodied in our everyday language. Each of these is a **re-presentation** of experience in discursive form. Processes of any kind are semiotically transformed, into meanings. (On the nature of language, and of scientific theory in relation to a general theory and typology of systems, see Lemke 1990, 1993.)

For example: consider the context of glass cracking. We might **explain** this, in commonsense terms, in some such dialogue:

The glass suddenly cracked!
– Well, you shouldn't have pressed so hard on it.

We might then go on to **predict**:

Don't press so hard on that glass – it'll crack!

We might then **generalize** this to:

Glass cracks more quickly the harder you press on it.

This could then be **technicalized**:

The rate of glass crack growth depends on the magnitude of the applied stress.

Note that these are not the same in meaning (they are **not** *synonymous*). For one thing, they differ in various ways on the interpersonal dimension: different speaker/writer and different audience. But in addition, when the theory has been technicalized we have created new abstractions, virtual entities such as *rate, crack growth, magnitude, applied stress*, which (a) can be measured (quantified) and (b) can be taxonomized (put into a systematic relationship one with another); and this enables us to express the experience mathematically. Thus there has been a significant expansion of the relevant semantic space. But mathematics is still a semiotic system, ultimately derived from natural language grammar; and all these variants are alike in this respect: they are *transformations of experience into meaning*.

Let me express this by saying that they are all *metaphors* for the phenomena they are representing. Now, a theory of *language*, in this respect, is no different: it is also a metaphor of experience. But in another respect a theory of language does differ from other theories, because language is itself a semiotic system. Hence a theory of language is a theory **whose domain is another system of the same kind as itself**. It is "language turned back on itself" as my teacher J. R. Firth used to express it. So a theory of language is metaphoric not only in a general sense but also more specifically, in that it may "copy" many of the features of that which it is theorizing.

This then relates to Parts 2 and 3 above, on the *metafunctions* and the *properties* of language.

(i) A grammar is, as we saw, not only a means of **thinking** (construing experience) but also a means of **doing** (enacting social processes and relationships). This is exactly what scientific theories are: they enable us to understand the world in order to act on it – to solve problems and to carry out tasks. Much of linguistic theory, in the West, has been ideologically linked with philosophy rather than with science: it has been promoted as a way of understanding, without any particular applications. Systemic linguistics, on the other hand, is more in the context of science and technology; it has been developed primarily as something to be applied. The major applications, up to now, have been (a) in education and (b) in natural language processing; as well as (c) in various other fields of research.

(ii) The more specific question that arises is, how far our grammatics may "copy" the particular properties that we have found in language itself. If it is to theorize about grammar in ways that are useful in application to specific problems and tasks, does this mean merely that it should **take account of** these properties? or should it actually **mimic** them, so that it is itself comprehensive, extravagant, telescopic, non-autonomous, variable and indeterminate? I shall comment briefly on these; and then, in the final sections, discuss one or two features of the theory, relevant to the question of "natural language as metalanguage", which do "copy" some of the properties of language itself, although at a rather more technical and abstract level. (A brief historical outline of systemic linguistics is found in Halliday 1994.)

(1) Systemic grammatics is comprehensive in that it is not dedicated to any one branch of the study of language. It is not an "all-purpose" theory (there are tasks to which it is not well-suited, those requiring a high degree of idealization and formalism), but any particular investigation is validated as part of the general interpretation of language (just as, in grammar, any particular clause, as representation of experience, derives its meaning from the grammatical system as a whole).

(2) It is extravagant in that it is not constrained by a requirement of "simplicity"; there are always more resources available than are necessary for any one task, and what is locally simpler often turns out to be globally much more complex. It thus provides various ways for representing a grammar (as networks of options, as structures, as syntagms, etc.), just as a grammar provides various ways for representing experience.

(3) It is telescopic in that it views language historically – on three different dimensions: the evolution of each language as a system, the development of language by each human child, and the unfolding of language in each individual text (referred to as phylogenesis, ontogenesis and logogenesis).

(4) It is non-autonomous in that it is located within a general theory of semiotic (meaning-making) systems (and beyond that in a general systems typology); and makes reference to theory and practice in other areas where language is involved, such as literacy education and artificial intelligence.

(5) It is variable in that it accommodates considerable theoretical leeway; there is no notion of orthodoxy or "received" doctrine (it has its dialects and its registers: different modellings of the relation between semantics and grammar, of register and genre, of exchange structure in dialogue and so on).

(6) It is indeterminate in that its categories are typically fuzzy; the boundary between grammar and semantics is inherently blurry and

shifting: similarly the line between grammar and lexis (vocabulary), and between the system and the instance – just as in language itself, these all arise from the freedom of the observer to vary the perspective, to move around within the phenomena being observed.

One should not make too much of analogies of this kind. But in the present context, where natural language is itself being considered as metalanguage (for "intelligent computing"), it is relevant to examine not only (i) its own properties that enable it to function in this way (i.e. as a theory of human experience; cf. Part 2 above), but also (ii) how these properties are themselves recapitulated, in more general and abstract terms, in the grammatics (the "meta-metalanguage" – but still a form of natural language, even if partially designed!) that is used to theorize it.

I will look at just three procedures: (i) systemizing (modelling proportionality); (ii) networking (modelling delicacy); (iii) quantifying (modelling probability). Each of these is exploiting, at a technical level, resources that are an integral part of the semantics of natural language.

4.2 Systemizing: modelling proportionality in grammar

A language has often been represented as an inventory of syntactic structures: i.e. a closed, stable and well-formed set. But this is of little relevance to the way people talk and write. Instead we may represent a language as open-ended, variable and indeterminate: hence, not as batteries of structures but as dimensions of meaningful choice. The term used for any one such dimension of choice is **system**; by "systemizing" I mean what the grammatics (or rather, the grammarian) does in charting systems in a grammar.

Let us take a very simple example. We might say, "Every clause in English is either positive or negative"; e.g. *it's Tuesday / it isn't Tuesday*. We set this up as a system:

This states that there is a **proportionality** such that *it's Tuesday : it isn't Tuesday :: the baby's asleep : the baby isn't asleep :: I was laughing : I wasn't laughing :: have you been told? : haven't you been told? :: ...* The system is called "polarity" (the name we give to the choice); the terms (features) are "positive / negative"; and the entry condition is "clause" (i.e. all clauses must make this choice).

It is immediately obvious that such a statement is hedged around with massive indeterminacy. It raises innumerable questions about clauses such as (a) *nobody was laughing, you've never been told*, which seem to be both positive and negative; (b) *without telling you*, which seems to be neither; (c) *how do you do?*, which has no negative equivalent; (d) *it may be Tuesday*, which seems to be in between; and so on. What are the principles involved?

The essential principle is one of **compromise**. The grammatics compromises, in categorizing the grammar, in exactly the same way that the grammar compromises in categorizing experience: it looks both "from above" (at meaning, or function) and "from below" (at outward appearance, or form); compromising between the two – but with a slight bias towards the first, when the two conflict. Thus when we "decide" (without conscious reflection, of course) whether to refer to some object as a *car* or as a *bus*, we take account of its function (carrying private or public passengers) and also of its form (size, number of seats, etc.); and if the two conflict, the functional categorization tends to predominate (that is, in actual language use; if you ask subjects experimentally, forcing them to reflect consciously on the issue, they tend to shift priority on to the form). Similarly our grammatics looks at the grammar from these two opposite perspectives: "from above" (the **meaning** of the category), and "from below" (the **form** of the category). But here there is also a third perspective, "from round about" (taking account of other, related systems within the grammar itself). So, for example, in (a) *you've never been told*: looking from below, we find that the form makes it seem positive; but looking from above, functionally, it appears negative. (There is an internal contradiction between this clause and the meaning 'so now you know'.) Looking from the same level, we find that the natural question tag is positive: *you've never been told, have you?*; and since question tags typically reverse the polarity (*it's Tuesday, isn't it? / it isn't Tuesday, is it?*) we might be inclined to decide that the clause *you've never been told* is negative.

Thus the grammatics always adopts a **trinocular vision**, and systemizing involves continuing compromise. However, it would be wrong to imply that the overriding goal is to reach a definitive answer. Sometimes the criteria are clear: we find **typical** members of a category (now often referred to as "prototypical", but the meaning is the same) – and there are significantly many of these, so that the general notion of "category" is a valid one. But very often the criteria conflict; the boundaries of the system are indeterminate, so that what is "in" from one perspective will be "out" when seen from another. Here the question of category membership is simply undecidable; we have two (or more) alternative interpretations.

This then opens up the more significant question: what are the consequences of interpreting one way or the other? For example, it might be that the clause in question formed part of a chain of dialogic reasoning or problem solving, where one interpretation would be strongly foregrounded. In general, however, when an item has more than one "address" within the grammar, its meaning is a composite of them all.

Indeterminate categories of this kind may be in a state of transition, moving into or out of a particular grammatical system; for example, lexical items in process of being grammaticized, like *keep / go on* [*doing*] becoming durative phase in English (cf. the earlier *going to* [*do*] becoming secondary future tense). Such mixed lexical / grammatical status is not necessarily unstable, however; items can remain there indefinitely, exploiting the dual potential it provides (cf. semi-prepositions in English such as *concerning, owing to, on behalf of*). Thus "systemizing" does not mean forcing categorical decisions; it means setting up proportionalities which best reveal the latent meaning potential that is involved.

4.3 Networking: modelling "delicacy" (progressive differentiation)

Systems do not operate in isolation; they are associated in complex ways, shown in systemic grammatics as **system networks**. Consider the following examples:

> this is the best plan
> this is probably the best plan
> this is not the best plan
> this is probably not the best plan

We characterize these as a system network with **realizations** (see Figure 10.7). Suppose now we want to bring in the further alternatives:

> this is certainly (not) the best plan
> this is possibly (not) the best plan

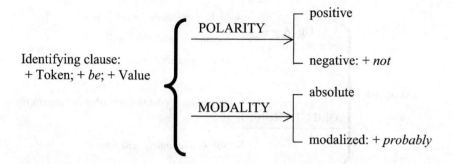

Figure 10.7

– we extend the network as in Figure 10.8. As this suggests, all features are open-ended in **delicacy** (that is, there are always further choices in meaning available).

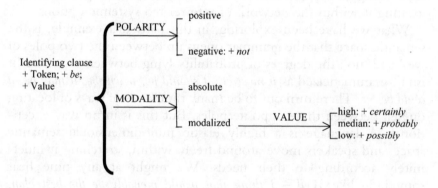

Figure 10.8

Suppose now we want to include *this must be / will be / may be* the best plan. These are structurally very different; functionally, however, they are closely related – they express the same three degrees of probability, but in a subjective rather than an objective form. We now have the picture as shown in Figure 10.9. Next, we might want to take account of:

I know that's the best plan
I think that's the best plan

and perhaps

I'm not certain that's the best plan

233

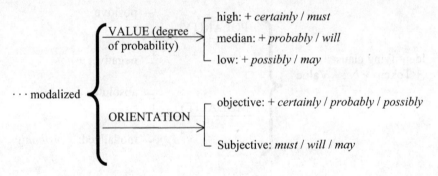

Figure 10.9

– where the subjectivity is made more explicit by the use of *I* (*I know*, etc.). Again, it does not matter that these are syntactically very distinct, provided the proportionalities are constant: each time, we are investigating a more delicate distinction within the grammar, and locating it within the network of interrelated systemic options.

What we have been exploring, in this particular example, is the semantic space that the grammar opens up between the two poles of 'yes' and 'no': the degrees of probability lying between 'it is' and 'it isn't', grammaticized as *it must be, it should be, it will be, it may be, it could be, . . .* There turn out to be many thousands of ways of locating oneself between these opposite poles. But this is in no way exceptional. A language is a highly elastic multidimensional semantic space, and speakers move around freely within, stretching it indefinitely according to their needs. We might at any time hear something like *Well – I think that would probably be the best plan, wouldn't it?* Our grammatics will represent this in the form of a **selection expression** showing what paths the speaker has chosen to follow through the network.

Figure 10.10 shows just a few more degrees of meaningful distinction. Note that all of these (and many more!) represent ordinary everyday usage in the language. The grammatical system is open, not closed; the complexity we are modelling is real – but, as the model shows, it results from the proportional intersection of a number of choices each of which, taken by itself, is in fact remarkably simple.

A system network models by progressive approximation. The principle is that of variable delicacy: there is no fixed endpoint where the grammar stops. Theoretically, every instance is different from every other instance – every token is a distinct type. The network allows the investigator to decide where to cut off. For example, the clause written as *perhaps that's the best plan* shows many hundreds, even thousands, of variations in meaning according to the intonation and rhythm; how many of these distinctions we choose to recognize will depend on the task in hand. (For documentation concerning the use of systemic models in natural language processing (text generation and parsing), see Matthiessen and Bateman 1992, Fawcett *et al.* 1993.)

4.4 Quantifying: modelling probability in grammar

The grammar of a natural language is characterized by overall quantitative tendencies. If we systemize some set of options, saying "if *a*, then choose either *x* or *y*" (e.g. "every clause is either positive or negative"), we imply "with a certain measure of probability attached to each". We can assign probabilities to the features in a network – provided we have some idea of what they are.

Quantitative analysis of a sample of about 1½ million clauses of English showed the following tendencies in the systems of polarity and type of "finiteness" (verbal deixis):

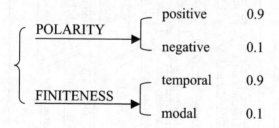

Assuming the two sets of probabilities are not associated, this would give the following prediction for any 1,000 clauses taken at random:

	positive	negative	total
temporal	810	90	900
modal	90	10	100
total	900	100	1000

We do not yet know much about the typical probability profiles of grammatical systems. It seems that some choices are roughly equally balanced, while others are decidedly skew; the latter (the skew) are

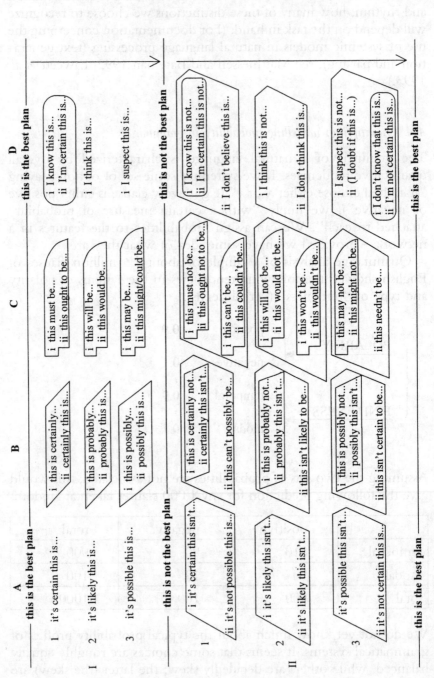

Figure 10.10 Note: Further distinctions within modality (see key to figure)

Key to Figure 10.10:

1   Columns: orientation and manifestation
      A   objective explicit
      B   objective implicit
      C   subjective implicit
      D   subjective explicit

2   Blocks: polarity
      I   positive
      II   negative

3   Rows: value
      1   high
      2   median
      3   low

4   ⬳ : thematization (in objective implicit)
      i   Subject as Theme
      ii   modality as Theme

5   ⬰ : Modal "tense" (in subjective implicit)
      i   neutral
      ii   oblique

6   ▭ : clause type (in subjective explicit)
      i   modality as mental process
      ii   modality as attribute

7   ⬯ : negation type (in negative)
      i   direct negative
      ii   transferred negative

likely to be those described qualitatively as having one term **unmarked**: e.g. in polarity, positive is the unmarked term. Now that we have access to large-scale corpuses of languages such as English, it will become possible, with the aid of parsing programs, to investigate the quantitative patterning displayed by the principal systems in the grammar. (See Halliday and James 1993/Chapter 6, this volume.)

The above refers to **global** probabilities. In any given context, however, these may be significantly perturbed. For instance, in the same sample the proportion of future tenses was found to be very low: only about one in twenty of the whole. But investigating the register of weather forecasting we found future tense as frequent as the sum of past and present together. Thus the **local** probabilities, for a given situation type, may differ significantly from the global ones.

I remarked above that it is this "resetting" of probabilities that characterizes functional (register) variation in language. This is how people recognize the "context of situation" of a text. It is useful therefore to be able to model the grammar in probabilistic terms.

Once again the grammatics appears as a copy of the grammar. In section 4.3 we saw how the grammar opens up the semantic space between 'it is' and 'it isn't', providing a rich resource whereby speakers express their ongoing construal of experience. Just as the grammar models features of reality as 'more or less likely', so the grammatics models features of grammar in similar fashion. But this is not surprising, since "probability" as a theoretical construct is just the technicalizing of "modality" from everyday grammar. It is in daily life that we learn to model reality in tendencies rather than in categorical terms. This general principle, whereby our most abstract meanings have their origin in the grammar of daily life, is what makes it possible for natural language to function as metalanguage. It is doing so all the time.

Notes

1. 'Fuzzy grammatics: a systemic functional approach to fuzziness in natural language' in the Proceedings of FUZZ-IEEE/IFES '95 (International Joint Conference of the Fourth IEEE International Conference on Fuzzy Systems and the Second International Fuzzy Engineering Symposium, Yokohama, 20–24 March 1995).
2. The point is an important one. If information was simply communicated by language (instead of being created by language), language would not have the power to function as a basis for intelligent computing (cf. Ellis 1993).

Chapter Eleven

COMPUTING MEANINGS: SOME REFLECTIONS ON PAST EXPERIENCE AND PRESENT PROSPECTS (1995)

It is the privilege of an old person to be allowed to look back in time – even perhaps in a context such as this, when addressing specialists in computing. Computing is, after all, one of the most future-oriented of all present-day human activities! But it happens to be just forty years since I had my first encounter with computational linguistics. This was in an early project in machine translation, which was the main purpose that was envisaged for linguistic computing at the time. I was Assistant Lecturer in Chinese at Cambridge; and I was delighted at being asked to be a member of the Cambridge Language Research Unit, along with Margaret Masterman, who directed it, R. H. Richens, plant geneticist, and A. F. Parker-Rhodes, whose extensive interests ranged from botany to mathematical statistics. That was a fairly brief excursion, since I left Cambridge shortly afterwards; but since then I have had further encounters from time to time, as the field of linguistic computing has developed and expanded to its present high-energy state. Of these the most notable, for me, were the times I spent working with Sydney Lamb, first at Berkeley then at Yale, in the 1960s, and then later, in the 1980s, working with William Mann and his group at the Information Sciences Institute of the University of Southern California.

Looking back over this period, I seem to see a change of direction taking place roughly every fifteen years. The first turning point, of course, was the idea of computing with language at all; we can date this in round figures from 1950, when the idea of using a computer to translate from one language to another began to be taken seriously. The approach was essentially mathematical, in that machine

239

translation was seen as a problem to be solved by applying to language the same logical methods that had gone into the design of the computer itself. There was, at least among mainstream researchers, no serious concern with language as a distinct type of phenomenon, one which might need to be investigated theoretically in terms of its own systemic traits.

Then in and around the mid-1960s a significant transformation took place. Language came more sharply into focus; it began to be treated as a phenomenon *sui generis*, with linguistics replacing logic as the theoretical point of departure from which to engage with it. In Russia, and perhaps in Japan, this transformation was fairly gradual; but in North America and western Europe it was more catastrophic, because 1965 was the year in which the US Air Force officially pronounced machine translation a failure and withdrew the funding from the major translation projects. American researchers who continued computing with language carried on their activities under other headings; taking over "artificial intelligence" as a unifying concept, they addressed some more specific computational tasks that were not tied directly to translating, such as parsing, abstracting, question-answering or expert systems and the like. Terry Winograd's major contribution *Understanding Natural Language* belongs to this time; so does the earliest work in computing our own system networks (forming paradigms, implementing realizations and so on) which was done by Alick Henrici at University College London (see Winograd 1972; Henrici 1966 [Halliday and Martin 1981]).

The third turning point came around 1980, when a new generation of computers made it possible to build systems that approached somewhat closer the complexity of natural language. Computational linguists now had at their disposal the necessary speed, memory and processing power that made parsing and generating look like more realistic goals. Before that time, computational grammars had remained fairly simple: limited to "toy" domains, syntactically constrained, and accommodating only rather gross distinctions in meaning; whereas one could now begin to conceive of "writing the grammar of a natural language in computable form", with account taken of considerations from linguistic theory. For linguists this meant that the computer now became, for the first time, a tool for linguistic research, a means of finding out new things about language: it made it possible on the one hand to test grammatical descriptions (which were becoming too complex to be tested manually) and on the other hand to build a large-scale corpus – not only to assemble and manage it but to access it and interrogate it from many different angles. Two very large systemic grammars of English for text generation were developed during this period: the Penman "Nigel" grammar built up by Christian Matthiessen under William Mann's direction at I.S.I., and the "Communal" grammar compiled by Robin Fawcett at the University of Wales (Matthiessen and Bateman 1992; Fawcett *et al.* 1993).

Fifteen years from 1980 brings us up to 1995; so are we now moving through another turning point? I suspect we may be, in that the status of language – that is, its general relationship to computing – is once again undergoing a major shift. It seems that language is being relocated at the very centre of the computing process itself. In order to explore this further, I would like to refer explicitly to the notion of "computing meanings" that I used in the title of my talk. But first let me say what I do not mean. I am not referring here to the rather overworked concept of the "information society". It is no doubt true, as we have been being told for the past two decades, that the exchange of goods-&-services is rapidly being overtaken by the exchange of information as the dominant mode of socio-economic activity; and this is certainly relevant, since information is prototypically made of language. But it is relevant as the **context** of the change I am referring to; it is not the nature of the change itself. What I have in mind is what Professor Sugeno calls "intelligent computing", which he defines as computing that is based on natural language. In Sugeno's view, if we want to move forward to the point where the computer becomes truly intelligent, we have to make it function, as people do, through the medium of language. And this critically alters the relationship of language to computing.

Let me then briefly return to the past, and use the concept of "computing meanings" to track the shifting relationship between the two. In the 1950s, there was no direct engagement between them at all; it was taken for granted that translating meant selecting from lists of possible formal equivalents – that it was an engineering job, in other words. The prevailing metaphor was that of a code: as Warren Weaver conceived of it, a Russian text was simply an English text with different coding conventions. There was no conception of language as the systemic resources that lay behind a text; hence no need to construct any kind of theoretical model of language. This is not to imply that nothing of value was achieved; on the contrary, there was a great deal of essential analytical work, especially in lexis and morphology: see for example Delavenay's

(1960) *Introduction to Machine Translation*. But meaning was taken as given, rather than problematized; this was not yet "computing with meanings".

In the second phase, language emerged as a computable object, needing to be modelled in its own right; the concept of "a grammar", a description of a language as written by a linguist, came to be accepted – or at least tolerated as a necessary nuisance. But such a descriptive grammar had no direct place in the computing process; the computational grammar was purely procedural, a program for parsing strings of words. (There was little text generation during this phase; one of the few such projects was the systemic generator developed in Edinburgh by Anthony Davey (1978).) On the other hand, as implied by the label "computational linguistics" which came into favour during this period, these were computing operations performed on language; the way the strings of words were manipulated was designed to establish what they meant. There had clearly been a move in the direction of computing with meanings.

It was in the third phase, after about 1980, that developments took place which the phrase "computing with meanings" could more accurately describe. By this time computational grammars came to take the form of descriptive, or "declarative", representations, and researchers sought to develop generalized forms of representation suited to their computational needs. It was accepted that these had to accommodate large-scale grammars with reasonable detail and complexity, not just the dedicated and simplified grammars of the earlier phase. The move from procedural to declarative, and the shift in scale and in depth of focus, changed the relationship once again: the value of a piece of wording was, for the first time, being interpreted in terms of *agnation*, its locus in the total meaning potential of the language. It would seem accurate now to characterize computational linguistic operations as operations on meaning.

Perhaps I could gloss this with a story from personal experience. Back in the 1960s, the working assumption was, "If we can't compute your grammar, your grammar must be wrong". This was not, let me make it clear, arrogance on the part of individual computer specialists; simply a conviction that the computer defined the parameters of human understanding. To me it seemed that the constraints set by current technology, and even more those set by current theories of logic, at that particular moment in human history, were quite irrelevant for evaluating models of grammar; this was the main reason why I moved away from the scene, for the second and (as I thought) the final time. So when in 1980 William Mann came to see me – I was working at U.C. Irvine – and asked me to write a systemic grammar of English for his forthcoming text generation project (the "Penman" I mentioned earlier), I challenged him on this point: how much would I have to "simplify" (that is, distort) the grammar in order to make it computable? Bill Mann's answer was, "If I can't compute your grammar, I'll have to learn how". He later added an interesting comment: "I don't always understand why linguists describe things the way they do; but I've come to realize they always have a reason". It was clear then that the relationship of language to computing had moved on.

There is a serious point underlying this little anecdote. Of course we, as grammarians, had to learn to write our descriptions in computable form: that is, to make them fully explicit. This was an important exercise, from which we learnt a great deal. But to make them explicit is not the same demand as to make them **simple**. Language is not simple; it is ferociously complex – perhaps the single most complex phenomenon in nature; and at least some of that complexity had to be accounted for. To take just one example: what was referred to under the general label "constituency" is not a single, undifferentiated type of structure (like a "tree"), but a highly variable array of different meaning-making resources, with highly complex interrelations among them. Unfortunately the linguists themselves had made the problem worse: the prevailing ideology, at least in America, but also perhaps in western Europe and in Japan, was the structuralist one deriving out of Bloomfield via Chomsky; and this was highly reductionist, in that, in order for natural language to be represented as a formal system, much of the rich variation in meaning had to be idealized out of the picture. But not only was it reductionist – it was also authoritarian: for linguists of this persuasion, the standard response to anyone who disagreed with them was, "Either your grammar is a notational variant of my grammar, or else your grammar is wrong". So computer scientists who ventured across the frontier into linguistics, in that second phase, might reasonably conclude that a natural language could be modelled as a well-formed system conforming to a recognizable mathematical-type logic. This period in mainstream linguistics was an age of syntax, in which a grammar could be reduced to an inventory of well-defined structural forms.

But by the time of what I am calling the third phase, the

orientation of linguistics had changed. Much more attention was now being paid to semantics, both by linguists working from within the Chomskyan paradigm and by those who had remained outside it. Thus the concept of "computational linguistics" already implied something closer to "computing meanings"; it implied a system that fully engaged with natural language, parsing and generating text in operational contexts. Machine translation once again figured prominently on the agenda, as the four components of a speech-to-speech translation program fell into place: recognition + parsing + generation + synthesis were all seen to be possible, and such systems now began to appear on the market – not perhaps doing all that was claimed for them, but performing adequately for a limited range of tasks. The general encompassing term was now "natural language processing".

But these continue to appear as two distinct activities: computing, and language processing. There is still the awkward disjunction between computing in general, and meaning. Computational linguistics, or natural language processing, or generation and parsing, are separate operations from computing in the general sense. And this has some strange consequences. I recently visited Japan, to attend the international conference on fuzzy systems chaired by Professor Sugeno. There were many interesting exhibits, from industry and also from LIFE, the Laboratory for International Fuzzy Engineering, which was just coming to the end of its own life cycle. One of the latter was FLINS, the Fuzzy Natural Language Communication System; this was a question-answering system incorporating an inference engine, which reasoned by taking the special case, assigning it to a general class and inferring a course of action therefrom. One very interesting feature of this system was the use of traditional proverbs to state the general proposition – this being precisely the function that proverbs had in our traditional societies. (My grandmother had a proverb for every occasion.) But what struck me particularly was that their inferencing procedures, which involved both symbolic and fuzzy matching, were totally insulated from their language processing; they had simply bought ready-made commercial systems for parsing and generating text. In other words, reasoning and inferencing were being treated as non-linguistic operations – although they were being entirely carried out through the medium of language. Notice what this implies: that there is no semantic relationship – no systematic relationship in meaning – between, say, the proverbial expression *more haste less speed* and (the verbal component of) an instance to which it relates as a general proposition, for example *Don't be in a hurry to overtake; it only slows you down. More haste less speed!*

This seems to be a scenario in which linguistics and computing inhabit two different worlds. Natural language is being seen as something to be separately processed, rather than as an inherent part of the computing process itself. And this is the difference, it seems to me, between the third phase and the subsequent fourth phase which we may now be entering. With "intelligent computing", the boundary between computing in general and natural language processing rather disappears: all computing could involve operating with natural language. Computing then becomes synonymous with computing meanings.

"Intelligent computing" is an important concept which could have very far-reaching consequences; so I would like to consider it here in a little more detail. As I mentioned earlier, Sugeno defines this as computing based on natural language; he also sometimes expresses it in simplified terms as "computing with words". Lotfi Zadeh, the founder of "fuzzy logic", used this same formulation in his talk at the conference, remarking that computing with words "enhances the ability of machines to mimic the human mind, and points to a flaw in the foundations of science and engineering". He also observed that, while human reasoning is "overwhelmingly expressed through the medium of words", people are only taught to compute with numbers – they are never taught how to compute with words. Commenting on the formulation "computing with words", Zadeh glossed "computing" as "computing and reasoning", and "words" as "strings of words, not very small".

We need to reformulate that last expression, in two steps as follows:

(1) for *words* (or *strings of words*), read *wordings*: words in grammatical structures, i.e. lexicogrammatical strings of any extent;
(2) for *wordings*, in turn, read *meanings*, again in the technical sense; that is, semantic sequences of any given extent.

Note that, in reformulating in this way, we are not questioning Sugeno's concept; we are recasting it in terms of semiotic practice. People reason and infer with **meanings**, not with wordings. (They don't store wordings, as is easily demonstrated when they repeat the steps along the way.) To put this in more technical terms: reasoning and inferencing are semantic operations.

Thus, if they are performed computationally, this will be done on semantic representations. But, at the same time, such semantic representations are related systemically to the lexicogrammatical ones. In other words, the meanings are **construed** in wordings. When people reason through talk, they are actually reasoning with **meanings**; but these meanings are not a separate "cognitive" universe of concepts or ideas – they are patterns of semantic (that is, linguistic) organization brought about, or "realized", by the wordings. They are reasoning in language, even though not, strictly speaking, in words.

There are in fact two noticeable disjunctions needing to be overcome, in the move into the intelligent computing phase. One is this one between language and knowledge, or rather between meaning and knowing, or meaning and thinking. Natural language processing systems typically operate with one kind of representation for language, a "grammar", and another, very different kind of representation for knowledge – a separate "knowledge base"; and the two different representations have then to be made to interact (see Figure 11.1). If we reconceptualize the knowledge base as a *meaning base* – as another level in the representation of language – the problem becomes more easily manageable: instead of two systems, one inside language and one outside (the grammatical and the conceptual), there is only one system, language, with two levels of representation, the grammatical (lexicogrammatical) and the semantic (see Figure 11.2) (cf. Halliday and Matthiessen 1999, 2000).

The second disjunction I have in mind is that between the *instance* and the *system* of which it is an instance. The grammar of a natural language is represented systematically: **either** conventionally, as a set of structures, **or**, in a systemic grammar, as a network of options – language as semiotic potential. On the other hand, reasoning and inferencing are operations performed on (representations

[cognitive]	knowledge	base
[linguistic]	grammar	discourse
	[linguistic]	[pragmatic]

Figure 11.1 The cognitive model

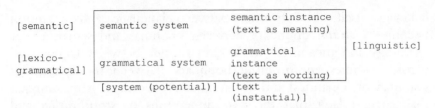

Figure 11.2 The semantic model

of) *instances*. Now, any instance is meaningful only by virtue of its **place** in, and its derivation from, the total *systemic potential*. But in computational reasoning and inferencing, the instances are typically presented as unrelated to the overall system of the language. They are handled as "discourse", with the implication that discourse is process, without any system behind it. If we reconceptualize discourse as "text" – as the instantiation of an underlying system – the problem of reasoning and inferencing may also become more easily manageable.

Each of these disjunctions corresponds to a major duality in Western thinking, enshrined in contemporary philosophy and philosophical linguistics. The first is the duality between language and mind, which is institutionalized in today's dichotomy between linguistics and cognitive science; the second is the duality of langue and parole, which in turn is institutionalized in today's dichotomy between linguistics and pragmatics. (See Ellis 1993, esp. chapter 5, and Matthiessen 1993, 1998 for relevant discussions.) These dualities are taken over into our intellectual pursuits – such as computational linguistics – without being problematized or even brought to conscious attention. But there are alternative strategies available, as I have remarked. Instead of two systems, one inside language (the grammatical) and one outside language (the conceptual, or cognitive), it is possible to operate with one system, language, having two related levels of representation, the (lexico)grammatical and the semantic; and instead of two classes of phenomena, one of langue (grammar) and one of parole (discourse), it is possible to operate with one phenomenon, language, having two degrees or phases of instantiation, that of system and that of text. The "knowledge base" becomes a "meaning base", which can then be described in a framework that is homologous to the grammar; and each instance of wording or meaning can be described by reference to the overall potential of the system.

In this way the boundaries are redrawn as boundaries within

language itself. The frontier between language and cognition becomes a **stratal** boundary between grammar and semantics, or wordings and meanings; while the frontier between langue and parole becomes an **instantial** boundary between the system (of grammar or semantics) and the instance (of wording or meaning). I shall suggest later that the two dimensions of **stratification** and **instantiation** can be used to define a matrix for locating computational linguistic representations. Meanwhile, a consequence of redrawing these frontiers as boundaries internal to language is that both of them become indeterminate, or "fuzzy". Since they are theoretical constructs for explaining, and managing, what is now being conceived of as a single unified semiotic system, namely language, this is not really surprising. But they are fuzzy in different ways.

Instantiation is a cline, modelling the shift in the standpoint of the observer: what we call the "system" is language seen from a distance, as semiotic potential, while what we call "text" is language seen from close up, as instances derived from that potential. In other words, there is only one phenomenon here, not two; langue and parole are simply different observational positions. But we can also position ourselves at an intermediate point along this cline, moving in from one end or from the other. I think that the critical intermediate concept, for our purposes, is that of **register**, which enables us to model contextual variation in language. Seen from the instantial end of the cline, a register appears as a cluster of similar texts, a **text type**; whereas seen from the systemic end, a register appears as a **sub-system**. Computationally it is possible to exploit these two complementary perspectives (see Figure 11.3).

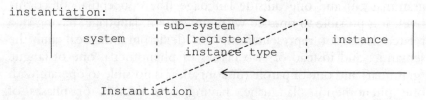

Figure 11.3 Instantiation

Stratification is a relationship of a different kind. The boundary between semantics and grammar is a true boundary; these are two distinct levels, or **strata**, within the content plane of natural language, and they have different realms of **agnation** – that is, the organization of grammatical space differs from the organization of semantic space (Martin and Matthiessen 1991). But we can draw this boundary at different places, shifting it "up or down" according to the task in hand. Furthermore, having defined the relationship between semantics and grammar in this way, we are then able to extend the same concept (known as *realization*) so as to model the relationship of language to the context of situation, interpreting the context also as a semiotic system (see Figure 11.4). Thus by deconstructing the two dualities and overcoming the disjunctions they set up, we gain additional freedom of movement on both the dimensions involved.

```
stratification:
                    context   [culture — situations]
                    semantics [semantic system  —  meanings]
                    -----------------------------------------------------
                    lexicogrammar [grammatical system — wordings]
```

Figure 11.4 Stratification

How is this relevant to the issue of "intelligent computing"? This concept, as defined by Sugeno and by Zadeh, involves using natural language as the "language" of the computer: natural language as the computational metalanguage. But this inevitably raises questions of representation. It is sometimes forgotten that the orthographic system of every (written) language already involves a large number of highly complex decisions about meaning – what meanings are to be distinguished, how they are to be interrelated, and so on; to take a very clear example, in the English writing system, if a semantic contrast is realized by the order of elements it will be registered in writing (*you can go / can you go*), whereas if it is realized by intonation or rhythm it is not (thus *you can go* represents a wide range of different kinds and degrees of emphasis, different modalities and so on). Since these decisions were taken a long time ago, without conscious reflection, we tend simply to forget about them; but the differences in meaning that are obscured in this way could be critical to the computational process. Even if we have a speech–recognition system which can accept spoken input, however, this does not eliminate the problem. Using natural language as metalanguage does not mean plucking isolated instances out of the air, as can be done with simple command control or question-answering systems. It means locating each instance within a defined realm of meaning potential, from which it derives its value in the given computational context – in other words, relating the instance to the system, or to some specified register or subsystem; and this requires engaging with the language in theoretical terms. We cannot just take language for granted as something we know all about in terms of common sense (which usually means, in practice, in terms of how our teachers used to talk about language in primary school). Intelligent computing will make stringent demands on the full range of complexity of natural languages; otherwise they would be of little use for the purpose. Therefore, it will require theoretical tools for describing and managing that complexity.

In other words, it will require what I have been calling a *grammatics*: a model of language which uses grammar as its underlying logic. Let me recall here Zadeh's reference to the "flaw in the foundations of science and engineering", and ask what Zadeh meant by this remark. The flaw, as Zadeh saw it, was that mathematics ruled, and that events were "quantized rather than granular": features that were characteristic of what he called "hard computing". We were now moving into an era of "soft computing", in imitation of human thinking which is "granular", a granule being defined as "a group of points with a fuzzy boundary". In other terms, "computational intelligence" (the analysis and design of intelligent systems, human-like in that they are based on approximate reasoning) takes over from "artificial intelligence" (which Zadeh characterized as analysis and design of physical systems); just as, in the industrial revolution, machine power augmented and transformed human muscular strength, so in the information revolution machine intelligence augments and transforms the power of the human brain (Zadeh 1995). Terano observed, in the same context (1995), that there is no mathematical model for macroscopic information processing; it is too "ill-structured". What then replaces mathematics in this new context? – the answer has to be, I think, **grammar**. When language comes to function not just as the **object** of computing but as its **instrument**, the intellectual foundation may have to shift, from mathematical logic to grammatical logic. Mathematics and grammar are both semiotic systems; but they constitute different, and in a sense complementary, kinds of logic: the logic of numbers and the logic of wordings and meanings – linguistic logic, in Sugeno's formulation.

As mathematics enables us to manage the complexity of numbers, so the grammatics enables us to manage the complexity of language. (And also, perhaps, to celebrate it! – we are often reminded of the aesthetic appeal of mathematics, but the aesthetic appeal of grammar has scarcely begun to be recognized, though it is certainly no less than that of numbers.) This means theorizing about language with an orientation towards working systems, in data fusion, contextual simulation and other such operations; not only mapping out the complexity but finding ways of ordering and operationalizing it. If I was seeking a research grant, I might dream up a "total language complexity management system".

In fact, of course, it will not be total; there are aspects of the complexity of language which we must be able to ignore, as irrelevant to the tasks in hand. So what are the aspects of linguistic complexity that do need to be taken into account, in practice, if one is computing with natural language? Here is a first guess, very tentative, in summary form. The first five points have been discussed already; the sixth and seventh remain to be explained.

1 *words* function by being organized into *wordings* (lexicogrammatical patterns);
2 *wordings*, in turn, construct semantic patterns, or *meanings*;
3 *meanings* relate systematically to features of the *context*;
4 particular *instances* of wording / meaning derive their value from their place in the *system* (relationships within the system network, or *agnation*);
5 the *system* accommodates *sub-systemic variation* (variation in *register*);
6 the *system* is organized *metafunctionally* (into zones of semantic space, which determine both the form of the grammar and its relationship to the context);
7 *meaning* involves three dimensions of history: *evolution* of the system, *unfolding* of the individual text, *development* of the human infant into adulthood (phylogenesis, logogenesis, ontogenesis).

I shall first discuss point no. 6; then, on the basis of 1–6, suggest a possible architecture for a linguistic module that might be used in intelligent computing. Finally I shall return to point no. 7, adding one further dimension to the total picture.

Let me return briefly to the notion of lexicogrammar (which we usually refer to simply as "grammar", for short). A grammar is a purely abstract semiotic construct that evolves as a distinct level, or *stratum*, in between the content and the expression; by "purely abstract" I mean that it has no direct interface with material phenomena (whereas the "lower" stratum, that of spoken or written expression, interfaces with the human body, and the "higher" stratum of the content, that of semantics, interfaces with human experience and human social processes). A stratified system of this kind – one with a grammar in it – has the special property that it can *constitute*; unlike simple sign systems, which reflect meanings that are already given, a stratified system **creates** meaning. It creates meaning, of course, in contexts of function; and because the meanings are then non-randomly related to features of these contexts, it can also create the contexts themselves.

The functional contexts of language fall into two major types; and the semiotic function that language is performing differs as between the two (see Table 11.1). On the one hand, language constitutes human experience; and in this aspect, its function is to *construe*: language **imposes order on** the world that lies around us, and that is located within ourselves. On the other hand, language constitutes human relationships; and in this aspect, its function is not to construe but to *enact*: language **brings about** our ongoing social interaction. The grammar integrates these two modes of meaning in such a way that every *instance* – everything we say or write, listen to or read – "means" in these two ways at once. These major functional types are referred to in systemic theory as *metafunctions*.

Table 11.1 The metafunctional components of meaning

metafunction	gloss
ideational:	construing experience (the "knowledge base")
experiential	construing categories
logical	construing relations among categories
interpersonal	enacting personal and social relationships (the "action base")
textual	creating flow of meaning (the "text, or discourse, base")

This interdependence of the two metafunctions, the *experiential* (or *ideational*, to give it its more inclusive name) and the *interpersonal*, has been central to the evolution of language, and to its persistence as a metastable system, constantly changing in interaction with its environment. The ideational mode of meaning comes closest to "meaning" in the everyday sense of the term ('content', especially 'referential content'). It is language as the **categorizing** and logical **construing of human experience**: that is, language taking over the material processes and conditions of human existence and transforming them into meanings. We usually become aware of this semiotic transformation only when we consider designed scientific or technical knowledge, where we have a clear sense of the semiotic energy involved (for example in writing a theoretical discussion such as the present one!). But all knowledge is like this. To "know" anything is to have transformed it into meaning; and what we call "understanding" is the process of that semiotic transformation.

The integration, by the grammar, of ideational and interpersonal meanings calls into being a third functional component, the *textual* metafunction, which creates a flow of meanings, a semiotic current by which the other components are activated in conjunction. We refer to this process, or more often to its output, by the name of "discourse". In commonsense terms, what makes it possible for humans to develop and use language, in the contexts of daily life, is that every linguistic act (every *act of meaning*) involves both talking about the world and acting upon those who are in it; and that this conjunction is achieved by creating a semiotic flow of events that parallels, and in some respects mimics, the material flow which constitutes its environment.

By a "linguistic module" for intelligent computing, I mean an operational map of the terrain, such that any step in the process of computing meanings can be located and defined within an overall theoretical framework. Such a module could be initially constructed as a simple matrix intersecting stratification and instantiation. For the purpose of illustration, I shall ignore the expression plane, and consider just the strata of lexicogrammar, semantics and context. On the instantiation cline, I shall include just the one intermediate category of "sub-system / type". This gives a framework consisting of nine cells, but with those of the centre column represented in two aspects (see Table 11.2).

Each of the nine cells defined in this way is in turn occupied by a structure of an analogous kind. If we take as prototypical the bottom left-hand cell (column "system", row "lexicogrammar", i.e. the lexicogrammatical system), this structure takes the form of another matrix, this time with the vectors of metafunction and rank. The metafunctions are common to semantics and grammar; shown here in their grammatical "order" (logical; experiential, interpersonal,

Table 11.2 Instantiation / stratification matrix

STRATI-FICATION \ INSTANTIATION	system	sub-system / instance type	instance
context	culture	institution / situation type	situations
semantics	semantic system	register / text type	[text as] meanings
lexico-grammar	grammatical system	register / text type	[text as] wordings

textual). The ranks are the structural units of the grammar (clause, phrase, group, word; each with its associated complex – clause complex, etc.).

The form of entry, in each cell of this inner matrix, is that of a system network. What this means is that the grammatical system of the given language is represented **paradigmatically**, in the form of a network of options, or alternative possibilities: either positive or negative, either past or present or future, either indicative or imperative, and so on; each set of options accompanied by its real-izations. The grammar is thus presented synoptically, as a resource. Operationally, the activity of meaning consists in tracing paths through this network; either "left to right", in the case of produc-tion (speaking or writing), or "right to left" in the case of under-standing (listening or reading). The network is open-ended: the more we know, or find out, about the grammar, the further we can extend it in delicacy, or depth of detail. Current systemic grammars of English in computational form have about a thousand sets of options (**systems**, in the technical sense).

The form taken by these inner matrices – the vectors involved, and the representational mode – will differ from one to another of the cells of the outer matrix. Table 11.3 gives a sketch of the overall organization of the content. Despite the architectural metaphor, and the solid lines separating the rows and the columns, this is not a building with rigid walls and floors; it is a multidimensional elastic space, within which are constituted the whole of human experience and social processes.

The left-hand middle cell is the semantic system. This we are not

Table 11.3 Instantiation / stratification matrix, with glosses

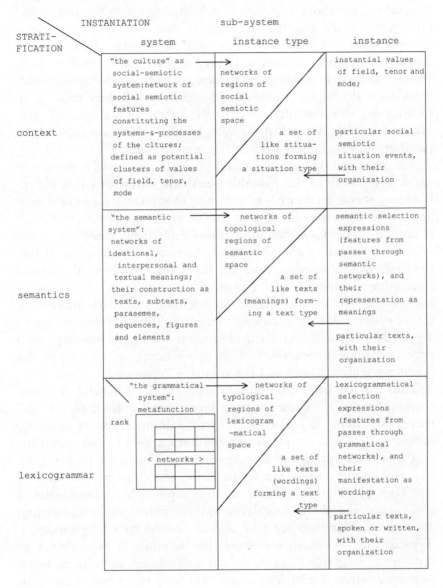

| | INSTANIATION | sub-system | |
STRATI-FICATION	system	instance type	instance
context	"the culture" as social-semiotic system:network of social semiotic features constituting the systems-&-processes of the cltures; defined as potential clusters of values of field, tenor, mode	networks of regions of social semiotic space ⟶ a set of like stitua-tions forming a situation type	instantial values of field, tenor and mode; particular social semiotic situation events, with their organization
semantics	"the semantic system": networks of ideational, interpersonal and textual meanings; their construction as texts, subtexts, parasemes, sequences, figures and elements	networks of topological regions of semantic space ⟶ a set of like texts (meanings) form-ing a text type	semantic selection expressions (features from passes through semantic networks), and their representation as meanings particular texts, with their organization
lexicogrammar	"the grammatical system": metafunction — rank — < networks >	networks of typological regions of lexicogram-matical space ⟶ a set of like texts (wordings) forming a text type	lexicogrammatical selection expressions (features from passes through grammatical networks), and their manifestation as wordings particular texts, spoken or written, with their organization

255

yet capable of modelling as a whole; we can, however, specify its internal organization, which is closely analogous to the function / rank matrix of the grammar but with its own distinctive categories – a "rank scale" of structural units such as, possibly, text, subtext, semantic paragraph, sequence, figure, element; and metafunctional regions defined in topological fashion, construing the activity patterns and ideological motifs of the culture (clusters relating to technology, to social hierarchy, to the sphere of activities of daily life, and so on). As with the lexicogrammar, these are represented paradigmatically, as networks of "meaning potential".

The left-hand upper cell is taken up with contextual networks: it contains a theory of the **possible semiotic situations** that collectively constitute a culture – taxonomies of institutions and of doings and happenings, manifested as possible clusterings of values of field, tenor and mode. Consider as an example the generalized institution of professionalism, with (as field) the thematic systems of medicine, the law, technical education and the like; (as tenor) the paired interactive processes involving professional and client, such as doctor and patient, lawyer and client, teacher and student; (as mode) the mixed patterns of spoken and written communication that constitute a professional exchange. Such clusterings are highly solidary, with strong coupling among the various components; in other cases, the couplings will be looser and less mutually constrained.

Thus the left-hand column as a whole is the *potential*: the total semiotic resources of the culture, represented systemically as networks. Stratifying it – sorting it out into doings (level of context), meanings (level of semantics) and wordings (level of lexicogrammar) – is a way of managing its complexity: splitting up meaning by dispersing it into a spectrum, to use Firth's metaphor from forty years ago (1957b). The right-hand column represents the *instantial*: a particular event (doing) involving some linguistic activity (meaning / wording). Here too we take account of the stratal organization. Typically in computational work the wording is represented in ordinary orthography; this has served well enough up to now, but it imposes arbitrary constraints which may need to be overcome. (For example, for input to a speech synthesizer the wording needs to include information concerning intonation and rhythm.) Semantic representations of the instance – the instance as meaning – are still quite unsatisfactory, and there is much work to be done in this respect. Likewise for the instantial *situation*: we tend to work with informal word-pictures, like the stage directions in the printed edition of a play; but the basic concept of situation as instance has advanced very little in recent decades. The sense of "context" is usually taken to include the situation **before** (and sometimes also **after**) what is selected as the instance of meaning / wording, on the grounds that, while we can "freeze" instances over as many frames as we like, there will always be a precursor and a sequel; and this is also taken to include the "co-text", the **text** preceding and following that which is under focus. (Note that the *instance* is the event itself. We may have a **record** of it, say on video, and then a replay or performance of it; but then the performance itself becomes the substantive event, the "original" being now an event of the second order.)

It may be helpful to distinguish recording from describing. When we **describe** an instance, we relate it across the row from right to left: that is, to our representation of the *system* at that stratum. This is a theoretical operation, different from the sort of running commentary that is sometimes offered by way of description. The form taken by such a description, in a systemic grammar, is called a "selection expression"; this states which of the features in the system network have been selected in the instance in question. The selection expression thus gives an account of the total *agnation* of the instance – how it relates to other possible instances. This is based on the *paradigmatic* principle, referred to earlier: the significance of a semiotic event lies in what it might have been, but was not.

Let me introduce here some snatches of a constructed text, in order to illustrate some of the points being raised. Items [in square brackets] represent "doings"; other text represents wordings; the interactants are a driving instructor and her pupil.

[Driving instructor and pupil in car; on public roads, in urban traffic; pupil driving]

[Pupil takes corner rather too fast]
Instr: You should have braked before turning. O.k.; go left here.
[Pupil again takes corner too fast]
Instr: Now what did I tell you just now?
Pupil: Sorry! You said I had to slow down at corners.

[Bus pulls out in front]
Instr: Brake!!
[Pupil stops car]

[On three-lane highway; pupil repeatedly changes lanes]
Instr: Don't be in a hurry to overtake; it'll only slow you down.
  More haste less speed!

[Bus appears from cross street; pupil swerves and misses it]
Instr: Why didn't you brake?
[Pupil slows down and draws into kerb]
Instr: You can't stop here – go on!
Pupil: But you told me to stop the car!

Consider for example the urgent command *Brake!!* This is a piece of wording, in orthographic representation; its locus is in the right-hand bottom corner cell. Moving up the column, we might give it a semantic representation along these lines: 'you = learner / listener = responsible person / agent + cause / stop + car + I insist'. Moving up to the top row, we might characterize the situation as: (preceding situation) [pupil driving, instructor sitting beside; a bus crosses in front]; (following situation) [pupil hits foot brake; car slows and stops]. Starting again from the instance of wording *Brake!!*, but now moving across the row to the left-hand column, we map the traversal in the form of a selection expression showing that this piece of wording realizes the following features, among others: (clause:) polarity: positive; mood: imperative: jussive; process type: material: action; voice: middle; (verbal group:) finiteness: non-finite; tense: neutral, and so on – the number of features depending on the **delicacy** (depth in detail) of our grammatics. The left-hand bottom cell itself, as already remarked, is the locus of (our representation of) the lexicogrammatical system as a whole.

The situation, in any given instance, will be one of a set of similar situations, constituting a "situation type". Of course, all such sets are fuzzy; we determine their boundaries according to the task in hand, assigning some "membership function" to non-core, borderline cases: if the situation type is characterized as "driving lessons", such a peripheral instance might be one where the trainee is learning to drive a bus, or a train, where the instructor is an amateur rather than a professional, and so on. Likewise, the text, in any given instance, will be one of a set of similar texts – we refer to it as a "text type". Such "types" share common features; this is what enables us to make predictions in the way we do all the time in daily life, both from the text to the situation and from the situation to the text.

Descriptively, the type is the instantial manifestation of a sub-system, shown in our middle column in Table 11.2 as **register**. A "sub- system" is a complex category, not definable as a subset. It is not simply the full system network with some of its arteries sealed off. Some systemic options may be effectively ruled out, especially at the level of context; people do not mix up their patterns of cultural activity – or if they do (if, for example, the instructor and the pupil start playing chess in the middle of the driving lesson), this **constitutes** a change of register. But semantically, and even more lexicogrammatically, sub–systems are characterized mainly in terms of probabilities. Seen from the "system" end, a register is a **local** resetting of the **global** probabilities that characterize the system as a whole. So, for example, in instructional situations direct imperative may take over as the most favoured selection of mood, as in *Brake!!*; but that does not mean closing off the other moods: the instructor also uses wordings such as declarative *You should have braked*, interrogative *Why didn't you brake?*, or indirect, projected imperative as in *I told you to brake*. Subsystemic variation is thus a selective highlighting of features of the overall system. (At the level of the grammar, where we are able to model the system as a whole, subsystemic variation in register can be represented in these terms, as further, largely quantitative patterning superimposed upon it. But at the level of the semantics, it may be that each register will be modelled, initially at least, in its own terms, following the usual practice of domain-specific representations.)

Let me now return to the points enumerated earlier (as "aspects of linguistic complexity" to be accounted for), and add brief illustrations by making reference to the "driving instruction" mini-text.

(1) Words are organized into wordings (lexicogrammatical patterns). We can represent these patterns in structural terms, so as to show the grammar "at work" in the construction of meaning. Table 11.4 shows part of the structural make-up of *You should have braked before turning*.

(2) Wordings construct meanings (semantic patterns). Notice that when reasoning about 'what did I do wrong?', the pupil **rewords** *you should have braked before turning* as *(you said) I had to slow down at corners*. These two wordings could be related through the grammar, showing rather complex patterns of agnation. But the pupil is reasoning with meanings, not with wordings; and it is probably more effective to relate them at the semantic level. Thus, *you / I* are dialogic alternants for the same interactant, the pupil, functioning in both cases as (i) Actor / Agent, (ii) Subject and (iii) Theme: semantically, as the doer, as the one held to account, and as the point of origin of the message. Secondly, *should have ...ed* and *had to ...* are both high value obligations; the former relating to a past event, the latter relating to the situation in general (*had to* is projected into a past tense form by "sequence of tenses" following *said*). Thirdly, in *brake | slow down*,

Table 11.4 The grammar at work (showing metafunctions)

	You	should	have	braked	before	turning
logical	α. (primary clause)				xβ (secondary)	
	clause nexus: hypotactic / enhancing : temporal					
experiential	Actor	Process			Conjunction	Process
	clause: material				*clause: material*	
interpersonal	Subject	Finite	Predicator			Predicator
	Mood		Residue			Residue
	clause: finite : declarative/ modulated : high / neutral key				*clause: non-finite*	
textual (1)	Theme	Rheme			Theme	Rheme
	clause: unmarked theme				*clause: structural theme*	
textual (2)	Given ⟵———————————— New ⟵———————————— New					
	information unit: complex (major + minor focus)					

one process has been replaced by another one designating its intended effect. Fourthly, in *before turning | at corners* a spatial process defined by temporal location has been replaced by a spatial location in which this process takes place.

(3) Meanings relate to features of the context. We may represent the context as a construction of three variables: field, tenor, and mode. The *field* is 'what is going on': the nature of the social process, as institutionalized in the culture. The *tenor* is 'who are taking part': the role and status relationships of the interactants. The *mode* is 'what the text is doing': the rhetorical functions and channels assigned to language in the situation. By modelling the context in these terms we can display the "resonance" between contextual and linguistic features: typically, the field is realized in ideational meanings, the tenor in interpersonal meanings and the mode in textual meanings.

There is a note to be added at this point. The critical factor here is the modelling of language in "stratal" terms, such that the concept of a *semiotic system* comes to include not only meanings but also the environment in which meanings are exchanged. It seems likely that, in intelligent computing, the "knowledge base" of artificial intelligence will be replaced by a "meaning base", and the external world of referents by a world located at the interface between semiotic and material events (this is the meaning of "context"). In this way particular operations in meaning, such as reasoning from a general to a particular case, inferring the situation from instances of discourse, or deriving information from a variety of different sources, may be located and managed within an overall conceptual framework.

(4) Instances derive value from their place within the system. For example, the features enumerated above in the selection expression for the wording *Brake!!* are all represented paradigmatically in the system network for the grammar of English (cf. Matthiessen 1995). See Figure 9.1 in Chapter 9 (p. 211) to see a network for the English verbal group, incorporating about 70,000 alternatives. Each instance of a verbal group may be represented as a pass through this network, showing the option selected at each of the possible choice points. Thus *[you] should have braked!* is "finite: modal: high / oblique / obligation; secondary tense: past; contrast: event / (force:) neutral; polarity: positive; voice: active"; agnate to:

— You should **brake!** [secondary tense: past | neutral]
— You shouldn't have **braked!** [polarity: positive | negative]
— You could have **braked!** [modal value: high | low]
— You **should** have braked! [contrast location: event | auxiliary]
— You didn't **brake**. [polarity; deixis: modal | temporal]
    etc. etc.

The pupil understands the meaning of the particular instance, as spoken by the instructor, from its location in this multidimensional grammatical space.

(5) The system accommodates variation in register. We could characterize the context of the driving lesson, as institution, in something like the following terms:

Field: Learning, under instruction; a skill: (mechanical operation: driving a car).
Tenor: Instructor: professional (power = knowledge: can give orders); learner: client (power = authority: can withdraw custom).
Mode: Spoken; instructional: action-oriented; mainly monologic.

The corresponding register is likely to foreground ideational meanings to do with the field, such as active processes of locomotion with explicit agency; interpersonal meanings to do with the tenor, such as imperatives, or declaratives modulated by obligation; and textual meanings to do with the mode, such as clausal information units with learner as theme and focus on the process or the vehicle. (Compare what was said about "resonance" under (3) above.)

(6) The system is organized metafunctionally. The different components of the meaning are integrated by the grammar into a single wording, as illustrated in Table 11.4. The multiple layers of structure (whose actual difference is rather greater than appears when they are represented in this unified compositional format) are displayed so as to suggest how this integration is achieved. Each structural layer contributes one band of meaning, which we could bring out informally in a hybrid grammatico- semantic commentary:

You should have **braked** before **turning**

Ideational: logical:
   sequence of two processes linked by temporal succession, the subsequent process made dependent on (i.e., construed as conditioning environment of) the prior one;

Ideational: experiential:
   (1) material process: action: 'make + stop / slow'; active participant 'the learner'; time: past;
   (2) material process: action: 'make + turn'; same active participant;

Interpersonal:
   (1) statement of unfulfilled obligation: high (strong); force: neutral (moderate); person held accountable: 'the listener';
   (2) [meanings carried over from (1)];

Textual:
   (1) theme 'you (learner/listener)'; focus 'brake (action)';
   (2) theme: prior location in time; focus 'turn (action)';
   (1 & 2) message complete: one information unit, with major + minor focus.

(7) Meaning involves three dimensions of history, a point to which I said I would return at the end. Up to now I have freeze-framed both the instances and the systemic categories, taking them out of history; it is useful to hold them still while we examine them. But, of course, semiotic processes, just like material processes, take place in time. There is always a diachronic dimension. Meaning has a history; and when computing with meanings, one may need to take account of the axis or dimension of time. The problem is, that there is more than one dimension of time involved – more than one distinct kind of history. In terms of the matrix I have been using, each of the two outer columns has a separate history of its own.

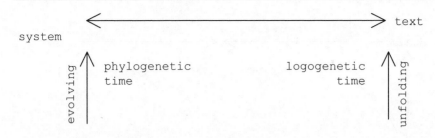

Figure 11.5 Phylogenesis and logogenesis

On the one hand, the system has a history: a language ***evolves***. Its evolution is that of what Edelman (1992) refers to as higher-order consciousness: the evolution of the human brain. On the other hand, the instance also has a history: a text ***unfolds***. Its unfolding is the individuation of the (in principle unique) semiotic act. The evolution of the system is "phylogenesis"; we refer to the unfolding of the text as "logogenesis" (see Figure 11.5). When we locate ourselves, as observers, in between the system and the text, we adopt one orientation or the other; so register, as noted already, appears either as variation in the system or as similarity in text type. There are thus two historical perspectives on register variation in language. On the one hand, a register is something that evolves, as a distinct sub-system (say, the language of science); on the other hand, a register is something that unfolds, as an accumulation of related text (say, the discourse of science; with "intertextuality" throughout – all scientific texts in English as one macrotext unfolding since the time of Newton and beyond) (see Figures 11.6 & 11.7). This dual historical perspective sets the parameters for any particular instance. If we consider reasoning, then the individual speaker (or "meaner") is typically reasoning within these historically determined limits: to take the same trivial (though not so trivial) example of the driving lesson, within the limits of the language of driving instruction as it has evolved, and of a particular sequence of driving instruction texts as these have unfolded.

Figure 11.6 Two angles on register

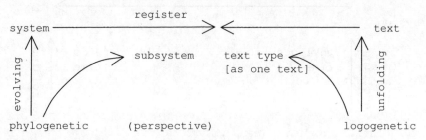

Figure 11.7 Historical angles on register

But this, in turn, directs us on to a third dimension of history, that of "ontogenesis": the development of the meaning subject from birth through childhood and adolescence into the adult state. The individual human being has his/her own history, which is neither evolution nor unfolding but growth, maturation and eventual decay. This history of **development** defines a third set of limits within which the act of meaning is located (see Figure 11.8). (I have presented these historical parameters as "limitations" on the semiotic processes involved. But it is better, I think, to see them as enabling rather than constraining. What sets limits on the production and interpretation of discourse is simply the set of conditions that makes such discourse possible in the first place.)

It might seem that the developmental, ontogenetic perspective is the least relevant to intelligent computing; but I am not so sure. Every instance embodies some aspects of developmental history; what is important here is not the difference between one human being and another (the significance of this I think is often exaggerated) but rather what is common to the developmental history of the group, the paths traversed by all members in building up their meaning potential (Halliday 1975/2004; Painter 1984). This particular historical dimension is important because the development of language proceeds epigenetically, broadly recapitulating the trajectory of its evolution; and the discourse of adult life tends to comprise meanings from each phase along the way. If I may project our driving instruction text back into the history of the child, to the time when he is given his first wheeled vehicle to propel himself on, here is a brief sample of the instructions that might be offered:

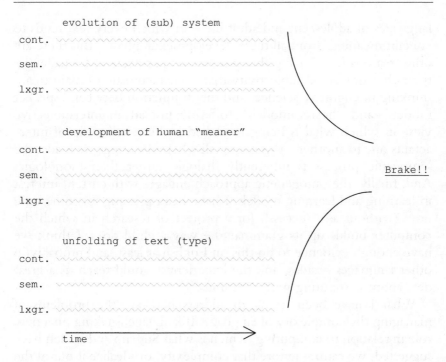

Figure 11.8 The three histories of an instance

(age)

> 1   Don't go too fast! You'll hit something.
>
> 2   You shouldn't go so fast. If you go too fast, you won't be able to stop.
>
> 5   You'd better slow down! The faster you go, the harder it is (the longer it takes) to stop.
>
> 9   It's important to keep at a low speed. Faster speed makes stopping much more difficult.
>
> 13+   Low speed maintenance is essential. Braking distance increases more rapidly at high speeds.

These examples are constructed so as to illustrate the one most significant movement that underlies the development of the typical adult discourse of the age of information: the progression from the general, through the abstract, to the metaphorical. Generalization (the move from "proper" to "common" meanings) is the condition of entry from infant protolanguage into the mother tongue; abstractness is the gateway into the literate discourses of primary education; and metaphor (in the grammatical sense, particularly in the form of nominalization) is the gateway into the technical languages of adolescent and adult life – in which every text tends to contain meanings from all these developmental phases. But there are other reasons for stressing the ontogenetic perspective. It challenges the rather one-sided subjectivity that is characteristic of mainstream thinking in cognitive science, and the disjunction between "speaker models" and "hearer models", offering instead an intersubjective view in which what is being modelled is the relationship of inter-actants one to another – this is after all where meanings are made: the semogenic process is inherently dialogic rather than monologic. And, finally, the ontogenetic approach engages with current interest in learning and learning models. I have been pressing for some time now (without any success!) for a project of research in which the computer builds up its grammar the way a child does. I think we have enough evidence to do this, in English at least, and probably in other languages besides; and the experience would teach us a great deal about computing with meanings.

What I have been trying to address here are the problems of managing the complexity of language. If language is taking on a new role in relation to computing, which is what Sugeno and Zadeh have suggested, we cannot ignore that complexity, or idealize it out of the picture, because it is precisely the complexity of language that makes it operationally effective. Up to the present, language has been represented in the computer through the intermediary of designed systems, forms of representation based on a logic that is itself deriv-ative of language. But this involves a fairly massive loss of infor-mation, a serious semiotic seepage over a wide area. It is now being suggested that language itself will become the primary computational resource; this should not only help to preserve the level of infor-mation but also make it possible to exploit the positive features of natural language – its multiplicity of functions, its elasticity, its sys-tematic variation and so on. These are highly relevant to specific tasks of the kind that Sugeno has identified, such as data fusion (integrating information from language with that from numbers, symbols, images and non-linguistic sounds), fuzzy reasoning (as in his example of playing Go) and construing the context of situation by inference from the text. But even if the metalinguistic role is taken over directly by natural language, this still involves some form of representation. (It is useful to recall that ordinary orthography is ultimately a representational device, even if "written language" has now evolved into a system in its own right.) In particular, if, as I have suggested, computing with words really means computing with meanings, some form of *semantic* representation becomes crucial. I have not tried to tackle this problem here (cf. Halliday and Martin 1993, chapter 2, for some relevant discussion; also Halliday and Matthiessen 1999). What I have attempted, in the latter part of this chapter, is to outline a conceptual framework in which to locate representations of meaning – by reference one to another, and to whatever is "above" and "below". At least I have found it helpful for myself, in trying to follow the sometimes tortuous paths through computational linguistics. It is easy to lose one's way in the labyrinth of language.

SYSTEMS OF THE ENGLISH CLAUSE: A TRIAL GRAMMAR FOR THE PENMAN TEXT GENERATION PROJECT

INFORMATION SCIENCES INSTITUTE, UNIVERSITY OF SOUTHERN CALIFORNIA

CLAUSE SYSTEMS

000–999

systems 200–299   MOOD
systems 300–499   TRANSITIVITY
systems 500–599   PERSPECTIVE

000	# System:	CLAUSE
	Condition:	Node
	Input:	start
	Outputs:	1 clause 0.9

M. + Residue
    Residue (+ Predicator)
    + Process + Medium
    + Theme
    + ^Theme
    + Culmination
    Process / Predicator

2 clausette 0.1

systems 200–299   201–209: mood type

200   # System: MOOD
      Condition: Node
      Input: clause
      Outputs: 1 finite 0.9   M. + Mood
                                                  Mood (+ Finite)
                                                  Mood ^ Residue

                  2 non–finite 0.1

201   # System: MOOD TYPE
      Condition: Node
      Input: finite
      Outputs: 1 indicative 0.9   M. Mood (+ Subject)
                  2 imperative 0.1

202   # System: INDICATIVE TYPE
      Condition: Node
      Input: indicative
      Outputs: 1 declarative   M. Subject ^ Finite
                  2 interrogative

203   # System: INTERROGATIVE TYPE
      Condition: Node
      Input: interrogative
      Outputs: 1 yes/no   M. Finite ^ Subject
                  2 wh-   M. + WH
                                                  Wh ^ Finite

204   # System: WH-FUNCTION
      Condition: Node
      Input: wh-
      Outputs: 1 wh- subject   M. Wh / Subject
                  2 wh- other   M. Wh / Residual
                                                  Finite ^ Subject

205   # System: NON-FINITE TYPE
      Condition: Node
      Input: non-finite
      Outputs: 1 perfective   M. Predicator : infinitive
                  2 imperfective   M. Predicator : participle

206   # System: NON-FINITE SUBJECT
      Condition: Node
      Input: non-finite
      Outputs: 1 subject presupposed 0.9
                  2 subject specified 0.1   M. + Subject

269

209	# System:	MOODLESS TYPE	
	Condition:	Node	
	Input:	clausette	
	Outputs:	1 call	M. + Vocative
		2 greeting	M. + Greeting
		3 exclamation	M. + Exclamation

<u>MOOD</u>		systems 200–299	211–219: <u>residual elements</u>

211	# System:	RESIDUALITY	
	Condition:	Node	
	Input:	clause	
	Outputs:	1 .... n no-residual	
		one-residual	M. + $Residual_1$
		two-residual	M. + $Residual_1$ + $Residual_2$
		...	M. + ...

NOTE: This is not an independent system. Its function is to insert as many Residuals as are called for by conflation messages in other systems.

<u>MOOD</u>		systems 200–299	221–229: <u>subject person</u>

221	# System:	SUBJECT PERSON	
	Condition:	Node	
	Input:	finite	
	Outputs:	1 interactant subject	
		2 other subject	

222	# System:	INDICATIVE INTERACTANT SUBJECT	
	Condition:	And	
	Inputs:	indicative And interactant subject	
	Outputs:	1 speaker subject	M. Subject : 'I' : <u>I</u>
		2 addressee subject	M. Subject : 'you' : <u>you</u>
		3 speaker-plus subject	M. Subject : 'we' : <u>we</u>

223	# System:	INDICATIVE SUBJECT PRESUMPTION	
	Condition:	Or And	
	Inputs:	declarative And speaker subject	
		Or	
		Interrogative And addressee subject	
	Outputs:	1 subject explicit 0.9	
		2 subject implicit 0.1	M. @ Subject

224   # System: IMPERATIVE INTERACTANT SUBJECT
      Condition: And
      Inputs: imperative And interactant subject
      Outputs: 1 oblative   M. + Subject
                                                       Subject : 'I' : let me
                   2 jussive   M. + Subject
                                                       Subject : 'you'
                   2 suggestive   M. + Subject
                                                       Subject : 'us' : let's

225   # System: IMPERATIVE SUBJECT PRESUMPTION
      Condition: Node
      Input: jussive
      Outputs: 1 subject implicit 0.9
                   2 subject explicit 0.1   M. Subject : 'you' : you

226   # System: INDICATIVE OTHER SUBJECT
      Condition: And
      Input: indicative And other subject
      Outputs: 1 pronominal subject   M. Subject : other pronoun
                   2 nominal subject   M. Subject : nominal group

227   # System: IMPERATIVE OTHER SUBJECT
      Condition: And
      Input: imperative And other subject
      Outputs: 1 proper subject 0.9   M. Subject : n gp : proper
                   2 common subject 0.1   M. Subject : n gp : common

MOOD   systems 200–299   231–239: tagging

231   # System   DECLARATIVE TAG
      Condition: Node
      Input: declarative
      Outputs: 1 untagged 0.9
                   2 tagged 0.1   M. & Moodtag
                                                       Residue ^ Moodtag
                                                       Moodtag (+ Tagfinite + Tag-
                                                       subject)
                                                       Tagfinite = Finite
        [interactant subject Or pronominal subject] Tagsubject = Subject
                            [nominal subject]   Tagsubject = other pronoun★

      ★in number and gender concord with Subject

271

232 # System   IMPERATIVE TAG
     Condition: Node
     Input: imperative
     Outputs: 1 untagged 0.9

                2 tagged 0.1   M. & Moodtag
                                                 Residue ^ Moodtag
                                                   Moodtag (+ Tagfinite +
                                                   Tagsubject)
                          [oblative]   Tagfinite : <u>shall</u>
                                            Tagsubject : <u>I</u>
                          [jussive]   Tagfinite : <u>will</u>
                                            Tagsubject : <u>you</u>
                        [suggestive]   Tagfinite : <u>shall</u>
                                            Tagsubject : <u>we</u>

233 # System   TAG POLARITY
     Condition: Node
     Input: tagged
     Outputs: 1 reversed 0.9   M. Tagfinite : (polarity) $\neq$ Finite
                2 constant 0.1   M. Tagfinite : (polarity) = Finite

<u>MOOD</u>   systems 200–299   241–249: <u>polarity</u>

241 # System   POLARITY
     Condition: Node
     Input: finite
     Outputs: 1 positive   M.
                       [indicative] Finite : positive
                       [imperative]
                2 negative   M.
                       [indicative] Finite : negative
                       [imperative] Finite : 'don't'
                                     'don't' ^ Subject

242 # System   POLARITY MARKING: POSITIVE
     Condition: Node
     Input: positive
     Outputs: 1 unmarked positive 0.9   M.
                       [indicative] Finite: : reduced
                       [imperative]
                2 marked positive 0.1   M.
                       [indicative] Finite : : non-reduced
                       [imperative] Finite : 'do' : <u>do</u>
                                     'do' Subject

243 # System   POLARITY MARKING : NEGATIVE
     Condition: Node
     Input: negative
     Outputs: 1 unmarked negative 0.9   M.
                                        [indicative] Finite : : reduced
                                        [imperative] 'don't' : reduced : <u>don't</u>
                     2 marked negative 0.1   M.
                                        [indicative] Finite : : non-reduced
                                        [imperative] 'don't' : non-reduced : <u>do not</u>

244 # System: NON-FINITE POLARITY
     Condition: Node
     Input: Non-finite
     Outputs: 1 positive
                     2 negative   M. + <u>not</u>
                                                    <u>not</u> ^ Predicator

<u>TRANSITIVITY</u>   systems 300–499   300–319 : <u>transitivity type</u>

301 # System: AGENCY
     Condition: Node
     Input: clause
     Outputs: 1 middle   M. Medium / Subject
                                                    Process : class 01
                                                    Process : active
                     2 effective   Process : class 02

302 # System: BENEFACTION
     Condition: Node
     Input: effective
     Outputs: 1 non-benefactive 0.9
                     2 benefactive 0.1   M. + Participant – Beneficiary

303 # System: RANGE
     Condition: Node
     Input: middle
     Outputs: 1 non-ranged 0.9
                     2 ranged 0.1   M. + Participant – Range

304 # System   EXTENT
     Condition: Node
     Input: clause
     Outputs: 1 non-extent 0.9
                     2 extent 0.1   M. + Circumstance – Extent

305	# System:	EXTENT-TYPE	
	Condition:	Node	
	Input:	extent	
	Outputs:	1 duration	M. Extent – Duration
		2 distance	M. Extent – Distance

306	# System:	LOCATION	
	Condition:	Node	
	Input:	clause	
	Outputs:	1 non-location 0.9	
		2 location 0.1	M. + Circumstance – Locative

307	# System:	LOCATION-TYPE	
	Condition:	Node	
	Input:	location	
	Outputs:	1 time	M. Location – Temporal
		2 place	M. Location – Spatial

308	# System:	MANNER	
	Condition:	Node	
	Input:	clause	
	Outputs:	1 non-manner 0.9	
		2 manner 0.1	M. + Circumstance – Manner

309	# System:	MANNER-TYPE	
	Condition:	Node	
	Input:	manner	
	Outputs:	1 means	M. Manner – Means
		2 quality	M. Manner – Quality
		3 comparison	M. Manner – Comparison

310	# System:	CAUSE	
	Condition:	Node	
	Input:	clause	
	Outputs:	1 non-cause 0.9	
		2 cause 0.1	M. + Circumstance – Cause

311	# System:	CAUSE-TYPE	
	Condition:	Node	
	Input:	cause	
	Outputs:	1 reason	M. Cause – Reason
		2 purpose	M. Cause – Purpose
		3 behalf	M. Cause – Behalf

312   # System: ACCOMPANIMENT
      Condition: Node
      Input: clause
      Outputs: 1 non-accompaniment 0.9
                    2 accompaniment 0.1   M. + Circumstance –
                                                 Accompaniment

313   # System: MATTER
      Condition: Node
      Input: clause
      Outputs: 1 non-matter 0.9
                    2 matter 0.1   M. + Circumstance – Matter

314   # System: ROLE
      Condition: Node
      Input: clause
      Outputs: 1 non-role 0.9
                    2 role 0.1   M. + Circumstance – Role

TRANSITIVITY   systems 300–499   321–330: material processes

320   # System: PROCESS-TYPE
      Condition: Node
      Input: clause
      Outputs: 1 material   M. + Actor
                                                 Process : class 10

                    2 mental   M. + Senser
                                                 Senser / Medium
                                                 Process : class 20

                    3 verbal   M. + Sayer
                                                 Sayer / Medium
                                                 Process : class 30

                    4 relational   M. + Be-er
                                                 Be-er / Medium
                                                 Process : class 40

322   # System: HAPPENING
      Condition: And
      Inputs: material And middle
      Outputs: 1 behavioural   M. Actor / Medium
                                                 Actor : conscious
                                                 Process : behaviour

                    2 eventive   M. Actor / Medium
                                                 Actor : non-conscious
                                                 Process : event

323 # System: DOING
     Condition: And
     Inputs: material And effective
     Outputs: 1 creative   M. Actor / Agent
                                        + Goal
                                        Goal / Medium
                                        Process : creation
              2 dispositive   M. Actor / Agent
                                        + Goal
                                        Goal / Medium
                                        Process : disposal

324 # System: RANGE-TYPE
     Condition: And
     Inputs: material And ranged
     Outputs: 1 quality-range   M. Range : qualified
              2 quantity-range   M. Range : quantified

325 # System: BENEFACTION-TYPE
     Condition: And
     Inputs: benefactive And material
     Outputs: 1 recipiency   M. Beneficiary : recipient
              2 cliency   M. Beneficiary : client

<u>TRANSITIVITY</u>   systems 300–399   341–359: <u>mental processes</u>

341 # System: SENSING
     Condition: Node
     Input: mental
     Outputs: 1 perceptive   M. Process : perception
              2 reactive   M. Process : reaction
              3 cognitive   M. Process : cognition

342 # System: PERCEPTION-TYPE
     Condition: Node
     Input: perceptive
     Outputs: 1 seeing   M. Process : visual
              2 hearing   M. Process : auditory
              3 other-perceiving M. Process : other-perceptual

343 # System: REACTION-TYPE
     Condition: Node
     Input: reactive
     Outputs: 1 liking   M. Process : like
              2 disliking   M. Process : dislike
              3 fearing   M. Process : fear

344	# System:	COGNITION-TYPE	
	Condition:	Node	
	Input:	cognitive	
	Outputs:	1 opining	M. Process :
		2 understanding	M. Process : epistemic
		3 remembering	M. Process : mnemonic
345	# System:	PHENOMENALITY	
	Condition:	And (Or)	
	Input:	mental And (ranged Or effective)	
	Outputs:	1 phenomenal	M. + Phenomenon
			Phenomenon : thing
		2 metaphenomenal	M. + Phenomenon
			Phenomenon : metathing
346	# System:	METAPHENOMENALITY	
	Condition:	Node	
	Input:	metaphenomenal	
	Outputs:	1 factive 0.9	M. Phenomenon : : fact
		2 reportive 0.1	M. Phenomenon : : report
347	# System:	347	
	Condition:	And	
	Inputs:	ranged And phenomenal	
	Output:		M. Phenomenon / Range
348	# System:	348	
	Condition:	And	
	Inputs:	effective And phenomenal	
	Output:		M. Phenomenon / Agent

TRANSITIVITY		systems 300–399	361–369: verbal processes
361	# System:	SAYING	
	Condition:	And	
	Input:	verbal And non-ranged	
	Outputs:	1 indicating	M. + Beta
			Beta : finite
		2 imperating	M. + Beta
			Beta : perfective
362	# System:	INDICATING	
	Condition:	Node	
	Input:	indicating	
	Outputs:	1 declaring	M. Beta : : declarative
		2 interrogating	M. Beta : : interrogative

364	# System:	SPEECH-RANGE	
	Condition:	And	
	Inputs:	verbal And ranged	
	Outputs:	1 texting	M. + Text-name
			Text-name / Range
		2 languaging	M. + Language-name
			Language-name / Range
365	# System:	ADDRESS	
	Condition:	Node	
	Input:	verbal	
	Outputs:	1 non-address 0.9	
		2 address	M. + Addressee

TRANSITIVITY   systems 300–399   371–389: relational processes

371	# System:	TYPE OF BEING	
	Condition:	And	
	Inputs:	relational And middle	
	Outputs:	1 ascriptive	M. Be-er : Carrier
			Carrier / Subject
			+ Attribute
		2 existential	M. Be-er : Existent
			Existent / Range
			+ there; there / Subject
			Process : 'be'
372	# System:	372	
	Condition:	And	
	Inputs:	relational And middle	
	Output:	Equative	M. Be-er : Identified
			+ Identifier
373	# System:	RELATION TYPE	
	Condition:	Or	
	Inputs:	ascriptive Or equative	
	Outputs:	1 intensive	M. Process : 'be like'
			+ Value
		2 circumstantial	M. Process : 'be at'
			+ Circumstance
		3 possessive	M. Process : 'have'
			+ Possession

374 # System: ATTRIBUTE STATUS
Condition: And
Inputs: intensive And middle
Outputs: 1 property attribute   M. Value / Attribute
Attribute : nominal group :
(Head / Epithet)

2 class attribute   M. Value / Attribute
Attribute : nominal group :
(Head / Thing)

375 # System: IDENTIFICATION DIRECTION
Condition: And
Inputs: intensive And effective
Outputs: 1 decoding   M. + Token
Identified / Token
Identifier / Value

2 encoding   M. + Token
Identified / Value
Identifier / Token

376 # System: CIRCUMSTANCE AS ATTRIBUTE
Condition: And
Inputs: circumstantial And middle
Outputs: 1 circumstantial ascription   M. Circumstance / Process
2 circumstantial attribute   M. Circumstance / Attribute

377 # System: CIRCUMSTANCE AS IDENTITY
Condition: And
Inputs: circumstantial And effective
Outputs: 1 circumstantial equation   M. Circumstance / Process
2 circumstantial identity   M. Circumstance / Identified
+ $Circumstance_2$
$Circumstance_2$ / Identifier

378 # System: CIRCUMSTANCE TYPE
Condition: Node
Input: circumstantial
Outputs: 1 extent   M. Circumstance : Extent
2 location   M. Circumstance : Location
3 cause   M. Circumstance : Cause
4 manner   M. Circumstance : Manner
5 accompaniment   M. Circumstance : Accompaniment
6 matter   M. Circumstance : Matter
7 role   M. Circumstance : Role

379   # System: POSSESSION AS ATTRIBUTE
        Condition: And
        Inputs: possessive And middle
        Outputs: 1 possessive ascription   M. Possession / Process
                    2 possessive attribute   M. Possession / Attribute

380   # System   POSSESSION AS IDENTITY
        Condition: And
        Inputs: possessive And effective
        Outputs: 1 possessive equation   M. Possession / Process
                    2 possessive identity   M. Possession / Identified
                                            + $Possession_2$
                                            $Possession_2$ / Identifier

<u>PERSPECTIVE</u>   systems 500–599   500–519 : <u>theme</u>

501   # System: TEXTUAL THEME
        Condition: Node
        Input: clause
        Outputs: 1 no textual theme
                    2 textual theme   M. Theme (+ Textual)
                                        ($ \$ \; ^\wedge \;$ Textual)

502   # System: INTERPERSONAL THEME
        Condition: Node
        Input: clause
        Outputs: 1 no interpersonal theme
                      2 interpersonal theme   M. Theme (+ Interpersonal)
                                          ($ \$ \; ^\wedge \; $ / Textual / $^\wedge$ Interpersonal)

503   # System: 503
        Condition: Node
        Input: clause
        Output: M. Theme (+ Topical)
                                          (Topical $^\wedge$ $\$$)

504   # System: THEME MARKING (DECLARATIVE)
        Condition: Node
        Input: declarative
        Outputs: 1 unmarked declarative theme 0.9 M. Topical / Subject
                    2 marked declarative theme 0.1   M. Topical / (Residual-Culminative)

505   # System: THEME MARKING (YES/NO)
        Condition: Node
        Input: yes/no
        Outputs: 1 unmarked yes/no theme 0.9   M. Topical / Subject
                                           Interpersonal / Finite
                    2 marked yes/no theme 0.1   M. Topical / (Residual-Culminative)

506 # System: THEME MARKING (WH-)
     Condition: Node
     Input: wh-
     Outputs: 1 unmarked wh- theme 0.9   M. Topical / Wh
                  2 marked wh- theme 0.1   M. Topical / (Residual-Culminative)

507 # System: THEME MARKING (IMPERATIVE)
     Condition: Node
     Input: imperative
     Outputs: 1 unmarked imperative theme   M.
                                 [subject implicit]   Topical / Predicator
                                 [all others]   Topical / Subject
                                 [negative]   Interpersonal / Finite 'don't'
                                 [marked positive]   Interpersonal / Finite 'do'
                  2 marked imperative theme   M. Topical / (residual-Culminative)

PERSPECTIVE   systems 500–599   520–539 : voice

521 # System: EFFECTIVE-VOICE
     Condition: Node
     Input: effective
     Outputs: 1 operative 0.9   M. + Participant – Agent
                                                Agent / Subject
                                                Medium / Residual
                                                Process : active
                  2 receptive 0.1   M. Process : passive
                                 [non-benefactive]   Medium / Subject

522 # System: BENEFACTIVE-VOICE
     Condition: And
     Inputs: receptive And benefactive
     Outputs: 1 medioreceptive   M. Medium / Subject
                  2 benereceptive   M. Beneficiary / Subject

523 # System: AGENTIVITY
     Condition: Node
     Input: receptive
     Outputs: 1 non-agentive 0.9
                  2 range-receptive 0.1   M. + Participant – Agent
                                                Agent / Residual

524 # System: RANGE-VOICE
     Condition: Node
     Input: ranged
     Outputs: 1 range-operative 0.9   M. Medium / Subject
                                                Process : active
                  2 range-receptive 0.1   M. Range / Subject
                                                Process : passive

525 # System: RANGE-MEDIATION
      Condition: Node
      Input: range–receptive
      Outputs: 1 non–mediated 0.9   M. @ Medium
                 2 mediated 0.1   M. Medium / Subject => Residual

531 # System: BENEFACTIVE-CULMINATION I
      Condition: And
      Inputs: benefactive And operative
      Outputs: 1 ben–med   M. Beneficiary $^\wedge$ Medium
                                       Beneficiary / (Residual–
                                       Complement)
                 2 med–ben   M. Medium $^\wedge$ Beneficiary
                                       Beneficiary / (Residual–Adjunct)

532 # System: BENEFACTIVE-CULMINATION II
      Condition: And
      Inputs: benefactive And operative
      Outputs: 1 med–ag   M. Medium $^\wedge$ Agent
                 2 ag–med   M. Agent $^\wedge$ Medium

533 # System: BENEFACTIVE-CULMINATION III
      Condition: Node
      Inputs: medioreceptive
      Outputs: 1 ben–ag   M. Beneficiary $^\wedge$ Agent
                                        Beneficiary / (Residual–
                                       Complement)
                 2 ag–ben   M. Agent $^\wedge$ Beneficiary
                                       Beneficiary / (Residual–Adjunct)

General principle of ordering in the Residue: Complements before Adjuncts.

However this is not exceptionless (e.g. *I was given by my sister a beautiful Chinese brooch*) nor is it exhaustive (i.e. it doesn't arrange Complements or Adjuncts relative to each other)

So we specify ordering by transitivity functions.

Ordering of Process, Medium and Participants already fully specified:

1) whichever is mapped on to Subject comes first;
2) Process comes second;
3) others ordered by voice systems (520–539).

except as modified by selection of wh- other or marked theme (also specified)

Ordering of Circumstances: adopt ordering   (each of which
as follows: puts just one
   Extent Location Manner Cause Accompaniment   element before the
   Matter Role   Subject, rest unaltered)
   except as modified by wh- other or marked theme.

Note however that we do need to specify mapping on to Complement or Adjunct for purposes of next stage (rewriting Functional expression as syntagm of classes).

General principles:

1) Process / Predicator
2) Medium & Participants:
   either (a) – / Subject (specified by voice systems)
   or (b) if not – / Subject, then:
      Medium / Complement
      Agent / Adjunct
      Beneficiary:
         either (i) – / Complement (if immediately following Process)
         or (ii) – / Adjunct (otherwise)
      Range:
         either (i) – / Adjunct (if following Process but not immediately)
         or (ii) – / Complement (otherwise)

3) Circumstance:
   all / Adjunct

Whatever Residual (Complement or Adjunct) comes out last in the sequence, conflate with Culminative. Then leave it where it is (unspecified), or
    put first (specified as output of feature
            <u>marked theme</u>: Topical / (Residual-Culminative)

BIBLIOGRAPHY

Aijmer, K. and Altenberg, B. (eds) (1991) *English Corpus Linguistics: Studies in Honour of Jan Svartvik*. London: Longman.

Asher, R. E. (ed.) (1994) *The Encyclopedia of Language and Linguistics*. Oxford: Pergamon Press.

Baker, M., Francis, G. and Tognini-Bonelli, E. (eds) (1993) *Text and Technology: in Honour of John Sinclair*. Amsterdam: Benjamins.

Bateman, J. and Matthiessen, C. M. I. M. (1991) *Systemic Linguistics and Text Generation: Experiences from Japanese and English*. London and New York: Frances Pinter.

Benson, J. D. and Greaves, W. S. (eds) (1985) *Systemic Perspectives on Discourse*. Vol. 1. Norwood NJ: Ablex.

Biber, D. (1992) 'Using Computer-based Text Corpora to Analyze the Referential Strategies of Spoken and Written Texts' in J. Svartvik (ed.), *Directions in Corpus Linguistics: Proceedings of Nobel Symposium 82*. New York: Mouton de Gruyter.

Brazil, D. (1995) *A Grammar of Speech*. Oxford: Oxford University Press.

Carter, R. (2002) 'Language and creativity: the evidence from spoken English'. The Second Sinclair Open Lecture, University of Birmingham.

Carter, R. and McCarthy, M. (1995) 'Grammar and the spoken language'. *Applied Linguistics* 16. 141–58.

Cloran, C. (1989) 'Learning through language: the social construction of gender', in R. Hasan and J. R. Martin (eds). 111–51.

Cloran, C. (1994) *Rhetorical Units and Decontextualization: an Enquiry into Some Relations of Meaning, Context and Grammar*. Monographs in Systemic Linguistics 6. Nottingham: University of Nottingham.

Collins COBUILD English Dictionary (1995). London: HarperCollins.

Collins, P. C. (1987) 'Cleft and pseudo-cleft constructions in English spoken and written discourse'. ICAME Journal 11, 5–17.

Davey, A. (1978) *Discourse Production: A Computer Model of Some Aspects of a Speaker*. Edinburgh: Edinburgh University Press.

Davidse, K. (1991) 'Categories of experiential grammar', doctoral thesis, Katholieke Universiteit Leuven.

Davidse, K. (1992a) 'Transitivity/ergativity: the Janus-headed grammar of actions and events', in M. Davies and L. Ravelli (eds), *Advances in Systemic Linguistics: Recent Theory and Practice*. London: Frances Pinter. 105–35.

Davidse, K. (1992b) 'Existential constructions: a systemic perspective'. *Leuven Contributions in Linguistics and Philology* 81. 71–99.

Davidse, K. (1992c) 'A semiotic approach to relational clauses'. *Occasional Papers in Systemic Linguistics* 6. 99–131.

Davidse, K. (1994) 'Fact projection', in K. P. Carlon, K. Davidse and B. Rudzka-Ostyn (eds), *Perspectives on English: Studies in Honour of Professor Emma Vorlat*. Leuven: Peeters. 259–86.

Davidse, K. (1996) 'Ditransitivity and possession', in R. Hasan, D. Butt and C. Cloran (eds), *Functional Descriptions: Linguistic Form and Linguistic Theory*. Amsterdam/Philadelphia: Benjamins. 85–144.

Davidse, K. (1999) *Categories of Experiential Grammar*. Monographs in Systemic Linguistics. Nottingham: University of Nottingham.

Delavenay, E. (1960) *Introduction to Machine Translation*. London: Thames & Hudson.

Edelman, G. (1992) *Bright Air, Brilliant Fire: on the Matter of the Mind*. New York: Basic Books; London: Allen Lane.

Eggins, S. and Slade, D. (1997) *Analysing Casual Conversation*. London: Cassell.

Ellis, J. M. (1993) *Language, Thought and Logic*. Evanston IL: Northwestern University Press.

Elmenoufy, A. (1969) 'A study of the role of intonation in the grammar of English'. PhD thesis. University of London.

Fawcett, R. P. and Perkins, M. (1981) 'Project report: language development in 6- to 12-year-old children'. *First Language* 2. 75–9.

Fawcett, R. P. and Tucker, G. (1990) 'Demonstration of GENESYS: a very large, semantically based systemic functional grammar'. Proceedings of COLING 90, 1.

Fawcett, R. P., Tucker, G. and Lin, Y. Q. (1993) 'How a systemic grammar works', in H. Horacek and M. Zock (eds), *New Concepts in Natural Language Generation*. London: Pinter.

Fawcett, R. P. and Young, D. J. (eds) (1988) *New Developments in Systemic Linguistics*. Vol. 2. London: Pinter.

Firth, J. R. (1935) 'The technique of semantics'. *Transactions of the Philological Society*. Reprinted in Firth 1957b.

Firth, J. R. (1951) 'Modes of meaning'. *Essays and Studies* (The English Association). Reprinted in Firth 1957b.

Firth, J. R. (1957a) 'A synopsis of linguistic theory'. *Studies in Linguistic Analysis* (Special volume of the Philological Society), Oxford: Blackwell. Reprinted in F. R. Palmer (ed.) (1966) *Selected Papers of J. R. Firth 1951–1959* (Longman Linguistics Library). London: Longman.

Firth, J. R. (1957b) *Papers in Linguistics 1934–1951*. London: Oxford University Press.

FUZZ-IEEE/IFES '95 (1995) Proceedings of the International Joint Conference of the Fourth IEEE International Conference on Fuzzy Systems and the Second International Fuzzy Engineering Symposium. Yokohama: LIFE [Laboratory for International Fuzzy Engineering Research].

Gerot, L., Oldenburg, J. and van Leeuwen, T. (eds) (1988) *Language and Socialization: Home and School*. Proceedings from the Working Conference on Language in Education, Macquarie University, 17–21 November 1986. Sydney: Macquarie University.

Ghadessy, M. (1994) *Register Analysis: Theory and Practice*. London: Pinter.

Gross, M. (1972) *Mathematical Models in Linguistics*. Englewood Cliffs, NJ: Prentice-Hall.

Halliday, M. A. K. (1956) 'Grammatical categories in modern Chinese'. *Transactions of the Philological Society*. 177–224. In Collected Works, Vol. 8.

Halliday, M. A. K. (1959) *The Language of the Chinese 'Secret History of the Mongols'* (Publications of the Philological Society 17). Oxford: Blackwell. In Collected Works, Vol. 8.

Halliday, M. A. K. (1961) 'Categories of the theory of grammar'. *Word* 17.3. 242–92.

Halliday, M. A. K. (1966) 'Some notes on "deep" grammar', *Journal of Linguistics* 2. In Collected Works, Vol. 1.

Halliday, M. A. K. (1975) *Learning How to Mean: Explorations in the Development of Language*. London: Edward Arnold. In Collected Works, Vol. 4.

Halliday, M. A. K. (1976) *System and Function in Language*. London: Oxford University Press.

Halliday, M. A. K. (1985/1994) *An Introduction to Functional Grammar*. London: Edward Arnold [2nd edn 1994].

Halliday, M. A. K. (1991) 'Towards probabilistic interpretations'. This Volume, Chapter 3.

Halliday, M. A. K. (1992a) 'Language as system and language as instance: the corpus as a theoretical construct'. This Volume, Chapter 5.

Halliday, M. A. K. (1992b) 'The history of a sentence: an essay in social semiotics', in Vita Fortunati (ed.), *Bologna, la cultura italiana e le letterature stranieri moderne*, Vol. 3. Ravenna: Longo Editore. In Collected Works, Vol. 3.

Halliday, M. A. K. (1993) 'Quantitative studies and probabilities in grammar'. This Volume, Chapter 7.

Halliday, M. A. K. (1994) 'Systemic theory' in R. E. Asher (ed.), *The Encyclopedia of Language and Linguistics*. Oxford: Pergamon Press. In Collected Works, Vol. 3.

Halliday, M. A. K. (1998) 'On the grammar of pain'. *Functions of Language* 5. 1–32. In Collected Works, Vol. 7.

Halliday, M. A. K. (2002) 'Judge takes no cap in mid-sentence: on the complementarity of grammar and lexis'. The First Sinclair Open Lecture. University of Birmingham, Department of English.

Halliday, M. A. K. and Hasan, R. (1976) *Cohesion in English*. London: Longman.

Halliday, M. A. K. and Hasan, R. (1985) *Language, context and text: a social semiotic perspective*. Geelong, Victoria: Deakin University Press.

Halliday, M. A. K. and James, Z. L. (1993) 'A quantitative study of polarity and primary tense in the English finite clause'. This Volume, Chapter 6.

Halliday, M. A. K. and Martin, J. R. (eds) (1981) *Readings in Systemic Linguistics*. London: Batsford Academic.

Halliday, M. A. K. and Martin, J. R. (1993) *Writing Science: Literacy and Discursive Power*. London: The Falmer Press.

Halliday, M. A. K. and Matthiessen, C. M. I. M. (1999) *Construing Experience through Meaning*. London: Cassell.

Halliday, M. A. K. and Matthiessen, C. M. I. M. (2000) *Systemic Linguistics: a First Step into the Theory*. Macquarie University: National Centre for English Language Teaching and Research.

Halliday, M. A. K., Gibbons, J. and Nicholas, H. (eds) (1990) *Learning, Keeping and Using Language*. Selected Papers from the 8th World Congress of Applied Linguistics, Sydney, 16–21 August 1987. Amsterdam/ Philadephia: Benjamins.

Hasan, R. (1980) 'What's going on: a dynamic view of context', in J. E. Copeland and P. W. Davis (eds), *The Seventh LACUS forum*. Columbia, SC: Hornbeam Press. 106–121.

Hasan, R. (ed.) (1985) *Discourse on Discourse*. Applied Linguistics Association of Australia, Occasional Papers 7.

Hasan, R. (1986) 'The ontogenesis of ideology: an interpretation of mother–child talk', in T. Threadgold *et al*. (eds). 125–46.

Hasan, R. (1987a) 'The grammarian's dream: lexis as most delicate grammar', in Halliday and Fawcett (eds), *New developments in systemic linguistics: theory and description*. London: Pinter.

Hasan, R. (1987b) 'Offers in the making: a systemic-functional approach. MS.

Hasan, R. (1988) 'Language in the processes of socialization: home and school', in L. Gerot, J. Oldenburg and T. van Leeuwen (eds). 36–95.

Hasan, R. (1991) 'Questions as a mode of learning in everyday talk', in T. Lê and M. McCausland (eds), *Language Education: Interaction and Development*. Launceston: University of Tasmania. 70–119.

Hasan, R. (1992) 'Rationality in everyday talk: from process to system', in J. Svartvik (ed.), *Directions in Corpus Linguistics*. Berlin: de Gruyter.

Hasan, R. (1999) 'Speaking with reference to context', in M. Ghadessy (ed.), *Text and Context in Functional Linguistics*. Amsterdam and Philadelphia: Benjamins. 219–328.

Hasan, R. and Cloran, C. (1990) 'Semantic variation: A sociolinguistic interpretation of everyday talk between mothers and children', in M. A. K. Halliday, J. Gibbons and H. Nicholas (eds).

Hasan, R. and Fries, P. (eds) (1995) *On Subject and Theme: a discourse functional perspective*. Amsterdam and Philadelphia: Benjamins.

Hasan, R. and Martin, J. R. (eds) (1989) *Language development: Learning language, learning culture*. (Advances in Discourse Processes 27.) Norwood NJ: Ablex.

Henrici, A. (1966/1981) 'Some notes on the systemic generation of a paradigm of the English clause', in M. A. K. Halliday and J. R. Martin (eds).

Huddleston, R. D., Hudson, R. A., Winter, E. O. and Henrici, A. (1970) *Sentence and Clause in Scientific English*. London: Communication Research Centre, University College London [for Office of Scientific and Technical Information].

Hunston, S. (1993) 'Evaluation and ideology in scientific English', in M. Ghadessy (ed.), *Register Analysis: Theory and Practice*. London: Pinter. 57–73.

Hunston, S. and Francis, G. (2000) *Pattern Grammar: a Corpus-Driven Approach to the Lexical Grammar of English*. Amsterdam and Philadelphia: Benjamins.

Kingdon, R. (1958) *The Groundwork of English Intonation*. London: Longman.

Kress, G. (ed.) (1976) *Halliday: System and Function in Language: Selected Papers*. London: Oxford University Press.

Leech, G. (2000) 'Same grammar or different grammar? contrasting approaches to the grammar of spoken English discourse', in S. Sarangi and M. Coulthard (eds), *Discourse and Social Life*. London: Longman. 48–65.

Lemke, J. L. (1984) *Semiotics and Education*. Toronto: Victoria University. (Toronto Semiotic Circle Monographs, Working Papers and Pre-publications, no. 2.)

Lemke, J. L. (1990) 'Technical discourse and technocratic ideology', in M. A. K. Halliday, J. Gibbons and H. Nicholas (eds).

Lemke, J. L. (1993) 'Discourse, dynamics, and social change', *Cultural Dynamics* 6.1–2. 243–76.

Léon, J. (2000) 'Traduction automatique et formalization du langage: les tentatives du Cambridge Language Research Unit (1955–1960)', in P. Desmet, L. Jooken, P. Schmitter and P. Swiggers (eds), *The History of Linguistics and Grammatical Praxis*. Louvain/Paris: Peeters. 369–94.

Mann, W. C. (1985) 'An introduction to the Nigel text generation grammar', in J. D. Benson and W. S. Greaves (eds). 84–95.

Mann, W. C. and Matthiessen, C. M. I. M. (1983) 'Nigel: a systemic grammar for text generation'. Marina del Rey, CA: Information Sciences Institute, University of Southern California.

Martin, J. R. (1985) 'Process and text: Two aspects of human semiosis', in J. D. Benson and W. S. Greaves (eds). 248–74.

Martin, J. R. (1991) 'Life as a noun', in E. Ventola (ed.), *Recent Systemic and other Functional Views on Language*. Berlin: Mouton de Gruyter.

Martin, J. R. (1992) *English Text: System and Structure*. Amsterdam: Benjamins.

Martin, J. R. (1993) 'Life as a noun: arresting the universe in science and humanities', in M. A. K. Halliday and J. R. Martin. 221–67.

Martin, J. R. (1998) 'Beyond exchange: appraisal systems in English', in S. Hunston and G. Thompson (eds), *Evaluation in Text*. Oxford: Oxford University Press.

Martin, J. R. and Matthiessen, C. M. I. M. (1991) 'Systemic typology and topology' in F. Christie (ed.), *Literacy in Social Processes*. Darwin, N.T. (Australia): Northern Territory University, Centre for Studies of Language in Education.

Martin, J. R. and Rose, D. (2003) *Working with Discourse: Meaning Beyond the Clause*. London: Continuum.

Matthiessen, C. M. I. M. (1983) 'Choosing primary tense in English'. *Studies in Language* 7.3. 369–430.

Matthiessen, C. M. I. M. (1985) 'The systemic framework in text generation' in J. D. Benson and W. S. Greaves (eds). 96–118.

Matthiessen, C. M. I. M. (1988) 'A systemic semantics: the chooser and inquiry framework', in J. D. Benson, M. J. Cummings and W. S. Greaves (eds), *Systemic Functional Approaches to Discourse: Selected Papers from the Twelfth International Systemic Workshop*, Norwood, NJ: Ablex. Also as ISI/RS–87–189.

Matthiessen, C. M. I. M. (1989) Review of M. A. K. Halliday's 'Introduction to Functional Grammar'. *Language* 65.

Matthiessen, C. M. I. M. (1992) 'Interpreting the textual metafunction', in M. Davies and L. Ravelli (eds), *Advances in systemic linguistics: recent theory and practice*. London: Pinter. 37–82.

Matthiessen, C. M. I. M. (1993a) 'The object of study in cognitive science in relation to its construal and enactment in language'. *Cultural Dynamics*. 6. 1–2.

Matthiessen, C. M. I. M. (1993b) 'Register in the round: diversity in a unified theory of register analysis', in M. Ghadessy (ed.), *Register Analysis: Theory into Practice*. London and New York: Frances Pinter.

Matthiessen, C. M. I. M. (1995) *Lexicogrammatical Cartography: English Systems*. Tokyo and Taipei: International Language Sciences Publishers.

Matthiessen, C. M. I. M. (1996) 'Systemic perspectives on tense in English', in M. Berry, C. S. Butler and R. P. Fawcett (eds), *Grammatical Structure: a Systemic Perspective*, Norwood NJ: Ablex [Meaning and Choice in Language, Vol. 2].

Matthiessen, C. M. I. M. (1998) 'Construing processes of consciousness: from the commonsense model to the uncommonsense model of cognitive science', in J. R. Martin and R. Veel (eds), *Reading Science: Critical and Functional Perspectives on Discourses of Science*. London: Routledge.

Matthiessen, C. M. I. M. (1999) 'The system of TRANSITIVITY: an exploratory study of text-based profiles'. *Functions of Language* 6.1. 1–51.

Matthiessen, C. M. I. M. (2002) 'Combining clauses into clause complexes: a multifaceted view', in J. Bybee and M. Noonan (eds), *Complex Sentences in Grammar and Discourse: Essays in Honour of Sandra A. Thompson*. Amsterdam and Philadelphia: Benjamins. 235–319.

Matthiessen, C. M. I. M. (n.d.) 'Fuzziness construed in language: a linguistic perspective'. [mimeo]

Matthiessen, C. M. I. M. and Bateman, J. M. (1992) *Systemic Linguistics and Text Generation: Experiences from Japanese and English*. London: Pinter.

Matthiessen, C. M. I. M. and Nesbitt, C. (1996) 'On the idea of theory-neutral descriptions', in R. Hasan, C. Cloran and D. G. Butt (eds), *Functional Descriptions: Theory in Practice*. Amsterdam and Philadelphia: Benjamins. 39–85.

McNeill, D. and Freiberger, P. (1993) *Fuzzy Logic*. Melbourne: Bookman Press.

Michalske, T. A. and Bunker, B. C. (1987) 'The fracturing of glass'. *Scientific American* 247.6.

Nesbitt, C. and Plum, G. (1988) 'Probabilities in a systemic grammar: the clause complex in English', in R. P. Fawcett and D. J. Young (eds), *New Developments in Systemic Linguistics, 2: Theory and Application*. London and New York: Pinter. 6–38.

Painter, C. (1984) *Into the Mother Tongue: a Case Study in Early Language Development*. London: Pinter.

Plum, G. and Cowling, A. (1987) 'Social constraints on grammatical variables: tense choice in English', in R. Steele and T. Threadgold (eds), Vol. 2. 281–305.

Polkinghorne, J. C. (1990) *The Quantum World*. Harmondsworth: Penguin Books [1st edn London: Longman, 1984].

Quirk, R. and Crystal, D. (1964) *Systems of Prosodic and Paralinguistic Features in English*. The Hague: Mouton.

Quirk, R., Greenbaum, S., Leech, G. and Svartvik, J. (1985) *A Comprehensive Grammar of the English Language*. London: Longman.

Reichenbach, H. (1947) *Elements of Symbolic Logic*. New York: Macmillan.

Shannon, C. E. and Weaver, W. (1963 [1949]) *The Mathematical Theory of Communication*. Urbana: University of Illinois Press.

Sinclair, J. M. (1966) 'Beginning the study of lexis', in C. E. Bazell *et al.* (eds), *In Memory of J. R. Firth*. London: Longman. 410–30.

Sinclair, J. M. (1985) 'Lexicographic evidence', in R. Ilson (ed.), *Dictionaries, Lexicography and Language Learning*. Oxford: Pergamon; London: The British Council.

Sinclair, J. M. (ed.) (1987) *Looking Up: an Account of the COBUILD Project in Lexical Computing*. London and Glasgow: Collins ELT.

Sinclair, J. M. (1991) *Corpus, Concordance, Collocation*. Oxford: Oxford University Press.

Sinclair, J. M., Daley, R. and Jones, S. (1970) *English Lexical Studies, Report No. 5060*. Office of Scientific and Technical Information, London.

Sinclair, J. M., Hanks, P., Fox, G., Moon, R. and Stock, P. (1987) *Collins Cobuild English Language Dictionary*. London: Collins.

Steele, R. and Threadgold, T. (eds) (1987) *Language Topics*. Vols 1 and 2. Amsterdam/Philadelphia: Benjamins.

Stubbs, M. (1996) *Text and Corpus Analysis: Computer-Assisted Studies of Language and Culture*. Oxford: Blackwell.

Stubbs, M. (2001) *Words and Phrases: Corpus Studies of Lexical Semantics*. Oxford: Blackwell.

Sugeno, M. (1993) 'Intelligent fuzzy computing'. Paper presented at PacLing [Pacific Conference on Computational Linguistics].

Svartvik, J. (1966) *On Voice in the English Verb* (Janua Linguarum Series Practica, 63). The Hague: Mouton.

Svartvik, J. (ed.) (1992) *Directions in Corpus Linguistics: Proceedings of Nobel Symposium 82, Stockholm, 4–8 August 1991*. Berlin: Mouton de Gruyter.

Svartvik, J. and Quirk, R. (eds) (1980) *A Corpus of English Conversation*. Lund: C. W. K. Gleerup [Lund Studies in English].

Threadgold, T., Grosz, E. A., Kress, G. and Halliday, M. A. K. (eds) (1986) *Semiotics, Ideology, Language*. Sydney: Sydney Association for Studies in Society and Culture (Sydney Studies in Society and Culture 3).

Tognini-Bonelli, E. (2001) *Corpus Linguistics at Work*. Amsterdam and Philadelphia: Benjamins [Studies in Corpus Linguistics 6].

Ure, J. (1971) 'Lexical density and register differentiation', in G. E. Perren and J. L. M. Trim (eds), *Applications of Linguistics: Selected Papers of the Second International Congress of Applied Linguistics*. Cambridge: Cambridge University Press.

Winograd, T. (1972) *Understanding Natural Language*. Edinburgh: Edinburgh University Press.

Zadeh, L. (1995) 'Fuzzy logic and its applications'. Paper presented at FUZZ-IEEE/IFES '95.

Zipf, G. K. (1935) *The Psychobiology of Language*. Boston: Houghton Mifflin.

INDEX

adjective   16–17, 86, 100, 122, 172
adverb(ial)   16–17, 219–20
agnation   95, 224, 242, 248, 251, 257, 259
ambiguity, ambiguous   114, 153, 172, 214, 226–7
anaphora   224

Bateman, John   142, 209, 237, 241
biological   60–1, 128, 199
brain   202, 205, 224, 250, 263

Cambridge Language   138, 239
   Research Unit
Cantonese   18, 76
cause-and-effect   61–2
children   44–5, 50–1, 63, 73, 75, 81, 84, 90–2, 136, 138, 141–2, 161, 175, 177, 184, 189, 204, 207, 209, 224, 229, 264, 266
Chinese   7–10, 12–13, 15–16, 23, 28–9, 31–2, 45, 64, 68, 76–7, 81, 131–2, 134, 138, 164, 209, 220, 239
Chomsky, Noam   63, 146, 243–4
class
   middle-   49, 50, 140–1
   social-   49–51, 141
   word-   11, 15–7
   working-   49, 50, 140–1
clause(s)   25, 28–32, 44, 50, 52–4, 59, 63, 65–6, 67, 71–2, 77–8, 80–1, 83, 87–8, 91, 93, 95–100, 102–3, 105–7, 110, 112, 116, 118–19,

122–3, 125–6, 131–2, 134, 136–7, 140–2, 144–8, 150–2, 163, 168–9, 172, 175–7, 202, 207, 214, 216–21, 224, 229–32, 237–8, 254, 258
Cloran, Carmel   54, 94, 142, 177
COBUILD   59, 79, 93, 96, 100, 128, 143–4, 150, 161, 178
cognition   198, 217, 248
cognitive science   43, 247, 266
collocation(s)   11, 26, 30, 32, 72, 78–9, 85, 122, 144, 165, 178
comparative   7, 9, 15, 21, 24–8, 31–3
conjunction   15, 115–16, 172, 176, 225, 253
consciousness   50, 196, 199, 201, 205, 216, 263
constituent(s)   44, 97, 138, 162–3
construal   173, 205, 210, 223, 238
construe   43–6, 50, 73, 85, 90, 92, 96, 136, 146, 149, 176–7, 198, 200–2, 204–6, 208, 213, 216, 218–23, 225, 228, 246, 252–3, 256, 262
conversation   50, 77–8, 132, 134–5, 141, 157, 161–2, 164–5, 167, 176–8, 207, 224
corpus   45, 50, 59, 63–4, 66–7, 71–4, 76–80, 82–4, 87, 89–93, 95–7, 103, 105–6, 116, 122–3, 127–8, 130–1, 139–41, 143–4, 146, 149, 151, 153, 155–8, 160–178, 207, 238, 241
   -based   84, 139, 143, 156, 173
   -driven   166, 173–4

creativity 165–6
cryptotypic 95, 146
culture(s) 44, 60, 167, 175, 206, 209,
    224–5, 256, 260

deictic 100, 102, 147, 238
deixis 49, 56, 83, 97, 99, 100, 102,
    105, 127–8, 133, 135, 140, 147–9,
    225, 237, 261
delicacy 54, 57, 81, 83, 166, 208,
    230, 233–4, 254, 258
diachronic 60–1, 67, 90, 262
dialect(s) 59, 76–7, 84, 140, 144, 160,
    225, 229
dialogue 78, 86, 126, 158, 161, 165,
    169, 175–8, 207, 214, 227, 229
dictionary 11–12, 15, 25–6, 29, 33,
    78–9, 93, 143–4, 203, 217
discourse 12, 50, 76, 78, 84, 86, 131,
    137, 158–9, 162–4, 167, 169–70,
    172, 175, 177, 196, 198, 201, 204,
    207–9, 213–14, 216–17, 221,
    224–5, 247, 261, 263–5

Edelman, Gerald 199, 263
Eggins, Suzanne 161, 165, 167, 170,
    176
enact 200–1, 204, 206, 208, 213,
    216, 219, 222–3, 228, 252
English 7, 9–10, 12–13, 15–16,
    18–19, 23, 25–32, 46–8, 56, 63–6,
    68–72, 76–9, 81, 83–4, 88, 91, 93,
    95–6, 106, 110, 115, 125, 128,
    131–40, 142–5, 147, 149, 151,
    153, 156, 161–2, 164–8, 171–3,
    175, 178, 200, 202–3, 206,
    209–10, 215–16, 218, 220–4, 226,
    230, 232, 237–8, 241, 243, 249,
    254, 261, 263, 266
  Bank of 93, 144, 156
  Survey of – Usage 64, 84, 139
evolution 42–3, 45, 60, 72, 85–6,
    162, 172, 188, 201, 205, 224, 229,
    251–2, 263–4
  evolutionary 44, 60, 199, 224
experiential 96, 197, 201, 205,
    252–3, 262

Fawcett, Robin 95, 161, 209, 237,
    241
finite 15, 30, 44, 66, 91, 93, 97–100,
    105–7, 110, 112–16, 118–19, 125,
    127–8, 140, 144, 147–9, 151–4,
    202
  non- 55, 97, 100, 102–3, 106–7,
    112, 115, 147, 154, 258
Firth, J.R. 45, 64, 67, 70, 94, 133,
    145, 156, 174, 177–8, 205, 228,
    256
French 12, 32, 164, 168, 209
fuzzy 173–4, 196, 203–4, 213, 229,
    244, 248, 250, 258, 266

genre 93, 96–7, 126, 165, 229
German 123, 209
grammar 6, 9–11, 13, 15, 23–32, 45,
    52, 59–60, 62–74, 76–82, 84–5,
    89, 91–7, 122, 128, 130–4, 136,
    139–47, 155–6, 160, 162–3, 166–
    7, 171–4, 178, 197–203, 205–9,
    213–20, 222–6, 228–32, 234,
    235–8, 240–3, 246–54, 256–7,
    259, 261–2, 266
  "Nigel" 59, 81, 241
  paradigmatic 67, 92, 94
  probabilistic 57, 63, 67
  systemic 94–5, 147, 241, 243, 246,
    257
grammatics 45, 76, 92, 158, 167, 174,
    197, 204, 207, 213, 217, 223–32,
    234, 238, 250–1, 258
group
  nominal 107, 114, 145, 217,
    219–20, 238
  verbal 25, 28, 83, 91, 100, 112,
    128, 133, 137, 140, 145, 202,
    210, 218, 220, 258, 261

Hasan, Ruqaiya 50–1, 74, 94, 119,
    141–2, 177, 207, 218, 221
higher-order 199–202, 205, 263
Hjemslev, Louis 43, 62, 82
homonomy, homonyms 10, 12, 18,
    113, 164
Huddleston, Rodney 139, 156
Hunston, Susan 166–7, 173–4

hypotaxis, hypotactic 53–5, 71–2, 88–9, 141, 169, 172

ideational 201, 208, 210, 213, 215–16, 218, 223, 238, 252–3, 260–2
imperative 78, 81, 83–4, 112, 115–16, 126, 134–5, 147–8, 154, 254, 258–9, 261
indeterminacy 164, 204–5, 207, 210, 226–7, 231
indicative 65, 78, 81, 83, 134–5, 254
infant 189, 199–200, 202, 217, 224–5, 251, 265
inference 244–7, 266
instantiation 44–5, 60–1, 64, 73, 82, 199, 247–8, 253
interface 164, 200, 225, 252, 261
interlingua 32–3
interpersonal 96, 165, 167, 197, 201, 205–6, 208, 210, 213, 215–16, 219, 223, 238, 252–3, 260–2
interrogative(s) 16, 68–9, 77, 81, 83, 87–8, 132–5, 259
intersubjective 222, 266
intonation 77–8, 97, 135, 163, 167, 170, 176, 178, 216, 220–1, 236–7, 249, 256
intransitive 30, 78, 135, 145
intricacy, intricate 168–9, 171, 176, 207, 214
iterative(ly) 46–7, 136–8, 206

Japanese 164, 209, 213, 215, 220

knowledge 42–3, 132, 158, 173, 196–8, 201, 207, 209–10, 246, 253, 261

Labov, William 51, 140
language 6–13, 15–16, 18–19, 20–8, 30–3, 43–6, 50, 52, 56, 59–66, 68–71, 73, 75–9, 81–2, 84–5, 89–91, 93, 95, 97, 103, 110, 126, 128, 130–9, 143–4, 155–78, 196–210, 212, 213–17, 220–1, 222–31, 234, 237–54, 260, 263–4, 266–7
  complexity (in/of) 203–4, 251, 266

computing with 239–40
construed in 190, 205, 222–3
context(s) of 84, 200, 252
description(s) of 23, 27, 173
natural 33, 70, 81, 197–200, 207, 209, 213–17, 222, 227–8, 230, 237–8, 240–1, 243–6, 248–9, 251, 266
power of 160, 177, 202
source of 18, 22, 30–2
spoken 77, 97, 144, 157–78, 197
target 7–12, 15–16, 22, 31–2
theory of 158, 213, 215, 228
written 97, 159–60, 162–4, 167–9, 171, 175, 177, 249
understanding of 63, 73, 135, 156, 177
variation in 61, 226, 238, 248, 263
langue 43, 45, 61, 82, 174, 247–8
learner(s) 23, 45, 93, 131–2, 136, 143, 210, 258, 261–2
Lemke, Jay 42–4, 62, 86, 201, 227
lexeme(s) 96, 103, 113
lexical 6, 11, 13, 16, 18–19, 23, 25–6, 28–32, 59, 64–5, 72, 78–80, 85, 87, 103, 110, 130, 133, 143, 149, 151–2, 166, 168, 171, 177, 202, 213–4, 232
  density 87, 168, 171, 214
  item(s) 6, 18, 25–6, 28–30, 32, 65, 72, 80, 85, 87, 130, 168, 171, 232
  probabilities 59, 133
  series 13, 16
  verb(s) 103, 110, 149, 151–2
lexicogrammar, lexicogrammatical 29, 44, 51, 60, 64–5, 72–3, 78–9, 82, 84, 156, 158, 165, 167, 170–1, 175–8, 203–6, 245–6, 251, 253, 256, 258–9
lexicographer(s) 65, 78, 168
lexis 6, 10–12, 15–16, 24–5, 28–30, 32, 60, 64–5, 74, 78, 130, 139, 143, 156, 166, 171, 230, 241
linguistics 12, 20–4, 26–7, 33, 45, 74, 77, 128, 130, 133, 135, 139, 156, 159, 161, 173–4, 196–7, 213, 227–9, 239–40, 242–5, 247, 267

linguist(s) 7, 19, 21–2, 24, 26, 45, 69, 78, 130, 136, 138, 156, 158–9, 169, 175, 197–8, 212, 240, 242–4
listener(s) 51, 72, 102, 176, 203, 210, 215–16, 221, 258, 262
literacy 136, 139, 229
literate 197, 207, 209, 265
locution 53, 71–2, 89, 141
logical–semantic 47, 53–5, 141, 176
logogenesis 229, 251

Mann, William 80, 142, 209, 239, 241, 243
Markov 72, 214
Masterman, Margaret 15, 239
mathematics 21, 42–3, 197, 228, 250–1
  mathematical 15, 21, 33, 45, 138, 207, 239, 243, 250
matrix 248, 253–4, 256, 262
Matthiessen, Christian 84, 94–5, 137, 142, 156, 169, 174, 178, 198, 203–4, 209, 221, 226–7, 237, 241, 246–7, 249, 261, 267
meaning 13, 17, 22, 24, 26, 28, 32, 46, 51, 65, 69, 73, 84, 96–7, 140, 142, 146, 150, 157, 163, 166–7, 171–3, 176–7, 198–203, 205–10, 214, 216–18, 222–3, 225–6, 228–33, 237, 240, 242–4, 246–54, 256–7, 259, 261–2, 264, 267
  potential 73, 157, 171, 176–7, 199–200, 207–8, 223, 232, 242, 250, 264
  meaning-creating 175, 224
  meaning-making 160–77, 229
mental 56, 68, 80, 83, 95, 146, 218, 238
metafunction(s) 165, 201, 206, 208, 215–16, 228, 252–3
metafunctional 44, 46, 201, 216, 218, 256
metalanguage 61, 213–4, 229–30, 238, 249
metaphor(s) 43, 62, 86–7, 95, 162, 206, 209–10, 223, 228, 241, 254, 256, 265
  metaphoric(al) 188, 206, 228, 265

metastable, metastability 44–5, 252
modal(s) 65, 79, 98–9, 102, 105, 112, 118, 127–8, 133, 140, 147–50, 152, 155, 226, 237–8, 261
modality 79–80, 83, 98, 100, 102, 105–6, 127, 140, 149, 160, 165, 208, 210, 238
monologic 169, 176, 210, 261, 266
monologue 126, 175–6, 207
mood 65, 83–4, 96, 106, 131–2, 134–5, 150–1, 165, 220, 238, 258–9
morpheme 28–31, 164
morphology 140, 163, 167, 241
narrative(s) 126, 140, 151, 165, 176
negative 45, 64, 67–9, 71, 77–8, 80, 83, 91, 95, 98–107, 110, 112, 119, 123, 125–7, 129, 131–5, 138, 144–55, 204, 216, 230–1, 237–8, 254, 261

Nesbitt, Christopher 52–6, 71–2, 88, 131, 141–2, 174–5
network 46–8, 50, 52–3, 59, 66, 73, 80, 92, 95, 128, 141–2, 144, 167, 177, 202–4, 208, 210, 223, 232–4, 237, 246, 251, 254, 257–8, 261
  system- 46, 52, 59, 66, 79, 92, 108–10, 144, 202–3, 232, 234, 251, 254, 257–8, 261
Newton, Isaac 158, 263
noun 16–17, 30, 83, 87, 100, 105, 114, 122–3, 131, 145, 153–4, 172

oblique 238, 261
ontogenesis, ontogenetic 44, 85, 210, 229, 251, 264, 266
orthography, orthographic 10, 27, 69, 97, 138, 146, 161, 163, 170, 249, 256, 258, 266

paradigmatic 43, 45, 64, 66–7, 92, 94, 122, 133, 138, 163–4, 174, 203, 257
parataxis, paratactic 53–5, 71–2, 88–9, 115, 141, 169, 172
parole 45, 61, 82, 174, 247–8

parse   67, 80, 95, 169, 237–8, 240, 242, 244
  parser(s)   59, 67, 100, 148
participle   110, 112, 153–4
passive   63, 65–9, 71, 74, 78, 81, 83, 86–8, 103, 131, 134–5, 138–9, 145
philosophy   21, 198, 228, 247
phonetics   77, 85
phonology   10, 24, 60, 76, 133, 140, 174, 225
phylogenesis   85, 229, 251
Plum, G.A.   49, 52–6, 71–2, 88, 131, 140–2, 175
plural   15, 23, 30, 32, 68, 83, 94–5, 122, 131, 145, 153
pragmatics   247
preposition(al)   16–19, 65, 79, 105, 219–20
probabilistic   42, 45, 50, 52, 57, 60–4, 67, 73, 77, 80, 91–2, 136, 156, 238
probability, probabilities   8–9, 11, 18, 25–7, 29, 31, 45–8, 50–2, 57, 59–60, 64–75, 80–5, 87–8, 91–2, 96–7, 102, 127–8, 130–6, 141–4, 156, 175, 178, 210, 214, 226, 230, 233–4, 237–8, 259
pronoun   16, 105–7, 151
prosody, prosodic(ally)   162–3, 167, 169–70, 220
protolanguage   199–200, 202, 225, 265
punctuation   96–7, 107, 115, 161–3

Quirk, Randolph   74, 76, 139, 158, 161–3, 185

recursive system(s)   46–7, 83, 91
redundancy   13, 15–16, 19, 46, 48, 68–70, 74, 81, 138–9, 142–3, 214
register(s)   29, 50–2, 56, 59–60, 63, 66, 68–71, 73, 81, 84–5, 87, 131, 134, 140, 144, 156, 160, 168, 175, 178, 225–6, 229, 238, 245, 250–1, 258–9, 261, 263
  register-based   84
  register-department   84

residue   220, 238
rhetorical   208, 214–15, 260
rhythm   162–3, 167, 170, 178, 237, 249, 256
Russian   10, 25, 28, 30, 164, 241

Sankoff, David   140
Saussure, Ferdinand de   43, 60–1, 82
semantic   46, 50–1, 53, 67, 77, 88, 136, 140–1, 145, 165, 171–2, 176–7, 196–9, 203–4, 207–8, 217–18, 224–6, 228, 234, 238, 244–7, 249, 251, 254, 256, 258–9, 262, 267
  choice(s)   50–1, 144
  feature(s)   50–1, 141
  patterns   51, 251, 259
  relation(s)   46, 88, 172, 207
  representation(s)   246, 256, 258, 267
  space   176, 203–4, 225–6, 228, 234, 238, 249
  system   199, 254
  variation   50–1, 140
semantics   44, 60, 84, 160, 166, 170, 174, 209, 215, 220, 223–5, 229–30, 244, 248–9, 252–3, 256, 259
semiotic   50–1, 65, 69–70, 73, 136, 170, 177, 198–202, 206, 227–9, 245–6, 248–53, 256–7, 260–4, 266
  potential   246, 248
  system(s)   44–5, 60–2, 69, 73, 86, 128, 156, 160, 198–200, 202, 224–5, 227–8, 248–50, 260
  transformation   201, 253
semiotics   43, 197
semogenesis, semogenic   43, 57, 72–3, 157, 164, 175, 177, 266
sentence(s)   8, 12–13, 16, 18, 27–31, 76–8, 87, 91, 163, 169, 176, 188, 196
Sinclair, John   59, 72, 78–9, 85, 93, 96, 134, 139, 143, 156, 171, 178
socio-semiotic   177
sociolinguistic   50, 52
speaker(s)   12–13, 68, 92, 102, 130, 132–3, 160, 165–7, 169, 175–6,

203, 207, 214, 216, 220–2, 226, 234, 238, 263
speech   16, 31, 56, 66, 72, 74, 77–8, 89, 100, 137, 140–1, 143, 158–70, 172, 175–8, 206, 220, 223, 225, 238, 244, 249, 256
strata(l)   60–1, 165, 225, 248, 253, 256
stratification   61, 248, 253
structuralism, structuralist   43–5, 60, 77, 136–7, 243
Stubbs, Michael   159, 166, 169, 171
Sugeno, Michio   196, 209, 213, 241, 244–5, 249–50, 266
Svartvik, Jan   63–4, 66, 69–70, 74, 81, 84, 94, 139, 156, 158, 161–3, 175, 185
synoptic   43–4, 65
syntagmatic   43–5, 138, 164, 203
syntax   7, 78, 171, 213, 225, 243
  syntactic   140, 196, 230
systemic   42, 50, 73, 75, 94–6, 122, 142, 145, 147–8, 163, 167, 174–6, 197, 207–8, 213, 216, 223, 227–9, 232–4, 237, 240–3, 246–8, 251–2, 254, 257–8, 262
  systemic-functional   140
    grammar   94–5, 147, 241, 243, 246, 254, 257
    grammatics   229, 232
    linguistics   228–9
    potential   167, 247
    theory   50, 94, 174, 252

taxis   53–6
taxonomy   48, 63, 144, 204
tenor   60, 208, 210, 256, 260–1
tense(s)   47, 68–9, 71, 83–6, 91, 97–100, 103, 126–8, 132, 135–7, 147–55, 223, 225, 238, 258–9
  English tense system   47, 91, 136–7
  future   98, 127, 148, 232, 238
  past   25, 110, 112, 140, 153, 259
  present   102, 110, 112, 116, 122, 136, 146, 151–3

primary   49, 83–4, 93, 97–8, 100, 102–3, 105–6, 112, 114, 116, 118–19, 126, 128, 137, 140, 144, 147, 149–52, 154–5, 174
secondary   83, 261
textual   116, 201, 208, 210, 213, 215–16, 221, 238, 253–4, 260–2
thesaurus   6, 11–12, 15–19, 26
tone   77, 135, 163, 224
transitivity   65, 68, 83, 95–6, 135
  transitive   78, 135, 145, 223
translation(s)   6–13, 18, 20, 22, 24–32, 138, 197
  machine   20, 138, 197, 214, 239–40, 242, 244
  mechanical   6–7, 9, 12, 15
  equivalence   6–11, 13, 15–16, 27
  equivalent(s)   8, 11, 18, 26, 28–9, 31
universal(s)   7, 25–7, 33

variant(s)   18–19, 51, 84, 88, 105, 153, 172, 202–3, 226, 228, 243
verb(s)   15–18, 27, 30–1, 63, 81, 86–7, 100, 103, 110–16, 118–19, 122–3, 126, 131, 133, 137, 139, 145, 147, 149, 151–5, 172, 202–3
Vietnamese   164, 203
vocabulary   11, 64, 78–9, 92, 130, 140, 163, 203, 230

Winograd, Terry   209, 240
word(s)   10–13, 15–18, 24–31, 55, 57, 59, 61, 72, 74, 76, 78–80, 83, 91, 93–4, 96–7, 103, 105–7, 110, 114–16, 122–3, 125, 130–1, 133, 136–7, 141, 143–6, 148–54, 156, 161, 163–4, 166–8, 171, 196, 198–9, 201, 203–4, 206, 241–2, 244–5, 244–6, 248, 251, 254, 256, 259, 266
wording(s)   64, 149, 165, 175–6, 199, 202, 242, 245–8, 250–1, 256–9, 261–2

Zadeh, Lotfi   245, 249–50, 266